The Questionmaster's Quizbook

D1643142

The Questionmaster's Quizbook

5000 questions arranged in 200 ready-to-use quiz rounds

Compiled and introduced by
David Self

Thorsons
An Imprint of HarperCollins*Publishers*

Thorsons
An Imprint of HarperCollins*Publishers*
77–85 Fulham Palace Road,
Hammersmith, London W6 8JB

Published by Thorsons 1990
5 7 9 10 8 6 4

© David Self 1990

David Self asserts the moral right to
be identified as the author of this work

A catalogue record for this book
is available from the British Library

ISBN 0 7225 2239 8

Typeset by Harper Phototypesetters Ltd,
Northampton, England
Printed and bound in Great Britain by
HarperCollinsManufacturing, Glasgow

Contents

Introduction

The first time I tried to organize a large-scale quiz was when I was a teacher. Most of my colleagues were off sick, suffering from some form of 'flu, and so, one wet afternoon, I was given the doubtful pleasure of occupying all the first- and second-year pupils in the school hall. An inter-class quiz seemed the best answer.

I seized two or three paperback quiz books and tried to improvise my way through the afternoon, skipping through the questions, looking for suitable ones, and trying to find the answers that were printed either upside down at the foot of each page, in small type at the back, or in closely-packed paragraphs of information in which it was all too easy to lose your way. 'Be quiet while I'm trying to find the answer,' is not what the efficient quiz-master is meant to say!

For my next attempt, I was better prepared. However this time the quiz was taking place on board an educational cruise ship and I had reckoned without the Bay of Biscay. As one of the party leaders on this cruise, I had volunteered to run the inter-schools quiz, seeing the chance to appear on stage as a suave, debonair quizmaster compering the rounds between the different schools. A force nine gale defeated all my efforts and it was a far from smooth, calm, and collected compere who kept making rapid exits from the stage between rounds to seek a plastic bowl.

Despite such disastrous starts, I have continued to be fascinated by quizzes and, more recently, have been the question-setter for such series as Radio 4's *Top of the Form*, Granada Television's *Square One*, and Anglia Television's version of *Sale of the Century* and *Gambit*. In fact, I set the questions for well over 150 editions of *Sale of the Century*. Because it averaged almost a hundred questions in each edition, that means I have set over 15,000 questions.

With that number, I have obviously run into some problems. For example, very early on in my time with the programme, I was foolish enough to set a question without checking it properly. It was this: 'For what do the initials S.O.S. stand?' I thought that was so obvious there was no need to check it. S.O.S. stands for 'Save Our Souls'. Everyone knows that! Certainly it was what the contestant said, and so he was given his three pounds. But then letters started arriving by the dozen. Hundreds wrote to tell me I ought to know better: S.O.S. does not stand for 'Save Our Souls'; the letters do not stand for anything. S.O.S. was invented as a distress signal just because those letters, represented in the Morse code by three dots, three dashes and three dots, make a particularly distinctive sound and are easily identified by any wireless operator who might be listening, and so when he hears that signal he knows someone is in distress.

Some of the problems were harder to predict. When I set a question asking what was unique about the planet Saturn, believing the right answer was that it was the only one to have rings around it, I was unaware that some astronomer was in the process of discovering that there are rings round the planet Uranus as well!

By the time that particular programme was transmitted, the rings *had* been discovered and astronomers from all over the country wrote in to tell me I was out of date — to which I could only reply, 'Thanks for the information, but I had been relying on a very recent encyclopedia.'

Relying on reference books is in some ways the only thing the question compiler can do, but such books are not without their errors. There was the time I set this question: 'If a ship runs up a yellow flag, what does it mean?'

My edition of the *Oxford Dictionary* assured me a yellow flag was displayed by a ship with infectious disease aboard, but I double checked in *Brewer's Dictionary of Phrase and Fable* and that also said, 'A yellow flag signifies contagious disease on board ship.' Not a bit of it though. After the programme, the letters poured in again. They came from retired admirals, from chief petty officers, from able seamen; the whole Navy seemed to write to me. Apparently, according to the International Code System Manual, volume one, a ship flying a yellow flag means, 'I have a clean bill of health and I require free pratique', or free clearance — quite the opposite in fact. A letter of complaint to the editor of *Brewer's* resulted in a charming apology ('You will doubtless be pleased to know that the entry has been revised for the following edition of our dictionary'), but this sort of experience has taught me that every answer must be checked and re-checked in different places.

All the questions in this book have been thoroughly researched. 'Topical' ones, and ones to which answers are likely to alter, have been omitted, and (while no guarantee can be given that a fact will not alter, say when a scientist makes a new discovery) it is hoped that quizmasters can rely on the answers supplied!

The book is intended for those responsible for running quizzes in social and sports clubs, village halls, hospitals, clubs, pubs, schools, the services, and the social sections of large firms. It is also hoped that it will provide many hours of entertainment as a family 'run-your-own-quiz' guide, and as a 'keep-the-family-happy-in-the-back-of-the-car' book!

It is in fact a book of quizzes for all occasions. It can provide plenty of fun for the family, amongst friends, or as a basis for school or 'public' contests, or when you just want to test your own knowledge.

The 200 quizzes in this book include many general knowledge quizzes, and also more specialized 'thematic' quizzes (Nos. 41–50, 91–100, and 141–50). You will find the answers on the page following each quiz. This means that you can refer to them easily, but you can also avoid any temptation to cheat! There is space on each page, which you can use either for filling in the answers or for keeping the scores — and if you do this lightly in pencil, you can use the book again and again.

It has often been said that an 'easy' question is one to which everyone knows the answer and a 'difficult' one is one to which *you* don't know the answer. An 'unfair' one is a question to which only one person happens to know the answer — and that's a fluke!

However, my experience adjudicating television quiz shows has taught me a lot about which questions most people are *likely* to know the answers to and which questions may cause more problems. With this in mind, the questions have been arranged in ascending order of difficulty in each quiz and the quizzes are also arranged in order of increasing difficulty.

The groups of 'thematic' quizzes separate easy, medium, more difficult, and difficult sets of questions.

There are 24 questions per quiz (plus a tie-breaker) arranged in two groups of 12 — so the quizzes are suitable for two teams (Team A and Team B) each of 3, 4, or 6 contestants.

- The questions are graded within each game — a pair of 'matched' easier ones for the first team-member, then getting progressively harder.

- The questionmaster can select from the 24 questions depending on the number of team-members and the degree of difficulty required.

- Phonetic pronunciations of tricky words are given; and, as well as the required answer, 'acceptable' variants are also included to eliminate argument and reinforce the questionmaster's authority!

- A tie-breaker question is provided for all games, to make 25 questions in all. These vary from the light-hearted to the trivial, and from the moderately difficult to Mastermind finalist standard!

- The questions appear on right-hand pages, with the solutions (and the tie-breaker) on the following (left-hand) page.

- In short, the intention is to provide quiz organizers with 200 quizzes ready for use 'straight from the book' without further sorting, checking, verifying etc.

Obviously the book can also be used in much simpler situations where, for example, individuals compete against each other.

In serious or public competitions, it is always as well to formulate the rules quite precisely and to publish these rules in advance of the competition.

A basic decision facing any quiz organizer is whether each question is 'open' to the first competitor who can offer an answer, or whether questions will be posed to contestants (or teams) in turn. The advantage of the first style is that it generates much more pace and excitement. For it to function efficiently, each individual contestant (or, in the case of team quizzes, each team) should have a buzzer or light which will indicate quite clearly who was first to offer an answer. In this type of quiz, a person should be required to answer as soon as he buzzes, otherwise he or she merely handicaps his or her opponents.

While quizzes in which questions are posed to contestants in turn may lack pace, they do provide a longer entertainment. They also allow each contestant to participate equally rather than favouring the fastest thinkers. This form may be more suitable when contestants are of different ages — but even here you can bring in a timing element or impose time limits for individual questions or sequences of questions. You can add variety by letting your teams confer in some rounds but not in others.

How you score is again up to you. You may want to award two points for a correct answer, one point for a 'half-correct' answer, one point for a corrected answer from the opposing team if a question is passed over, and nothing for a wrong answer. Or you may like to give a sequence of, say, six questions to one team (or person), and then to award a bonus for getting them all right.

In most quizzes an unanswered question or one answered wrongly is usually offered to the opposing team or to the other individual contestants. Because they have had longer to think, and possibly because their recollection has been helped by the previous attempt, the question will normally be easier for them than it was for the first person to answer. It may therefore be decided not to award as many points for answering someone else's question, or for answering second, as for answering your own question or for answering first.

In any quiz, the quizmaster needs to be able to decide immediately whether he or she can accept a particular answer or not. For this reason, questions must be precise and unambiguous. They must be phrased carefully so as to elicit brief and concise answers which are clearly either right or wrong and not matters for debate. It is hoped that the questions in this book will satisfy these demands and will therefore be helpful in running quizzes that are not interrupted by delays, arguments, or confusion! You should not therefore need an adjudicator, because the questions are deliberately straightforward, the answers short and to the point, and any alternative answers are supplied; but you may need a scorer, or someone to check the quizmaster's scoring!

The quizmaster should always make it clear whether he or she has accepted an answer or not. From an audience's point of view, it is also more interesting if they can see the score and not rely on the scorer's announcement at the end of each round. A simple scoreboard can be made in the style of the old-fashioned cricket scoreboard where the score was shown by numbers hung on nails.

And finally, you can make up other kinds of round to go with the quizzes here. You can show slides, photographs, or newspaper cuttings, for example of famous landmarks, famous people, or important recent or current events; you can play brief excerpts from records, or a pianist can play snatches of tunes; you can invent questions about current pop groups, radio and television series, or local personalities; and you can look at current events (see quiz No. 200). And if you look closely at the questions in this book, you will not only have the material for 200 ready-made quizzes but also the ideas for many, many more.

Remember, a quiz is always great fun for both contestants and audience, provided it is well organized and fair!

When it came to setting the questions for *Sale of the Century* I always had to bear in mind the producer's instructions; all the questions must be of reasonable general knowledge and they must be about everyday subjects the average person might fairly be expected to know about. This seems to me to be one of the attractive features of general knowledge quizzes, whether they are television programmes or quizzes arranged in village halls, pubs, schools, or the home: in fair competition they encourage us to show that we are informed about the world around us. Such information can be only for the good.

Sometimes though the wrong answers are much more fun. Easily my favourite 'wrong' answer came in the last series of *Sale of the Century*. The question was 'What is a *billet doux*?' and the contestant answered, 'It is something you sit on to wash . . . It's a sort of . . .' Then he stopped, went bright red and said, 'Oh help, no it's not.'

No. 1

a1   According to a song, to where in Ireland is it a long way?

b1   With which county do you particularly associate the song, 'On Ilkley Moor bah't 'at'?

a2   What do we call a young horse?

b2   What do we call the young of a deer?

a3   Which famous leader was nicknamed 'Boney'?

b3   What was the first name of the Russian Tsar nicknamed 'The Terrible'?

a4   How do you find the area of a rectangle?

b4   How many faces has a cube?

a5   What is Adam's Ale?

b5   For which drink is 'Mother's Ruin' a nickname?

a6   With which sport is Cardiff Arms Park chiefly associated?

b6   For what sport is Henley famous?

a7   What are dried in an oast-house?

b7   What do we call the building where whisky is made?

a8   If you were having a holiday on the island of Corfu, in which country would you be?

b8   In which group of islands is Tenerife?

a9   Which quiz master is known for saying 'I've started so I'll finish'?

b9   In which radio serial would you hear about Ambridge?

a10   What would you keep in a potting shed?

b10   What would you expect to find in a punnet?

a11   What is the capital of Austria?

b11   What is the capital of Canada?

a12   Which explorer is said to have introduced potatoes into this country?

b12   Who is generally said to be the first Englishman to sail round the world?

No. 1 Answers

a1	Tipperary
b1	*Yorkshire*
a2	A foal
b2	*Fawn*
a3	Napoleon Bonaparte
b3	*Ivan*
a4	You multiply its length by its breadth (or width)
b4	*Six*
a5	Water
b5	*Gin*
a6	Rugby Union
b6	*Rowing*
a7	Hops
b7	*Distillery*
a8	Greece
b8	*Canary Islands*
a9	Magnus Magnusson
b9	*'The Archers'*
a10	Garden implements, seedlings, plants
b10	*Fruit (especially soft fruit)*
a11	Vienna
b11	*Ottawa*
a12	Sir Walter Ralegh
B12	*Sir Francis Drake*

Tie-breaker

Q How many bones can you move inside your head?
A One (the lower jaw)

No. 2

a1 Of which country is the dragon a symbol?

b1 *Which musical instrument is a national emblem of Eire?*

a2 What is a gamp?

b2 *What kind of transport was a penny-farthing?*

a3 What fraction is 80 per cent?

b3 *What fraction is 75 per cent?*

a4 What kind of fruit is a satsuma?

b4 *Which fruit is dried to make prunes?*

a5 What is the capital of Spain?

b5 *What is the capital of Sweden?*

a6 On film, Huey, Dewey, and Louie are which cartoon character's nephews?

b6 *What is the name of the cartoon cat that never quite manages to catch Tweetie Pie?*

a7 What is the national anthem of France?

b7 *'Land of my Fathers' is an anthem of which country?*

a8 What would you expect to find in a creel?

b8 *What would you expect to find in a ewer?*

a9 In which sport do we talk about a half nelson?

b9 *How many events do you have to take part in, in a Pentathlon?*

a10 In which Italian city is the Colosseum?

b10 *In which Italian city would you find a leaning tower?*

a11 What name is given to the sign of the zodiac that is usually pictured as a scorpion?

b11 *The zodiac sign of Taurus is also known as the sign of the . . . what?*

a12 'Divorced, beheaded, died; Divorced, beheaded, survived'. To whose wives does this apply?

b12 *Which English king won the battle of Agincourt?*

No. 2 Answers

a1   Wales *or* China
b1   *Harp*
a2   Umbrella
b2   *Bicycle*
a3 $\frac{4}{5}$ (four fifths)
b3   *¾ (three quarters)*
a4   Orange (mandarin)
b4   *Plums*
a5   Madrid
b5   *Stockholm*
a6   Donald Duck
b6   *Sylvester*
a7   La Marseillaise
b7   *Wales*
a8   Fish (it's a fish basket)
b8   *Water (or other liquid)*
a9   Wrestling
b9   *Five*
a10   Rome
b10   *Pisa (There is another in Bologna)*
a11   Scorpio
b11   *The Bull*
a12   Henry VIII
b12   *Henry V*

Tie-breaker

Q   Which garment was made popular by the nineteenth-century women's rights leader, Amelia Bloomer?

A   *Bloomers* (accept: *knickers*)

No. 3

a1 Which flower do you associate with Remembrance Sunday?

b1 *Which country awards the Legion of Honour medals?*

a2 For what is a Black Maria used?

b2 *What do we mean if we say two people are like Darby and Joan?*

a3 Which Spanish musical instrument is made of two wooden shells?

b3 *What musical instrument would a tympanist play?*

a4 Which English king was known as the 'Lion Heart'?

b4 *Which English king was known as the 'Confessor'?*

a5 In which country is the port of Antwerp?

b5 *In which European country is the city of Strasbourg?*

a6 What is the principal ingredient of coleslaw?

b6 *Which fruit is dried to produce raisins?*

a7 How many sides has a rhombus?

b7 *How many sides has a quadrilateral?*

a8 In the television series 'Star Trek', which spaceship boldly goes where no man has gone before?

b8 *Who was the masked hero, helped by Tonto?*

a9 What is the capital of India?

b9 *What is the capital of Switzerland?*

a10 In former times, what did a gentleman keep in his fob pocket?

b10 *What would you lock up in a tantalus?*

a11 Which team game begins with a face off?

b11 *In which sport is there a hooker, a stand-off, and a scrum half?*

a12 In the First World War, what did soldiers refer to as 'Blighty'?

b12 *According to the First World War song, in what should you pack your troubles?*

No. 3 Answers

a1 Poppy
b1 *France*
a2 Transporting prisoners
b2 *They're happily married (and elderly)*
a3 Castanets
b3 *Drums (accept: percussion instruments)*
a4 Richard I
b4 *Edward (Eadward)*
a5 Belgium
b5 *France*
a6 Cabbage
b6 *Grapes*
a7 Four
b7 *Four*
a8 Enterprise
b8 *The Lone Ranger*
a9 New Delhi (*accept*: Delhi)
b9 *Berne*
a10 His watch
b10 *Wine, decanters*
a11 Ice hockey
b11 *Rugby (Union or League)*
a12 Home (England, Britain)
b12 *Your old kit bag*

Tie-breaker

Q Who is the patron saint of comedians?
A *St Vitus*

No. 4

a1   What is the traditional sign of a barber's shop?

b1   In war, what is indicated by a white flag?

a2   At home, what would you normally keep in a bunker?

b2   On a golf course, what would you find in a bunker?

a3   Which smoked fish is called a kipper?

b3   What type of fish are plaice, sole, and halibut?

a4   What do we call a young seal?

b4   What do we call a young elephant?

a5   Which sport is played on a grid iron?

b5   In which sport do the Barbarians compete?

a6   Which king led the Saxons at the Battle of Hastings?

b6   Of which kingdon was Alfred the Great a monarch?

a7   Which is the largest of the following: a gill, a gallon, or a bushel?

b7   Of what is A4 a size?

a8   By what method have criminals been executed in France since 1792?

b8   In which town can you see the Bayeux Tapestry?

a9   What is the capital of Luxemburg?

b9   Which town is the capital of Jamaica?

a10   From which country comes the Pasodoble dance?

b10   What kind of dance is the 'Blue Danube'?

a11   In music, which note follows soh?

b11   In music, which note follows ray?

a12   In which English county is the holiday resort of Bournemouth?

b12   In which English county is the holiday resort of Morecambe?

No. 4 Answers

a1 Red and white striped pole
b1 Surrender
a2 Coal
b2 Sand
a3 Herring
b3 Flat fish; salt water fish
a4 A pup
b4 A calf
a5 American football
b5 Rugby Union
a6 Harold
b6 Wessex
a7 Bushel (8 gallons)
b7 Paper
a8 By the guillotine
b8 Bayeux
a9 Luxemburg (City)
b9 Kingston
a10 Spain
b10 Waltz
a11 Lah
b11 Me
a12 Dorset
b12 Lancashire

Tie-breaker

Q Which English monarch was the first to use a flush water closet?
A *Elizabeth I*

No. 5

a1 Which two comedians wrote and sang the song, 'Underneath the Arches'?

b1 *Who made famous a song about the biggest aspidistra in the world?*

a2 From which country does the drink Sake come (say: sah-ki)?

b2 *From which country does the wine Chianti come?*

a3 In what is a sword sheathed?

b3 *What would you expect to find in a band-box?*

a4 Which sport would you be most likely to watch at Rosslyn Park?

b4 *Which sport has its headquarters at Newmarket?*

a5 What two colours are there on the Polish flag?

b5 *On which country's flag can you see the Star of David?*

a6 What have these in common: Job, Judges, and Habakkuk?

b6 *What have the following in common: Crown Derby, Spode, and Swansea?*

a7 Who was King of England when Guy Fawkes tried to blow up parliament?

b7 *To which king did a Pope give the title Defender of the Faith?*

a8 With which country do we associate flamenco dancing?

b8 *What do we call the West Indian form of dancing in which you bend over backwards while passing under a pole?*

a9 What one event is generally said to have brought the United States into the Second World War?

b9 *On which two Japanese cities did the Allies drop atomic bombs in the Second World War?*

a10 How many sides has a trapezium?

b10 *How many sides has a hexagon?*

a11 Which capital city stands on the River Liffey?

b11 *Which town is the capital of the Isle of Man?*

a12 On which main river does Bristol stand?

b12 *On which river does the border town of Berwick stand?*

No. 5 Answers

a1	Flanagan and Allen
b1	*Gracie Fields*
a2	Japan
b2	*Italy*
a3	Scabbard
b3	*Hats (especially ladies' hats)*
a4	Rugby Union
b4	*(Horse) racing*
a5	Red and white
b5	*Israel*
a6	Books of the Bible (all Old Testament)
b6	*Types of china*
a7	James I (1605)
b7	*Henry VIII*
a8	Spain
b8	*Limbo dancing*
a9	The Japanese attack on Pearl Harbor
b9	*Hiroshima and Nagasaki*
a10	Four
b10	*Six*
a11	Dublin
b11	*Douglas*
a12	Avon
b12	*Tweed*

Tie-breaker

Q In Mexico, is a cucaracha a dancing girl, a doll, or a cockroach?
A *Cockroach*

22

a1 According to the nursery rhyme, what happened to the nose of the maid who was hanging out the clothes?

b1 *According to the nursery rhyme, after Polly was told to put the kettle on, who was asked to take it off again?*

a2 If you were having a holiday on the Isle of Capri, in which country would you be?

b2 *If you were having a holiday on Miami Beach, in which country would you be?*

a3 Who is the mother of Lady Sarah Armstrong-Jones?

b3 *By what name is the Queen's youngest son known?*

a4 What are the five lines called on which music is written?

b4 *How many notes in an octave?*

a5 What have these in common: Grampian, Strathclyde, and Lothian?

b5 *What have these in common: German Bight, Faroes, Finisterre?*

a6 Which novelist created the detective Miss Marple?

b6 *Who wrote the original stories,* Tales of the Unexpected?

a7 What is the unit of currency in Spain?

b7 *What is the unit of currency in Italy?*

a8 What is measured in amperes?

b8 *What would you be measuring if you were using a protractor?*

a9 In which sport do lions play wallabies?

b9 *What do we call a period of play in polo?*

a10 What are Jonathans, Blenheims, and Codlings?

b10 *For which fruit is Seville famous?*

a11 What is a coniferous tree?

b11 *What is the bole of a tree?*

a12 Of which country is Baghdad the capital?

b12 *Name the capital of Iceland*

No. 6 Answers

a1 It was snapped off by a blackbird
b1 *Sukey*
a2 Italy
b2 *United States of America*
a3 Princess Margaret
b3 *Prince Edward*
a4 Staff/stave
b4 *Eight*
a5 All are Scottish regions or regional councils
b5 *They're all sea areas (in the shipping forecasts)*
a6 Agatha Christie
b6 *Roald Dahl*
a7 Peseta
b7 *Lira*
a8 Electric current
b8 *An angle*
a9 Rugby (Union)
b9 *Chukka*
a10 All are apples
b10 *Oranges*
a11 One that keeps its leaves/needles all year round; *or* one that has cones.
b11 *The trunk (accept: stem)*
a12 Iraq
b12 *Reykjavik*

Tie-breaker

Q What is the official language of Greenland?
A *Greenlandic (Danish is also used widely)*

No. 7

a1 According to the nursery rhyme, how high was the old woman tossed up in a basket?

b1 According to the nursery rhyme, around what kind of bush should we go on a cold and frosty morning?

a2 What do we call a young frog?

b2 What do we call the young of a swan?

a3 Which popular singer is known as 'Old Blue Eyes'?

b3 Which singer had war-time hits with 'We'll Meet Again' and 'The White Cliffs of Dover'?

a4 In which European country is the port of Bergen?

b4 In which African country is the city of Pretoria?

a5 Which king reigned in Britain at the start of the First World War?

b5 Whose husband was Prince Albert of Saxe-Coburg and Gotha?

a6 Who wrote the play, *Measure for Measure*?

b6 What is a mazurka?

a7 If an article costs £1.25, how much will 200 cost?

b7 If you add together a century and a gross, what do you get?

a8 What is the basic ingredient of the drink mead?

b8 What colour are the liqueurs, absinthe, and crème de menthe?

a9 Of which country is Buenos Aires the capital?

b9 What is the capital of Algeria?

a10 What is a monologue?

b10 What is doggerel?

a11 In rugby union, which country is represented by the All Blacks?

b11 In which sport have Floyd Patterson and Larry Holmes both achieved fame?

a12 What is the unit of currency in Ireland?

b12 What is the unit of currency in Denmark?

No. 7 Answers

a1 Seventeen times as high as the moon

b1 *Mulberry bush*

a2 Tadpole

b2 *Cygnet*

a3 Frank Sinatra

b3 *Vera Lynn*

a4 Norway

b4 *South Africa (Transvaal)*

a5 George V

b5 *Queen Victoria's*

a6 William Shakespeare

b6 *Dance (like a polka; Polish)*

a7 £250

b7 *244*

a8 Honey

b8 *Green*

a9 Argentina

b9 *Algiers*

a10 A speech (or scene or play) with only one actor

b10 *Bad, poor poetry*

a11 New Zealand

b11 *Boxing*

a12 Punt, or Irish pound

b12 *The krone*

Tie-breaker

Q About which bird is the rhyme that starts: 'One's sorrow, two's mirth, three's a wedding, four's a birth?'

A *Magpie*

No. 8

a1   If you were having a holiday in Valletta, in which country would you be?

b1   *If you were having a holiday in Paphos, in which country would you be?*

a2   In a nursery rhyme, which line comes before, 'The moon doth shine as bright as day'?

b2   *According to the nursery rhyme, when the king was in his counting house, what was the queen doing?*

a3   If you were playing a jew's harp, how would you be holding it?

b3   *To play a harmonica you use hands and mouth. What do you use to play a harmonium?*

a4   What would you expect to find in a cruet?

b4   *What is a coracle?*

a5   In public, which monarch said he could not carry on without the woman he loved?

b5   *Whom did Edward VIII marry on abdicating?*

a6   In Britain, how many hundredweight make a ton?

b6   *How many yards in a chain?*

a7   What do we call small chunks of meat cooked and served on a skewer?

b7   *What has been removed from dehydrated food?*

a8   What is the capital of Thailand?

b8   *What is the capital of Iran?*

a9   In which Shakespeare play do we meet Puck and Bottom?

b9   *What is the name of the pub in 'Coronation Street'?*

a10   How many cents are there in an American nickel?

b10   *How many edges are there around a 20p coin?*

a11   The zodiac sign of Capricorn is also known as the sign of the . . . what?

b11   *The zodiac sign of Cancer is also known as the sign of the . . . what?*

a12   What kind of weapon is associated with the name Winchester?

b12   *Which sport do you associate with Hickstead?*

No. 8 Answers

a1 Malta

b1 *Cyprus*

a2 'Girls and boys come out to play'

b2 *Eating bread and honey (in the parlour)*

a3 In your teeth

b3 *Hands and feet*

a4 Pepper and salt (oil and vinegar, mustard)

b4 *Small (wicker) boat (used in Wales and Ireland)*

a5 Edward VIII

b5 *Mrs Simpson (formerly Mrs Wallis Warfield)*

a6 Twenty

b6 *Twenty-two*

a7 Kebab

b7 *Water (accept: liquid)*

a8 Bangkok

b8 *Tehran*

a9 'A Midsummer Night's Dream'

b9 *Rover's Return*

a10 Five

b10 *Seven*

a11 The goat

b11 *The crab*

a12 Rifle (repeating rifle) (accept: gun)

b12 *Equestrianism, show-jumping*

Tie-breaker

Q What name do we give to the first Sunday after the full moon that happens on, or next after 21 March?

A *Easter Sunday*

No. 9

a1 In a song, whom did a jolly swagman want to come dancing with him?

b1 *Which song begins, 'Dashing through the snow, in a one horse open sleigh'?*

a2 In the rhyme, what was the weather like when Doctor Foster went to Gloucester?

b2 *In which nursery rhyme is a small girl terrorized by a spider?*

a3 Which Scottish king defeated the English at Bannockburn?

b3 *Which royal residence is by the River Dee in Aberdeenshire?*

a4 What do these have in common: Laxton, Worcester, Bramley?

b4 *What do KLM, TWA, and Pan-Am have in common?*

a5 What is ½ minus ⅓?

b5 *What is 15 per cent of £60?*

a6 From which country does the drink ouzo come?

b6 *With which country do you associate the drink pernod?*

a7 On which French river are the ports of Le Havre and Rouen?

b7 *On what river can you travel from Frankfurt to Cologne?*

a8 Which capital city stands on the River Tiber?

b8 *Of which country is Nairobi the capital?*

a9 Which tree is associated with Lebanon?

b9 *What kind of tree is an osier?*

a10 In *The Wind in the Willows*, who buys a motor-car and gets put in prison?

b10 *In which book does a parrot say, 'Pieces of eight, pieces of eight'?*

a11 What is the currency unit used in Norway?

b11 *What is the unit of currency in the Netherlands?*

a12 What sport is played by the Wasps?

b12 *In which sport do the Washington Redskins and Los Angeles Raiders compete?*

No. 9 Answers

a1	(Waltzing) Matilda
b1	*'Jingle Bells'*
a2	Raining
b2	*Little Miss Muffet*
a3	Robert the Bruce
b3	*Balmoral*
a4	All are apples
b4	*Airlines*
a5	$\frac{1}{6}$ (one sixth)
b5	*£9*
a6	Greece
b6	*France*
a7	Seine
b7	*Rhine*
a8	Rome
b8	*Kenya*
a9	Cedar
b9	*Willow*
a10	(Mr) Toad
b10	*'Treasure Island'*
a11	Kroner
b11	*Guilder*
a12	Rugby union
b12	*American Football*

Tie-breaker

Q In cricket, when the batsman misses the ball and the wicket-keeper fails to stop it, the batsman may score a run. What is that run then called?

A *A bye*

No. 10

a1   In which nursery rhyme do the king's men fail to revive the victim of a fall?

b1   *In a nursery rhyme, which amphibian went a-wooing?*

a2   With what is 'Tin Pan Alley' generally associated?

b2   *In which musical are there two gangs called the Sharks and the Jets?*

a3   Who was 'invested' at Caernarvon in July 1969?

b3   *What is the name of the royal residence in Norfolk?*

a4   What is Quantas?

b4   *Of which country is Lufthansa the national airline?*

a5   How many yards are there in one mile?

b5   *How deep is a fathom?*

a6   From what is sauerkraut made?

b6   *What is made from the cayenne plant?*

a7   In which country is Lake Bala?

b7   *What is Kangchenjunga?*

a8   In children's fiction, what is the name of the scarecrow of Scatterbrook?

b8   *Which children's author wrote about the Secret Seven and the Famous Five?*

a9   What is the unit of currency in Japan?

b9   *What is the unit of currency in Greece?*

a10   Who or what was Tommy Atkins?

b10   *What has now replaced Armistice Day?*

a11   If you were having a holiday in Marrakesh, in which country would you be?

b11   *If you were having a holiday in Sevastapol, in which country would you be?*

a12   In which sport are there slalom, sprint, and wild water events?

b12   *In which sport do you use an épée? (say: ay-pay)*

No. 10 Answers

a1	Humpty Dumpty
b1	*Frog*
a2	Music (area of New York where music is composed and sold)
b2	*'West Side Story'*
a3	Prince Charles
b3	*Sandringham (House)*
a4	Airline (Australian)
b4	*Germany*
a5	1760
b5	*6 feet (2 yards, approx. 2 metres)*
a6	Cabbage
b6	*Pepper*
a7	Wales
b7	*Mountain (third highest mountain in the world)*
a8	Worzel Gummidge
b8	*Enid Blyton*
a9	Yen
b9	*Drachma*
a10	A typical British soldier
b10	*Remembrance Day (Sunday)*
a11	Morocco
b11	*Ukraine*
a12	Canoeing
b12	*Fencing*

Tie-breaker

Q Which explorer and journalist was commissioned to find another explorer, David Livingstone, in Africa?

A (Sir Henry Morton) Stanley

No. 11

a1   What do we call a young goose?

b1   Whose child is a papoose?

a2   If all your great grandparents were alive, how many would you have?

b2   Is your fraternal relative your brother, uncle, or father?

a3   Apart from fishing, what would you be doing if you 'caught a crab'?

b3   If a ship is 'scuttled', what happens to her?

a4   In Dublin's fair city, who was selling cockles and mussels, alive, alive-o?

b4   What colour was the horse on which the fine lady was sitting at Banbury Cross?

a5   With what do you play a vibraphone?

b5   On which musical instrument would you be most likely to play a pibroch?

a6   With which country is the famous soldier Robert Clive chiefly associated?

b6   Which nurse was known as 'The Lady with the Lamp'?

a7   In the world of aviation, what is Mach 1 (say: Mack)?

b7   Which two countries worked together to develop the Concorde aircraft?

a8   What is 75 per cent of 600?

b8   What is 15 per cent of £20?

a9   In which country are the Cambrian Mountains?

b9   Into which sea does the River Tay flow?

a10   Which schoolboy (aged 13¾) has become famous for his diary?

b10   At which school was Billy Bunter supposedly a pupil?

a11   In swimming, which is generally the fastest stroke?

b11   In motor racing, what does the chequered flag signal?

a12   Which European country uses escudos and centavos as its currency?

b12   In which country are roubles and kopeks the official currency?

No. 11 Answers

a1	Gosling
b1	*North American Indians (accept: Red Indians)*
a2	Eight
b2	*Brother*
a3	Rowing
b3	*She is sunk; holes in it are made (or opened) so it will sink*
a4	Molly Malone
b4	*White*
a5	With small hammers
b5	*Bagpipes*
a6	India
b6	*Florence Nightingale*
a7	The speed of sound
b7	*Britain and France*
a8	450
b8	*£3*
a9	Wales
b9	*North Sea*
a10	Adrian Mole
b10	*Greyfriars*
a11	The crawl
b11	*The end of the race*
a12	Portugal
b12	*Russia (and several other countries within the Commonwealth of Independent States) (CIS)*

Tie-breaker

Q   What famous cricketing doctor is reputed to have kept his confinements waiting until after the close of play?

A   *Dr W. G. Grace*

No. 12

a1   What is an ostrich said to do when it thinks it is in danger?

b1   By what name is the Yeti often called?

a2   Of what is a Pontefract cake made?

b2   Which vitamin is plentiful in oranges and lemons?

a3   If you were having a holiday on the shores of Lake Como, in which country would you be?

b3   Which English seaside resort advertises itself as 'so bracing'?

a4   In mathematics, what is measured in cubic metres?

b4   In which branch of mathematics are numbers represented by letters?

a5   What happens in a vortex?

b5   With what would you play Russian Roulette?

a6   In aviation, what is meant by VTOL?

b6   By what nickname is a Boeing 747 generally known?

a7   In the First World War, what was designed by Lieutenant-Colonel Peter Nissen?

b7   In which was was the battle of Passchendaele?

a8   In which sport is Peter Alliss famous?

b8   In which sport has Ivan Lendl achieved fame?

a9   What is the capital of the Lebanon?

b9   Of which country is Tripoli the capital?

a10   About which wonderful wizard did Lyman Frank Baum write a children's book?

b10   After which famous German prison camp did Patrick Reid name one of his books?

a11   What is the date of the Queen's actual birthday?

b11   14 November is the birthday of which member of the Royal family?

a12   What was the surname of the composer whose first names were Johann Sebastian?

b12   For which Shakespearean play did Mendelssohn compose incidental music?

No. 12 Answers

a1   Bury its head (in fact, it doesn't)
b1   *Abominable Snowman*
a2   Liquorice
b2   *Vitamin C (there is also some vitamin B, but only a little)*
a3   Italy
b3   *Skegness*
a4   Volume
b4   *Algebra*
a5   Everything swirls round (like a whirlpool). (A vortex can be of any liquid or gas or matter)
b5   *A revolver (gun) (loaded in one chamber)*
a6   Vertical take-off (and landing)
b6   *Jumbo, jumbo jet*
a7   Nissen huts
b7   *First World War (1917)*
a8   Golf
b8   *Tennis*
a9   Beirut
b9   *Libya*
a10   *The Wizard of Oz*
b10   *Colditz* (The Colditz Story)
a11   21 April
b11   *Prince Charles*
a12   Bach
b12   A Midsummer Night's Dream

Tie-breaker

Q   Where in the world does the wind blow only from the north?
A   *At the South Pole*

No. 13

a1 Which legendary animal is like a white horse with a single horn?

b1 *According to the story, out of what was Cinderella's coach made?*

a2 What kind of drink is porter?

b2 *From which fruit is the West Country Scrumpy made?*

a3 If a river is said to be meandering, what is it doing?

b3 *In geography, what is a delta?*

a4 To which section of the orchestra does the tuba belong?

b4 *Who has the lowest voice: a tenor, a bass, or a baritone?*

a5 Who became ruler of Spain after winning the Spanish Civil War?

b5 *Who was the 'little corporal' who became dictator of France?*

a6 Which is the highest British mountain?

b6 *Into which sea does the River Mersey flow?*

a7 In Britain, how many hundredweight make a ton?

b7 *How many kilograms make one metric tonne?*

a8 What is meant by the old-fashioned word sward, or greensward?

b8 *If you had an escutcheon, what would be shown on it?*

a9 What precious stone denotes your 40th Wedding Anniversary?

b9 *What is your 60th anniversary called?*

a10 In tennis, what must a player do to win a game after the score is 'deuce'?

b10 *On which island are the TT Motor Cycle races held each June?*

a11 How many sides are there around a 50p piece?

b11 *How many old pence were there in a £?*

a12 Which novelist created 'The Mallens'?

b12 *Who wrote the book* The Devil Rides Out?

No. 13 Answers

a1 Unicorn
b1 *A pumpkin*
a2 (Dark brown, bitter) beer
b2 *Apples*
a3 Winding, flowing circuitously
b3 *Triangular mouth of a river, river mouth with several branches*
a4 Brass
b4 *A bass*
a5 Franco
b5 *Napoleon (Bonaparte)*
a6 Ben Nevis (4,406 feet, 1,342 metres)
b6 *Irish Sea*
a7 Twenty
b7 *1,000*
a8 Area of grass, lawn
b8 *Your coat-of-arms*
a9 Ruby
b9 *Diamond*
a10 Win two consecutive points
b10 *Isle of Man*
a11 Seven
b11 *240*
a12 Catherine Cookson
b12 *Dennis Wheatley*

Tie-breaker

Q What do we call an imaginary line which goes right round the earth and passes through the North and South Poles?

A *Meridian*

No. 14

a1   Which English city has given its name to a wheel chair and to a bun?

b1   *Which English county is traditionally the centre of the woollen industry?*

a2   In the nursery rhyme, what birds were baked in a pie for a king?

b2   *Which little girl was very nearly eaten by a wolf who was impersonating her grandmother?*

a3   Born in Rochdale, lived on the isle of Capri — which singer was this?

b3   *In the song, who stuck a feather in his hat and called it macaroni?*

a4   In former times, what was a gibbet used for?

b4   *In history, which Indian city is famous for its 'Black Hole'?*

a5   Besides batter, what must you have to make a toad-in-the-hole?

b5   *Besides fruit, what is the principal ingredient of a summer pudding?*

a6   In literature, how many Arabian Nights were there?

b6   *By what popular name is the painting* La Gioconda *usually known?*

a7   In which month does the Income Tax year begin for most people?

b7   *Which government department collects Value Added Tax?*

a8   The zodiac sign of Virgo is also known as the sign of the . . . what?

b8   *How is the zodiac sign of Libra pictured?*

a9   Of which country was Peter the Great the ruler, from 1682?

b9   *Of which country was Pandit Nehru a statesman?*

a10   Which body frames the rules by which horse-racing is organized?

b10   *Which sport is traditionally said to have started when William Webb Ellis picked up a ball (and ran with it)?*

a11   In what units is air pressure measured?

b11   *What is measured in decibels?*

a12   Reading is the administrative headquarters of which English county?

b12   *Taunton is the administrative headquarters of which English county?*

No. 14 Answers

a1   Bath
b1   *Yorkshire*
a2   (24) blackbirds
b2   *Red Riding Hood*
a3   Gracie Fields
b3   *Yankee Doodle*
a4   Hanging people
b4   *Calcutta*
a5   Sausages
b5   *Bread (sliced)*
a6   1001
b6   *Mona Lisa*
a7   April
b7   *HM Customs and Excise*
a8   Virgin
b8   *A pair of scales; a balance*
a9   Russia
b9   *India*
a10   Jockey Club
b10   *Rugby (Union)*
a11   Inches or millibars
b11   *Sound, noise*
a12   Berkshire
b12   *Somerset*

Tie-breaker

Q   By what name do we call the group of islands off the east coast of Spain which includes Majorca, Minorca, Ibiza and several smaller islands?
A   *The Balearics*

No. 15

a1   In which city can you see Nelson's flagship, the *Victory*?

b1   *In what town was Drake playing bowls when the Armada was sighted?*

a2   Which animal is associated with Paddy McGinty?

b2   *In legend, with what animal was Androcles very friendly?*

a3   A raga is a piece of music from which country?

b3   *From which country does Bouzouki music come?*

a4   What kind of fruit is a pearmain?

b4   *What kind of fruit is a Granny Smith?*

a5   In which war was the steel helmet adopted by the British Army for general use?

b5   *In the Second World War, what was a Doodle Bug?*

a6   For which sport is Sunningdale famous?

b6   *Which sporting event is held between Putney and Mortlake?*

a7   In Britain, in summer, what sort of weather does an anticyclone usually bring?

b7   *What is the common name for rain polluted by waste fumes in the air?*

a8   Which island is separated from the mainland by the Menai Straits?

b8   *In area, which is the largest of the Channel Islands?*

a9   Which war was America involved in, from 1965–73?

b9   *What was tested at Bikini Atoll in 1954?*

a10   Of which country was Eamon de Valera a statesman?

b10   *Of which country was Farouk a king?*

a11   What is measured on the Beaufort Scale?

b11   *What was once measured in rods, poles, or perches?*

a12   Who wrote *Pilgrim's Progress*?

b12   *What were the first names of the three Brontë sisters?*

No. 15 Answers

a1 Portsmouth
b1 Plymouth
a2 Goat
b2 A lion
a3 India
b3 Greece
a4 Apple
b4 Apple
a5 First World War
b5 V-1 Rocket (accept: rocket, pilotless plane, flying bomb)
a6 Golf
b6 Oxford/Cambridge boat race
a7 Dry, warm weather
b7 Acid rain
a8 Anglesey
b8 Jersey
a9 Vietnam war
b9 Hydrogen bomb (not atom bomb)
a10 Eire, Republic of Ireland
b10 Egypt
a11 Wind force (accept: wind speed)
b11 Area (accept: 'land' or 'ground' or 'fields')
a12 John Bunyan
b12 Emily, Charlotte, Anne

Tie-breaker

Q Ecuador, Peru and Chile are all South American countries. On which
ocean is the coast line of Chile?
A (South) Pacific

No. 16

a1   Who was Robin Hood's chaplain or priest?

b1   *Which words gave Ali Baba access to the cave of the forty thieves?*

a2   Which county used to be divided into Ridings?

b2   *In which English county is the district known as the Potteries?*

a3   In a song, which line follows this one; 'Rule Britannia, Britannia rule the waves'?

b3   *Which entertainer first made popular the song 'When I'm cleaning windows'?*

a4   Which ruler was murdered on the Ides of March in 44 BC?

b4   *In order to improve her complexion, which queen supposedly bathed in asses' milk?*

a5   With what kind of food would you be most likely to eat Tartare sauce?

b5   *If you bought a joint of silverside, what kind of meat would you have bought?*

a6   What is the county town of Shropshire?

b6   *What is the county town of Hampshire?*

a7   In films and comics, by what name is Bruce Wayne better known?

b7   *In fiction, what is the nickname of the character Simon Templar?*

a8   How much is an old half crown in new pence?

b8   *How much, in old money, was a tanner?*

a9   How many players are there in a hockey team?

b9   *In rugby union, how many players from each team normally form a scrum?*

a10   Austrian, Scots, and Corsican are all types of which tree?

b10   *Black, Italian, and Lombardy are all types of which tree?*

a11   How many square inches are there in a square foot?

b11   *How many pints are there in a quart?*

a12   What event took place in France on 14 July 1789?

b12   *In which year did Washington become the first American President?*

No. 16 Answers

a1	Friar Tuck
b1	*'Open Sesame'*
a2	Yorkshire
b2	*Staffordshire*
a3	'Britons never, never, never shall be slaves'
b3	*George Formby*
a4	Julius Caesar
b4	*Cleopatra*
a5	Fish
b5	*Beef*
a6	Shrewsbury
b6	*Winchester*
a7	Batman
b7	*The Saint*
a8	12½p
b8	*6d*
a9	Eleven
b9	*Eight*
a10	Pine
b10	*Poplar*
a11	144
b11	*Two*
a12	Storming of the Bastille
b12	*1789*

Tie-breaker

Q With which scientist was the equation $E = mc^2$ first associated?
A *Einstein*

44

No. 17

a1 Which English saint is traditionally associated with a dragon?

b1 *According to legend, whose drum sounds when England is threatened?*

a2 On which river does Balmoral stand?

b2 *Which city is overlooked by Arthur's Seat?*

a3 What kind of fruit is a russet?

b3 *What kind of fruit is a conference?*

a4 Which British decimal coin equals an old shilling?

b4 *Silver pieces were known as shekels by which people?*

a5 In a novel, whose companion was Man Friday?

b5 *Which novelist created the characters Bertie Wooster and Jeeves?*

a6 In which athletics field event does the winning team move backwards?

b6 *In which sport would you use crampons?*

a7 In which war was the sea battle of Jutland?

b7 *In the Second World War, what were Spitfires and Hurricanes?*

a8 On which island is the town of Limassol?

b8 *In which sea is the island of Jamaica?*

a9 A batsman scores 24, 48, and 36 in successive innings. What is his average?

b9 *If I'm offered 10 per cent off an item costing £120, how much will I have to pay?*

a10 Of which country was Marshall Bulganin a political leader?

b10 *Of which country was President Tito the leader?*

a11 Who composed the *1812 Overture*?

b11 *What nationality was the composer Debussy?*

a12 Which emperor supposedly fiddled while Rome burned?

b12 *What were the Egyptian pyramids built for?*

No. 17 Answers

a1 George (*accept*: Michael)

b1 *Drake's*

a2 Dee

b2 *Edinburgh*

a3 Apple

b3 *Pear*

a4 5p

b4 *Jews*

a5 Robinson Crusoe's

b5 *P. G. Wodehouse*

a6 Tug-o-war

b6 *Mountaineering/Rock-climbing*

a7 First World War

b7 *(Fighter) aircraft*

a8 Cyprus

b8 *Caribbean (accept: Atlantic Ocean)*

a9 36

b9 *£108*

a10 Soviet Union (USSR)

b10 *Yugoslavia*

a11 Tchaikovsky

b11 *French*

a12 Nero

b12 *Tombs (of the pharaohs); to house the possessions of the dead pharaohs*

Tie-breaker

Q In our solar system, which planet takes exactly one year to orbit the sun?

A *The Earth*

No. 18

a1   Back in 1955, who rocked around the clock?

b1   *Of the Beatles, by what name was the drummer known?*

a2   For what industry has Sheffield traditionally been famous?

b2   *In which county is Sherwood Forest?*

a3   Cobalt is a shade of what colour?

b3   *Of what colour is Georgian a shade?*

a4   Which general of ancient Carthage is associated with elephants?

b4   *In a Roman 'triumph', what kind of crown did the Roman general wear?*

a5   What kind of fruit is a Beauty of Bath?

b5   *In a restaurant, what are fruits de mer?*

a6   What is the square root of 169?

b6   *How many is half a gross?*

a7   Middlesbrough is the administrative headquarters of which English county?

b7   *Preston is the administrative headquarters of which English county?*

a8   What is a fandango?

b8   *What does an epicure enjoy?*

a9   Which London soccer club are known as the Hammers?

b9   *In which sport does the team Hull Kingston Rovers compete?*

a10   What is special about a deciduous tree?

b10   *What colour are the flowers of the horse chestnut tree?*

a11   How much is four shillings in new pence?

b11   *How much was 25p in pre-decimal money?*

a12   In which year did Queen Elizabeth II begin ruling?

b12   *To which king was Lady Elizabeth Bowes-Lyon married?*

No. 18 Answers

a1	Bill Haley (and the Comets)
b1	*Ringo Starr*
a2	Steel
b2	*Nottinghamshire*
a3	Blue
b3	*Green*
a4	Hannibal
b4	*Crown of laurel (or bay) leaves*
a5	Apple
b5	*Sea food*
a6	13
b6	*72*
a7	Cleveland
b7	*Lancashire*
a8	Dance (Spanish)
b8	*Good eating/drinking* (accept: *Good living*)
a9	West Ham United
b9	*Rugby League* (not *Rugby Union*)
a10	Sheds its leaves each year
b10	*(Creamy) white or red*
a11	20p
b11	*5 shillings*
a12	1952 (1953 was the year of her Coronation)
b12	*George VI*

Tie-breaker

Q Name two countries that border the Black Sea
A *Turkey, Bulgaria, Romania, Ukraine, Georgia*

No. 19

a1   With which pop star was 'Heartbreak Hotel' especially associated?

b1   *Who made famous 'Bridge over Troubled Water'?*

a2   In which group of islands is Fair Isle?

b2   *Skye, Mull, and Tiree all lie in which group of Scottish islands?*

a3   Who is father to Peter Mark Andrew and Zara Anne Elizabeth?

b3   *Who was father to Princess Alexandra and Prince Michael?*

a4   Eau-de-nil is a shade of what colour?

b4   *Of what colour is saffron a shade?*

a5   Who wrote *The Tale of Peter Rabbit*?

b5   *Which story book character swam in a pool of her own tears?*

a6   What fruit do we get from hawthorn?

b6   *What kind of fruit is an Orange Pippin?*

a7   What fraction of a mile is a furlong?

b7   *In Britain, how many pints make a gallon?*

a8   In November 1605, who was arrested in a cellar under the House of Lords, and later executed for treason?

b8   *In 753 BC which city was supposedly founded by Romulus and Remus?*

a9   What is special about the Mediterranean island of Stromboli?

b9   *With which Mediterranean island was the Mafia originally associated?*

a10   In the English football league, how many points does a team get for a win?

b10   *Normally, how many points do you have to score to win a game of table tennis?*

a11   How many new pence are there in a guinea?

b11   *In old money, how many farthings were there in a penny?*

a12   What kind of body in space has a long tail (made of dust and gas)?

b12   *What is measured in 'light years'?*

No. 19 Answers

a1   Elvis Presley
b1   *Simon and Garfunkel*
a2   Shetlands
b2   *(Inner) Hebrides*
a3   Captain Mark Phillips
b3   *The Duke of Kent*
a4   Green/Blue-green
b4   *Orange/yellow*
a5   Beatrix Potter
b5   *Alice (in Wonderland)*
a6   Haws
b6   *Apple*
a7   ⅛th (.125)
b7   *Eight*
a8   Guy Fawkes
b8   *Rome*
a9   Volcanic
b9   *Sicily*
a10   Three
b10   *21*
a11   105
b11   *Four*
a12   A comet
b12   *Distance in space*

Tie-breaker

Q   Which American President is supposed to have said, 'You can fool all of the people some of the time, and some of the people all of the time, but you cannot fool all the people all of the time?'
A   Abraham Lincoln

No. 20

a1   In which park is the Serpentine?

b1   In which park is London Zoo?

a2   From which country does Beef Stroganoff originate?

b2   What is a canapé?

a3   What is the black wood traditionally used for piano keys?

b3   From what animal does ivory come?

a4   What colour do you get if you mix blue and yellow paint?

b4   What colour do you get if you mix red and yellow paint?

a5   Which comic actor had a hit with 'Grandad'?

b5   In the world of pop music, which brothers 'Walked Right Back'?

a6   Which revolution began in 1917?

b6   What terrible disaster struck London in 1666?

a7   In Britain, what telephone number do you normally dial to get the operator?

b7   If 1, 2, 3, 4 are cardinal numbers, what are the equivalent ordinal numbers?

a8   Maidstone is the administrative headquarters of which English county?

b8   Matlock is the administrative headquarters of which English county?

a9   In which sport is the America's Cup competed for?

b9   In which sport do teams compete for the Ryder Cup?

a10   What is measured with an altimeter?

b10   What are recorded on seismographs?

a11   Who wrote the story of 'The Ugly Duckling'?

b11   Who wrote the famous novel about rabbits, Watership Down?

a12   Whose husband was Lord Darnley?

b12   Who was Queen of England and of Scotland from 1702?

No. 20 Answers

a1	Hyde Park (*accept*: Kensington Gardens)
b1	*Regent's Park*
a2	Russia
b2	*Piece of toast topped with a savoury (e.g. cheese, meat, fish)*
a3	Ebony
b3	*Elephants (also occasionally from the tusks of walruses and even rhinoceroses)*
a4	Green
b4	*Orange*
a5	Clive Dunn
b5	*The Everly Brothers*
a6	Russian Revolution
b6	*The Great Fire*
a7	100
b7	*First, second, third, fourth*
a8	Kent
b8	*Derbyshire*
a9	Yachting
b9	*Golf*
a10	Height or altitude
b10	*Earth tremors or earthquakes*
a11	Hans (Christian) Andersen
b11	*Richard Adams*
a12	Mary (Queen of Scots)
b12	*Anne*

Tie-breaker

Q What are you afraid of if you suffer from chrometophobia?
A Money

No. 21

a1   Where are the Crown Jewels kept?

b1   *What is the common name for the Central Criminal Court in London?*

a2   What colour is ochre?

b2   *What colour is magenta?*

a3   In which country is there an illegal drink called poitin (say: p'cheen)?

b3   *Originally, 'grog' was which drink?*

a4   What is a bivouac?

b4   *If you're out camping, what do you do if you 'tighten the guys'?*

a5   If Prince Harry were to become King, he would be called King Henry the . . . what?

b5   *When Prince Charles is King, he will be King Charles the . . . what?*

a6   Which archbishop was murdered in Canterbury cathedral?

b6   *Who is said to have introduced the habit of smoking into this country?*

a7   What sort of vehicle would you see on the Cresta Run?

b7   *Name a sport in which there is a slalom.*

a8   The zodiac sign of Gemini is also known as the sign of the . . . what?

b8   *What name is given to the sign of the zodiac which is usually pictured as a lion?*

a9   How many points has a snowflake?

b9   *When you write down in figures the number one million, how many noughts are there?*

a10   Of which country are the islands Hokkaido and Kyushu a part?

b10   *Of which country is Baffin Island a part?*

a11   Name the vet who wrote the books *All Creatures Great and Small* and *Let Sleeping Vets Lie*?

b11   *Who wrote the novels* Airport *and* Hotel?

a12   What is counterfeit money?

b12   *What do we call the place where our coins are made?*

No. 21 Answers

a1	Tower of London
b1	*The Old Bailey*
a2	Yellow or orange
b2	*(Purplish) red*
a3	Ireland
b3	*Rum (watered)*
a4	An encampment, camp site (usually temporary, overnight)
b4	*Adjust the ropes that hold it to the ground/tent pegs*
a5	Ninth
b5	*Third*
a6	Thomas à Becket, Becket of Canterbury
b6	*Sir Walter Ralegh*
a7	Toboggan
b7	*Skiing; canoeing*
a8	The Twins
b8	*Leo*
a9	Six
b9	*Six*
a10	Japan
b10	*Canada*
a11	James Herriot
b11	*Arthur Hailey*
a12	Forged, imitation money
b12	*The (Royal) Mint*

Tie-breaker

Q What would you fear if you suffered from terdekaphobia?
A *The number 13*

No. 22

a1 What is *café au lait*?

b1 *What kind of soup is a consommé?*

a2 Which island is described as 'emerald'?

b2 *What colour is ebony?*

a3 In which sport would you bowl a Yorker?

b3 *In which sport is the Wightman Cup competed for?*

a4 How are you standing if you've got your arms akimbo?

b4 *What do you do if you abscond?*

a5 In London, where is Poet's Corner?

b5 *In London, where is the statue commonly known as Eros?*

a6 After seven, which is the next highest prime number?

b6 *How many centimetres are there in 10 metres?*

a7 In the theatre, what is a walk-on part?

b7 *What is 'ham' acting?*

a8 In the modern three-core electric cable, which colour wire is connected to neutral?

b8 *In modern three-core electric cables, what colour is the earth?*

a9 Who wrote *The Hound of the Baskervilles*?

b9 *Who wrote the novel* Lord of the Flies*?*

a10 Lerwick is the administrative headquarters of which Scottish region?

b10 *Lewes is the administrative headquarters of which English county?*

a11 Who was the giant killed by the boy David?

b11 *In the Bible, who was found in some bulrushes?*

a12 Which British queen had seventeen children, all of whom died at an early age?

b12 *Which English queen never married?*

No. 22 Answers

a1	Milky coffee; coffee with milk in it
b1	*A clear soup*
a2	Ireland
b2	*Black*
a3	Cricket
b3	*Lawn tennis*
a4	Hands on hips, elbows pointing out
b4	*Run away, escape*
a5	Westminster Abbey
b5	*Piccadilly Circus*
a6	Eleven
b6	*1000*
a7	Part in which the actor has nothing (or almost nothing) to say
b7	*Crude acting; acting which is exaggerated or overdone*
a8	Blue
b8	*Green and yellow*
a9	(Sir Arthur) Conan Doyle
b9	*William Golding*
a10	Shetland
b10	*East Sussex*
a11	Goliath
b11	*Moses*
a12	Queen Anne
b12	*Elizabeth I*

Tie-breaker

Q   For what is Gerhard Mercator remembered?
A   *Map making (his projection of the world on maps) (accept: Mathematics or Geography).*

No. 23

a1   By what name is the clock tower in the Houses of Parliament popularly known?

b1   *Which bridge in London opens upwards to allow tall ships to pass through?*

a2   Of what colour is jonquil a shade?

b2   *Of what colour is russet a shade?*

a3   What is a labyrinth?

b3   *During the Trojan war, how did the Greeks first enter Troy?*

a4   Which saint has given her name to a firework?

b4   *After which saint is the chapel at Windsor Castle named?*

a5   From which animal do we get cat gut?

b5   *From which animal do we get vellum?*

a6   In boxing, at what 'weight' do you fight if you weigh over 12 stone 7 pound?

b6   *In what part of the world did the sport of surfing originate?*

a7   In Russia, what relation to you is your baboushka?

b7   *In South America, what is a gaucho?*

a8   Through what do fish breathe?

b8   *In order to reach their sprawning grounds, which fish leap up rivers?*

a9   What is the unit of currency in Australia?

b9   *In old money, how much was a 'bob'?*

a10   Which English king was excommunicated in 1538?

b10   *During whose reign was Magna Carta sealed?*

a11   Of which country is Phnom Penh the capital?

b11   *Within which other capital city is Vatican City?*

a12   What's the equivalent of a kilogram weight in pounds?

b12   *If you had 3½ pints of milk, approximately how many litres is that?*

No. 23 Answers

a1	Big Ben
b1	*Tower Bridge*
a2	Yellow (pale yellow)
b2	*Red/brown; golden brown (accept grey)*
a3	A maze
b3	*In a wooden horse*
a4	St Catherine
b4	*St George*
a5	The sheep (or horse or ass)
b5	*Calf (accept cow)*
a6	Heavyweight
b6	*Polynesia (accept Australia/Tahiti)*
a7	Grandmother
b7	*Cowboy (accept horseman)*
a8	Gills
b8	*Salmon*
a9	(Australian) dollar
b9	*One shilling (5p)*
a10	Henry VIII
b10	*King John*
a11	Cambodia (formerly the Khmer Republic later Kampuchea)
b11	*Rome*
a12	2.2 lb (2¼ lb)
b12	*Two*

Tie-breaker

Q   Supposedly, what did women spend their time doing while watching the victims of the guillotine in the French Revolution?

A   *Knitting*

No. 24

a1   In London, for what is Billingsgate famous?

b1   *What is sold at Smithfield market?*

a2   According to tradition, what is the only way to destroy a vampire?

b2   *In legend, what is a man who has been turned into a wolf called?*

a3   What is a jay walker?

b3   *What do you do if you 'tread the boards'?*

a4   The insides of which domestic items are often covered with teflon?

b4   *What household articles are made out of candlewick?*

a5   What colour are the flowers of the hawthorn?

b5   *When a tree has been felled, how can you tell its age?*

a6   For which of these games would you use a dice: ludo, whist, hopscotch, snakes-and-ladders?

b6   *In which card game would you stick, twist, or buy one?*

a7   In courts of law, at what age do you cease to be a juvenile?

b7   *At what age can you vote in local and parliamentary elections?*

a8   Who wrote the novel *Jane Eyre*?

b8   *Which woman novelist wrote* Pride and Prejudice*?*

a9   Kingston upon Thames is the administrative headquarters of which county?

b9   *Kirkwall is the administrative headquarters of which Scottish region?*

a10   What do the Latin words *Ave Maria* mean?

b10   *Which prayer is sometimes known as the* Pater Noster*?*

a11   In this country, who came to the throne on the death of George V?

b11   *In 1876 who became Empress of India?*

a12   What do you suffer from if you have halitosis?

b12   *In layman's language, what is dyspepsia?*

No. 24 Answers

a1 Fish, fish market
b1 *Meat*
a2 By driving a stake through its heart
b2 *Werewolf*
a3 A pedestrian who ignores traffic regulations
b3 *Act, go on stage*
a4 (Non-stick) pans
b4 *Bedspreads*
a5 White or pinkish red (*accept*: pink or red)
b5 *By counting the rings which show its annual growth*
a6 Ludo and snakes-and-ladders
b6 *Pontoon*
a7 Seventeen
b7 *Eighteen*
a8 Charlotte Brontë
b8 *Jane Austen*
a9 Surrey
b9 *Orkney*
a10 Hail Mary
b10 *The Lord's Prayer* or *Our Father*
a11 Edward VIII
b11 *Queen Victoria*
a12 Bad breath
b12 *Wind; indigestion*

Tie-breaker

Q Can you name two of the United States of America which have a Pacific coastline?

A *Alaska, Washington, Oregon, California, or Hawaii*

No. 25

a1   What is distinctive about gingham cloth?

b1   *What kind of handwork can involve purling?*

a2   Which street in London is particularly associated with the medical profession?

b2   *Which London street was once the home of many British newspapers?*

a3   In which sport are there 'maidens' and 'wides'?

b3   *With which sport do we associate Brands Hatch?*

a4   What is sometimes described as 'nine points of the law'?

b4   *What rank is a policeman who has three stripes on his arm?*

b5   What instrument would you use to measure the diameter of a cylinder?

b5   *What is the purpose of a thermostat?*

a6   Which American writer created Tarzan?

b6   *For what kind of books was Zane Grey famous?*

a7   Until its recent division, what was the capital of Yugoslavia?

b7   *What is the capital of Hungary?*

a8   What do Catholics call the string of beads they use when praying?

b8   *At which religious service is a font used?*

a9   Who was the first king to rule over both England and Scotland?

b9   *Which king is said to have written the piece of music called 'Greensleeves'?*

a10   If you're a Jeremiah, what sort of news do you bring?

b10   *What is the modern equivalent for the old-fashioned name Cathay?*

a11   In the UK, what is the voltage of the normal electricity supply?

b11   *For which domestic fuel are the charges calculated in therms?*

a12   From which cape in America is the American Space Shuttle launched?

b12   *Which is the oldest satellite orbiting the earth?*

No. 25 Answers

a1 It is striped or checked (made of cotton)
b1 *Knitting*
a2 Harley Street
b2 *Fleet Street*
a3 Cricket
b3 *Motor racing*
a4 Possession
b4 *Sergeant*
a5 Calipers
b5 *To maintain a constant temperature (to turn on and off a heater)*
a6 Edgar Rice Burroughs
b6 *Westerns (Cowboy stories)*
a7 Belgrade
b7 *Budapest*
a8 Rosary
b8 *Baptism (Christening)*
a9 James I of England (VI of Scotland)
b9 *Henry VIII*
a10 Bad news, gloomy news
b10 *China (Northern China)*
a11 240 volts (*accept*: 220–250v)
b11 *Gas*
a12 Cape Canaveral (formerly known as Cape Kennedy)
b12 *The moon*

Tie-breaker

Q Whose portraits appeared on the reverse of a special crown piece issued in 1981?
A *Prince of Wales and Lady/Princess Diana*

No. 26

a1   Name the patron saint of travellers.

b1   *Which saint is generally said to stand at the gates of heaven?*

a2   The zodiac sign of Aquarius is also known as the sign of . . . what?

b2   *What name is given to the sign of the zodiac which is usually pictured as a ram?*

a3   From which fruit is the drink kirsch made?

b3   *Which drink is known as* eau-de-vie?

a4   In which part of London each August is there a famous carnival?

b4   *In London in the 1960s, which street became the centre for fashionable, swinging clothes?*

a5   If you study calligraphy, in what are you interested?

b5   *What shaped teeth do pinking sheers have?*

a6   What was invented in 1851 by Isaac Singer?

b6   *With which invention is Sir Isaac Pitman chiefly associated?*

a7   In which century did William I reign?

b7   *Which king was the father of Edward VI?*

a8   Glasgow is the administrative headquarters of which Scottish region?

b8   *Ipswich is the administrative headquarters of which English county?*

a9   How many decades are there in a millennium?

b9   *In which month of the year is Michaelmas day?*

a10   Who painted *The Last Supper*?

b10   *Which Dutch painter cut off one of his own ears?*

a11   In which game do we use the terms 'pair', 'impair', and 'manqué'?

b11   *With which children's game do you associate salt, vinegar, mustard, pepper?*

a12   Which of these is not a metal: chromium, krypton, magnesium?

b12   *Which of these is not a metal: uranium, neon, copper?*

No. 26 Answers

a1 St Christopher (*accept*: St Anthony of Padua/St Nicholas)
b1 *St Peter*
a2 The water carrier
b2 *Aries*
a3 Cherry
b3 *Brandy*
a4 Notting Hill
b4 *Carnaby Street*
a5 Handwriting
b5 *V-shaped*
a6 Sewing machine
b6 *Shorthand*
a7 Eleventh
b7 *Henry VIII*
a8 Strathclyde
b8 *Suffolk*
a9 100
b9 *September (29 September)*
a10 Leonardo da Vinci
b10 *Vincent van Gogh*
a11 Roulette
b11 *Skipping*
a12 Krypton (it's a gas)
b12 *Neon (it's a gas)*

Tie-breaker

Q Whose theorem says that the square on the hypotenuse is equal to the sum of the squares on the other two sides?
A *Pythagoras'*

No. 27

a1   On which night of the year do American children traditionally play 'Trick or treat'?

b1   *Which saint's day falls on 17 March?*

a2   Which London park bears the name of a colour?

b2   *Where in London is Speakers Corner?*

a3   In snooker, which colour ball is worth four points?

b3   *Not counting jokers, how many playing cards are there in a standard pack?*

a4   What is the purpose of a chaperone?

b4   *What job is done by a concierge?*

a5   In which country were turkeys first found?

b5   *In which country did saunas originate?*

a6   What was invented by Charles Mackintosh in 1819?

b6   *What was invented by K. C. Gillette in 1901?*

a7   What is prestidigitation?

b7   *What is a patois?*

a8   Over which country did the king of the Hellenes rule?

b8   *Who was king of Great Britain from 1910 to 1936?*

a9   At what age can you first get a licence to drive a car in the UK?

b9   *What is the minimum school leaving age?*

a10   If you consulted *Debrett* on what would you be seeking information?

b10   *About what would you be seeking information if you consulted Gibbons' catalogue?*

a11   In which country was John Knox a religious leader?

b11   *Which English archbishop signs himself with the name Cantuar?*

a12   Of which country is Kabul the capital?

b12   *Of which country is Addis Ababa the capital city?*

No. 27 Answers

a1   Halloween (31 October)
b1   *St Patrick*
a2   Green Park
b2   *Marble Arch (accept: Hyde Park)*
a3   Brown
b3   *52*
a4   To protect a young lady; to escort an unmarried girl
b4   *He or she looks after a block of flats (or other buildings)*
a5   North America (and Mexico)
b5   *Finland*
a6   Waterproof rubber/mackintoshes
b6   *Safety razor*
a7   Conjuring, juggling, sleight of hand
b7   *Dialect, spoken language of an area*
a8   Greece
b8   *George V*
a9   Seventeen
b9   *Sixteen*
a10   The peerage (knights, peers, barons, lords, etc)
b10   *Postage stamps*
a11   Scotland
b11   *Archbishop of Canterbury*
a12   Afghanistan
b12   *Ethiopia*

Tie-breaker

Q   If an explorer pitched his tent in a place where all four walls pointed south, where would he be?
A   *At the North Pole (precisely!)*

No. 28

a1 Who or what live in a byre?

b1 *Where does an arboreal animal live?*

a2 Who is said to have rid Ireland of snakes?

b2 *What colour especially is associated with the Virgin Mary?*

a3 What does a pedometer measure?

b3 *What is measured by a chronometer?*

a4 Back in 1961, who was the first man in space?

b4 *Which astronaut was the first man to set foot on the moon?*

a5 In what building do Jews meet for worship?

b5 *Who wears a mitre?*

a6 What is adulation?

b6 *What is a carillon?*

a7 In which game does the term 'cannon' occur?

b7 *In which game is the term 'stalemate' properly used?*

a8 Which writer created the detective Hercule Poirot?

b8 *Which crime writer created the private eye Philip Marlowe?*

a9 Chelmsford is the administrative headquarters of which English county?

b9 *Exeter is the administrative headquarters of which English county?*

a10 What happens when red litmus paper is put in an alkaline solution?

b10 *What ingredient has been added to some water supplies to improve dental health?*

a11 In the theatre, what are the flies?

b11 *In the theatre, what is an aside?*

a12 Which day of the week is named after the Norse god Odin?

b12 *Which month of the year is named after the Roman god of war?*

No. 28 Answers

a1   Cattle

b1   *In trees*

a2   St Patrick

b2   *Blue*

a3   The distance someone walks

b3   *Time (used in navigation)*

a4   Yuri Gagarin

b4   *Neil Armstrong*

a5   Synagogue

b5   *Bishop (Archbishop)*

a6   Flattery, praise, excessive flattery

b6   *Set of bells (or chimes); or instrument which sounds like a set of bells*

a7   Billiards (*accept*: Russian pool)

b7   *Chess*

a8   Agatha Christie

b8   *Raymond Chandler*

a9   Essex

b9   *Devon*

a10   It turns blue

b10   *Fluoride*

a11   The tower above the stage (where scenery can be hoisted, etc.)

b11   *A remark meant for the audience to hear, but not the other characters on stage*

a12   Wednesday

b12   *March (Mars)*

Tie-breaker

Q   Name four of the countries that border the Baltic sea

A   *Denmark, Sweden, Finland, Russia (Russian Federation), Estonia, Latvia, Lithuania, Poland, Germany*

No. 29

a1   Which animal lives in a drey?

b1   *What is kept in an apiary?*

a2   In which novel do we meet Bob Cratchit and Marley's ghost?

b2   *What kind of animals were Comet, Cupid, Donder, and Blitzen?*

a3   What is or was an Albert?

b3   *What is a St Martin's Summer?*

a4   How many pieces are there in a standard set of dominoes?

b4   *In chess, what is another name for a rook?*

a5   What part of a theatre is the auditorium?

b5   *According to tradition, what was Sweeney Todd's job?*

a6   Britannia and King Neptune are shown holding the same type of weapon. What is it?

b6   *For what kind of building are Conway, Harlech, and Beaumaris all famous?*

a7   For what is Elizabeth Fry chiefly remembered?

b7   *Who discovered penicillin?*

a8   In the Bible, which man lost his strength when his hair was cut off?

b8   *Which of the Apostles is sometimes nicknamed 'Doubting'?*

a9   Who wrote the novel *Gone With the Wind*?

b9   *Who wrote the novel* Lady Chatterley's Lover*?*

a10   In 1926, which inventor gave the first public demonstration of television?

b10   *With what industry is the inventor Richard Arkwright associated?*

a11   Of which country is Sofia the capital?

b11   *Of which country is Nicosia the capital?*

a12   What does an anemometer measure?

b12   *What is meant by the word ferrous?*

No. 29 Answers

a1 Squirrel

b1 Bees

a2 'A Christmas Carol'

b2 Reindeer

a3 Watch-chain, frock coat

b3 Late spell of fine weather (St Martin's Day = November 11th)

a4 28

b4 Castle

a5 Where the audience sits

b5 Barber

a6 Trident

b6 Castles

a7 Prison reform; care of prisoners

b7 (Sir) Alexander Fleming

a8 Samson

b8 Thomas

a9 Margaret Mitchell

b9 D. H. Lawrence

a10 (John Logie) Baird

b10 Spinning (cotton) (he invented a spinning frame)

a11 Bulgaria

b11 Cyprus

a12 Wind speed

b12 Containing iron (as a divalent)

Tie-breaker

Q What disaster once killed more than half the inhabitants of the Derbyshire village of Eyam (say: Eem)?

A The (Great) Plague (1665)

No. 30

a1   What fruit do we get from a rose?

b1   *What is kelp?*

a2   In which sport might you have a caddie?

b2   *Which game is also known as checkers?*

a3   Which bird was the emblem of the Roman Empire?

b3   *What do the stars on the American flag represent?*

a4   In which month each year is Battle of Britain week?

b4   *In Britain, which month contains the longest day?*

a5   What would you see in a planetarium?

b5   *What is the science called that deals with stars and planets?*

a6   Which naturalist is the author of a series of famous animal books including *My Family and Other Animals*?

b6   *A book about the Von Trapp Family was made into a film musical. What was the film called?*

a7   In which field of science did Michael Faraday make discoveries?

b7   *What form of transport was invented by C. S. Cockerell?*

a8   Which is the county town of West Sussex?

b8   *What is the county town of Dorset?*

a9   In the Bible, who was in the belly of a whale or great fish?

b9   *Which book of the Bible tells us about the Jews leaving Egypt?*

a10   In the design of what was Sir Geoffrey de Haviland a pioneer?

b10   *In which industry did Sir Samuel Cunard achieve prominence?*

a11   Whose official residence is the Elysée Palace?

b11   *Who had a private retreat at Berchtesgaden?*

a12   What is the common name for calcium carbonate?

b12   *What is the name of the gas that bubbles in bottled fizzy drinks?*

No. 30 Answers

a1 Hips

b1 *Seaweed (dried, burnt)*

a2 Golf

b2 *Draughts*

a3 Eagle

b3 *The fifty states that now comprise the Union (the stripes represent the original thirteen states)*

a4 September

b4 *June*

a5 Models or projections of stars, planets, etc.

b5 *Astronomy*

a6 Gerald Durrell

b6 The Sound of Music

a7 Electricity

b7 *Hovercraft*

a8 Chichester

b8 *Dorchester*

a9 Jonah

b9 *Exodus*

a10 Aircraft

b10 *Shipping*

a11 French President

b11 *Hitler*

a12 Chalk (*or* Limestone, *or* Marble) (*not* Lime)

b12 *Carbon dioxide*

Tie-breaker

Q Which of Dickens's novels is about a boy who flees to London where he meets the Artful Dodger and a band of pickpockets?

A *Oliver Twist*

No. 31

a1   What do we call the young of a hare?

b1   *What is an elver?*

a2   What is a sampan?

b2   *What kind of vessel is a smack?*

a3   Who founded the Boy Scout movement?

b3   *Which Scottish explorer discovered the Zambezi river, found the Victoria Falls and discovered lake Nyasa?*

a4   What is a banshee?

b4   *What is or was a blunderbuss?*

a5   In which game do you use a shuttlecock?

b5   *In a bull fight, who kills the bull?*

a6   In politics, what is an MEP?

b6   *For what are the initials MBE an abbreviation?*

a7   In 1932, where was a famous harbour bridge opened?

b7   *Under which river is the Rotherhithe Tunnel?*

a8   Of what is geology the study?

b8   *What word is used for the science which deals with the structure of the body?*

a9   What was the name of the register of England compiled by order of William the Conqueror?

b9   *Whose famous book about cookery and household management first appeared in 1861?*

a10   Which religious organization leaves bibles in hotel rooms?

b10   *By what name are members of the Society of Friends often known?*

a11   Which month is named after the Latin word for the number eight?

b11   *On what day of the week must a month start in order for it to have a Friday the 13th?*

a12   Of which country is Montevideo the capital?

b12   *Of which country is Amman the capital?*

No. 31 Answers

a1	Leveret
b1	*A young eel*
a2	(Chinese/Japanese) boat (flat-bottomed)
b2	*(Small) sailing boat used for fishing*
a3	Lord Baden-Powell
b3	*(David) Livingstone*
a4	Ghost (howling ghost; signifies a death)
b4	*Gun (short barrel)*
a5	Badminton (*accept*: battledore and shuttlecock)
b5	*Matador*
a6	Member of the European Parliament
b6	*Member (of the Order) of the British Empire*
a7	Sydney
b7	*Thames*
a8	The earth's crust or surface (*accept*: rocks)
b8	*Anatomy*
a9	Domesday Book
b9	*Mrs Beeton's*
a10	Gideons
b10	*Quakers*
a11	October
b11	*Sunday*
a12	Uruguay
b12	*Jordan*

Tie-breaker

Q   Which range of hills forms the border between England and Scotland?
A   *The Cheviots*

No. 32

a1   What was the nickname of the American showman William F. Cody?

b1   *What was the surname of the legendary American bank and railroad robbers, Frank and Jesse?*

a2   If you cross the Channel from Newhaven by ferry, where in France do you normally dock?

b2   *Which ocean would you cross if you sailed from San Francisco to Sydney?*

a3   What size of bottle is a magnum?

b3   *For what drink is Jerez famous (say: Her'reth)?*

a4   On which day of the year do people go first-footing?

b4   *Which special day follows Shrove Tuesday?*

a5   How is the zodiac sign of Sagittarius usually pictured?

b5   *What name is given to the sign of the zodiac that is usually pictured as two fishes?*

a6   In chess, how many squares can the King move at a time?

b6   *How many black squares on a chess board?*

a7   In art or painting, what is a primer?

b7   *Origami is the Japanese art of . . . what?*

a8   Aberdeen is the administrative headquarters of which Scottish region?

b8   *Aylesbury is the administrative headquarters of which English county?*

a9   In France, what is *Le Figaro*?

b9   *What is a coup d'état?*

a10   According to the Book of Genesis, out of what did God make Eve?

b10   *In the Bible, which of Jacob's sons had a coat of many colours?*

a11   Who wrote the novels *Kidnapped* and *The Strange Case of Dr Jekyll and Mr Hyde*?

b11   *Whose mines were discovered by Allan Quartermain, Henry Curtis, and John Good?*

a12   For what is brimstone an everyday name?

b12   *Which chemical element is found in diamonds, coal, and soot?*

No. 32 Answers

a1   Buffalo Bill
b1   James
a2   Dieppe
b2   Pacific
a3   Holds two ordinary bottles (esp. of champagne) (2 'reputed' quarts)
b3   Sherry
a4   New Year's Day (1 January)
b4   Ash Wednesday
a5   An archer
b5   Pisces
a6   One
b6   Thirty-two
a7   A first coat of paint
b7   Paper folding (modelling with paper)
a8   Grampian
b8   Buckinghamshire
a9   (Daily) newspaper
b9   Seizure of power
a10 One of Adam's ribs
b10 Joseph
a11 Robert Louis Stevenson
b11 King Solomon's
a12 Sulphur
b12 Carbon

Tie-breaker

Q   What do we call the medieval period during which arts and letters suddenly began to flourish again?
A   *Renaissance*

No. 33

a1   When is the Blue Peter flag hoisted?

b1   What part of a ship is its prow?

a2   What is a chihuahua (say: shee-wah-wah)?

b2   What kind of dog is an Airedale?

a3   Why would you consult a gazetteer?

b3   Which department is responsible for making the official maps of Great Britain?

a4   With which industry is the Royal Smithfield Show concerned?

b4   What kind of farming is arable farming?

a5   Of what is a mullion a part?

b5   On which building would you be most likely to see a minaret?

a6   In politics, what is the opposite of a hawk?

b6   In British politics, which is the Lower House?

a7   Where would you find a gully, a slip, and a short leg?

b7   In the north of England, which game is played on a 'crown' green?

a8   What crime do you commit if you betray your country?

b8   What is larceny?

a9   Which English king was nicknamed 'Bluff King Hal'?

b9   Which English king was nicknamed 'Tum-Tum'?

a10   Trowbridge is the administrative headquarters of which English county?

b10   Truro is the administrative headquarters of which English county?

a11   As what kind of entertainer did Grock achieve fame?

b11   Which London theatre boasted during the war that 'We never close'?

a12   Which of Shakespeare's plays is about the Montagues and the Capulets?

b12   In which of Shakespeare's plays is the famous 'To be or not to be' speech?

No. 33 Answers

a1	When a ship is about to set sail (to leave port)
b1	*Front; bow; pointed part at front*
a2	Dog (Mexican, dwarf dog)
b2	*Terrier (accept: hunting)*
a3	To find out where a place is
b3	*Ordnance Survey*
a4	Farming; agriculture
b4	*To do with crops, growing of crops*
a5	A window (an upright divider)
b5	*Mosque*
a6	A dove
b6	*House of Commons*
a7	On a cricket field
b7	*Bowls*
a8	Treason
b8	*Theft; petty theft*
a9	Henry VIII
b9	*Edward VII*
a10	Wiltshire
b10	*Cornwall*
a11	Clown (mime artist)
b11	*Windmill*
a12	*Romeo and Juliet*
b12	Hamlet

Tie-breaker

Q In 1930 a famous British airship was destroyed in France on its first flight to India. What was it known as?

A *R101*

No. 34

a1   Every autumn, there are illuminations along which holiday resort's Golden Mile?

b1   *In what sport are championships held at the All England Club each June?*

a2   On board ship, what is a companionway?

b2   *On a ship, what are the scuppers?*

a3   Who was the first President of the United States of America?

b3   *Which American President had the first names Richard Milhous?*

a4   On what type of surface is the sport of curling played?

b4   *In golf, what is a divot?*

a5   Which book of the Bible tells us about the creation of the world?

b5   *Which is the last book of the Bible?*

a6   Which prime minister was nicknamed 'Dizzy'?

b6   *By what nickname was Louis Armstrong known?*

a7   Which important river links Austria to the sea?

b7   *On which river is the Lorelei rock?*

a8   In which art did Mrs Patrick Campbell achieve fame?

b8   *Who first defined the law of gravity?*

a9   Brasenose, Oriel, and Balliol are all colleges of which university?

b9   *Which university is situated at Colchester?*

a10   What is baccarat?

b10   *On which course is the Cesarewitch run?*

a11   What kind of heavenly body is named after Edmund Halley?

b11   *The Aurora Borealis is commonly known as what (say: Or-ror-a Bor-e-alis)?*

a12   Which religion celebrates the Feast of the Epiphany?

b12   *Of which religion is the Koran the sacred book?*

No. 34 Answers

a1 Blackpool
b1 *(Lawn) tennis*
a2 Steps; staircase
b2 *Holes to allow water to run off the deck*
a3 George Washington
b3 *Nixon*
a4 Ice
b4 *Piece of turf displaced by the player (when making a stroke)*
a5 Genesis
b5 *Revelation (of St John the Divine)*
a6 (Benjamin) Disraeli
b6 *Satchmo*
a7 Danube (to the Black Sea)
b7 *Rhine*
a8 Acting
b8 *Sir Isaac Newton*
a9 Oxford
b9 *University of Essex*
a10 A card-game; form of gambling
b10 *Newmarket*
a11 A comet (Halley's comet)
b11 *The Northern Lights*
a12 Christianity
b12 *Islam or Moslem*

Tie-breaker

Q Who was the sculptor of the famous statue, 'The Thinker'? (*Le Penseur*)
A *(Auguste) Rodin*

No. 35

a1   Where would you find a conning tower?

b1   *How many hulls has a catamaran?*

a2   From which wood were longbows made?

b2   *Where would you go to watch thespians at work?*

a3   What is a lacuna?

b3   *What is lapis lazuli?*

a4   What were Locomotion, Rocket, and Puffing Billy?

b4   *What have the Little Bear, the Great Bear, and the Swan in common?*

a5   What does *Hansard* record?

b5   *In Britain, after how long must an election be held?*

a6   Which country's elected parliament is known as the Dáil (*say*: Doyle)?

b6   *Name the two main political parties in the United States.*

a7   Which is the most sacred river of the Hindus?

b7   *On which river does Belfast stand?*

a8   Who wrote the play *A Winter's Tale*?

b8   *Who wrote the best selling novel* Jaws?

a9   According to the Book of Genesis, in how many days did God accomplish the creation?

b9   *In the Bible, who led the Israelites at the Battle of Jericho?*

a10   What crime is sometimes known as 'GBH'?

b10   *In education, for what do the initials GCSE stand?*

a11   In which sport are the Harlem Globe Trotters famous?

b11   *What game would you play at the Royal and Ancient Club, St. Andrews, in Scotland?*

a12   Which is the only star in our solar system?

b12   *Which constellation of stars is said to look like a hunter?*

No. 35 Answers

a1 On a submarine (or any warship)

b1 *Two*

a2 Yew

b2 *Theatre (they're actors)*

a3 A gap or space, where something is missing

b3 *Semi-precious stone (a silicate; blue in colour)*

a4 (Early) locomotives

b4 *All constellations (groups of stars)*

a5 What happens in parliament (both houses)

b5 *Five years*

a6 Eire (Ireland)

b6 *Democrat, Republican*

a7 Ganges

b7 *River Lagan*

a8 Shakespeare

b8 *Peter Benchley*

a9 Six

b9 *Joshua*

a10 Grievous Bodily Harm; wounding (or intending to wound) a person

b10 *General Certificate of Secondary Education*

a11 Basketball

b11 *Golf*

a12 The sun

b12 *Orion*

Tie-breaker

Q What name is popularly given to the Jacobite Rebellion led by Prince Charles Edward Stuart, and which was later crushed at Culloden?

A *The Forty-Five*

No. 36

a1   Which kind of spaniel is named after a king?

b1   *What kind of dog is a Bedlington?*

a2   What was a catacomb?

b2   *What do we call a place where leather is prepared?*

a3   In which sea is Jamaica?

b3   *In which country is the Corinth Canal?*

a4   What do we call a small stream that flows into a larger river?

b4   *What do you do if you dredge a river?*

a5   What have these in common: Tawny, Short-Eared, and Barn?

b5   *Edible, blue, and hermit are all types of which creature?*

a6   Which prime minister was nicknamed 'Supermac'?

b6   *Prime minister Gladstone was called the 'GOM'. What did these initials stand for?*

a7   In modern three-core electric cables, which wire is live?

b7   *How do bevel gears engage with one another?*

a8   Which decoration for conspicuous bravery was first awarded in 1856?

b8   *From which two countries did Anzac troops come?*

a9   In the theatre, what is an ad lib?

b9   *In the theatre, what is an angel?*

a10   Which British coin, no longer in use, was the colour of brass?

b10   *On a British coin, what is meant by the letters FD or Fid Def?*

a11   Name the gifts brought by the Wise Men to the child Jesus.

b11   *Before they became disciples of Jesus, what job was done by Peter and Andrew?*

a12   What is a sarcophagus meant to contain?

b12   *From which country do we get indian ink?*

No. 36 Answers

a1 King Charles Spaniel (King Charles II)
b1 *Terrier*
a2 Underground burial place, especially in Rome (*accept: underground gallery*)
b2 *Tannery*
a3 Caribbean
b3 *Greece*
a4 A tributary
b4 *Clear mud or silt from it*
a5 They're all kinds of owl
b5 *Crab (crustaceans)*
a6 Harold Macmillan
b6 *Grand Old Man*
a7 Brown
b7 *At right angles*
a8 Victoria Cross
b8 *Australia, New Zealand*
a9 A line not in the script; an improvised line
b9 *A backer; someone who puts money into a play*
a10 Threepenny (3d) piece
b10 *Defender of the Faith (Fidei Defensor)*
a11 Gold, Frankincense, and Myrrh
b11 *Fishermen*
a12 Dead body (it's a coffin, usually sculpted)
b12 *China*

Tie-breaker

Q Which Mediterranean island was the site of St Paul's shipwreck?
A *Malta*

No. 37

a1   Which month is 'fill-dike'?

b1   *According to the old saying, if the month of March comes in like a lion, how will it go out?*

a2   What is a poncho?

b2   *Who would wear a burnous?*

a3   In which country is the Taj Mahal?

b3   *Which country is popularly known as the Land of the Rising Sun?*

a4   What famous incident happened at Boston harbour in 1773?

b4   *What bird do Americans traditionally eat at Thanksgiving?*

a5   Are sponges animal, vegetable, or mineral?

b5   *Are jellyfish animal, vegetable, or mineral?*

a6   In the world of pop, which group was 'Glad All Over'?

b6   *In 1957, which skiffle star sang about 'Putting on the style'?*

a7   Of which country is Caracas the capital?

b7   *Kampala is the capital of which country?*

a8   At the coronation, who places the Crown on the sovereign's head?

b8   *In which building did Prince Charles marry Lady Diana Spencer?*

a9   In which Shakespeare play does an English prince fight at Agincourt?

b9   *In which Shakespeare play does a Scottish lord murder his king?*

a10   With which sport do you connect Jack Nicklaus?

b10   *In which sport did Sir Stanley Matthews achieve fame?*

a11   Who is the patron saint of mountaineers?

b11   *Which saint was born in the Italian town of Assisi?*

a12   In the world of medicine, for what do the initials ENT stand?

b12   *What is a greenstick fracture?*

No. 37 Answers

a1 February
b1 *Like a lamb*
a2 Cape with a slit for the head; blanket-like cloak
b2 *Arab*
a3 India
b3 *Japan*
a4 Boston Tea Party (tea thrown overboard)
b4 *Turkey*
a5 Animal
b5 *Animal*
a6 The Dave Clark Five
b6 *Lonnie Donegan*
a7 Venezuela
b7 *Uganda*
a8 Archbishop of Canterbury
b8 *St Paul's Cathedral*
a9 *Henry V*
b9 Macbeth
a10 Golf
b10 *Soccer*
a11 St Bernard
b11 *St Francis*
a12 Ear Nose and Throat
b12 *A partly broken (or bent) bone (especially in children)*

Tie-breaker

Q Which former airman won the VC in the Second World War and since retirement has devoted himself to the provision of houses for the sick and incurable?

A *Leonard Cheshire*

86

No. 38

a1   Which pop group once had a hit with 'Honky Tonk Woman'?

b1   *Which of the Beatles sang 'Imagine'?*

a2   What kind of apes live on the Rock of Gibraltar?

b2   *What two colours of squirrels are found in the UK?*

a3   In Cockney rhyming slang, what are 'mince pies'?

b3   *In Cockney rhyming slang, what is meant by a 'tea leaf'?*

a4   In cricket, which county plays at home at Trent Bridge?

b4   *Which county cricket team plays at home at Lords?*

a5   Which film star gave her name to a life jacket?

b5   *Which item of clothing would you throw down as a challenge to a duel?*

a6   In which country is Waterloo, the battlefield where Napoleon was defeated?

b6   *Of which European country are Madeira and the Azores a part?*

a7   Of which country was Catherine the Great an empress?

b7   *Which French king was husband to Marie Antionette?*

a8   What would you find in *Palgrave's Golden Treasury*?

b8   *In poetry, how many lines has a limerick?*

a9   Which city is the administrative capital of The Netherlands?

b9   *Of which country is Brazzaville the capital?*

a10   If a doctor specialized in geriatrics, for what sort of people would he care?

b10   *What happens to the pupils of your eyes when you enter a darkened room?*

a11   For how long is an American president elected?

b11   *Franklin D. Roosevelt — what did the 'D' stand for?*

a12   Which religion observes the Passover?

b12   *In which religion does the muezzin call the faithful to prayer?*

No. 38 Answers

a1   The Rolling Stones
b1   John Lennon
a2   Barbary Apes
b2   Red; grey
a3   Eyes
b3   Thief
a4   Nottinghamshire
b4   Middlesex
a5   Mae West
b5   Gauntlet
a6   Belgium
b6   Portugal
a7   Russia
b7   Louis XVI
a8   Poems, poetry
b8   Five
a9   The Hague
b9   Congo (People's Republic of the)
a10   Old people; elderly people
b10   They enlarge
a11   Four years (He can stand for re-election once)
b11   Delano
a12   Jewish (Hebrew)
b12   Islam (accept: Muslim) (NB The term Mohammedan is offensive to Muslims in this context)

Tie-breaker

Q   Which eighteenth-century English poet and artist is famous for his coloured engravings and for a poem beginning, 'Tyger, tyger . . .'?
A   (William) Blake

No. 39

a1 How would you recognize a Manx cat?

b1 *Which animal's tail is often called a brush?*

a2 On which part of the body would an epaulette be worn?

b2 *What are bespoke clothes?*

a3 In which country are there polders?

b3 *Of which country is the Yukon a part?*

a4 In which capital city is the statue of a small boy, the Mannekin Pis?

b4 *Which capital city is close to the seaside resort of Estoril?*

a5 Who wrote the play *The Importance of Being Earnest*?

b5 *Who wrote the play* Major Barbara?

a6 How many of Henry VIII's wives were executed?

b6 *In which building was young King Edward V and his brother murdered?*

a7 Which football team plays at home at Goodison Park?

b7 *Which soccer team plays at home at St James's Park?*

a8 Where in your body is your cranium?

b8 *Where in your body is your cornea?*

a9 What does an obdurate person find it difficult to do?

b9 *In which direction will a retrograde step take you?*

a10 Which religious sect was founded by John Wesley?

b10 *Which religious body's weekly magazine is called* The War Cry?

a11 What high office has been held by Andrew Jackson, Rutherford Hayes, and Harry S. Truman?

b11 *What toy is named after the American president Theodore Roosevelt?*

a12 In which Shakespeare play do we hear the words, 'Friends, Romans and Countrymen'?

b12 *In which Shakespeare play is a Danish prince visited by his father's ghost?*

No. 39 Answers

a1 It has no tail

b1 *Fox*

a2 The shoulder

b2 *Made-to-measure ones; specially ordered for an individual*

a3 Holland (land reclaimed from the sea)

b3 *Canada*

a4 Brussels

b4 *Lisbon (in Portugal)*

a5 Oscar Wilde

b5 *George Bernard Shaw*

a6 Two (Anne Boleyn and Catherine Howard)

b6 *The Tower (of London)*

a7 Everton

b7 *Newcastle*

a8 Head (top of the skull, above the brain)

b8 *Eye*

a9 Change his beliefs or feelings

b9 *Backwards*

a10 Methodists

b10 *Salvation Army*

a11 President of the USA

b11 *Teddy bear*

a12 Julius Caesar

b12 Hamlet

Tie-breaker

Q Before entering the sea, the River Rhine forms a complex delta. In which country is that delta situated?

A *Holland (Netherlands)*

No. 40

a1 In which football ground is the famous 'Kop'?

b1 *Which soccer team plays at home at the Dell?*

a2 Which animal is often measured in hands?

b2 *What can a cat do with its claws that a dog cannot do?*

a3 Over which river did prisoners build a bridge in a film starring Alec Guinness?

b3 *The film* Tora! Tora! Tora! *was about a Japanese attack on which American base?*

a4 Where on your body would you wear spats?

b4 *'Unmentionables' was a ninteenth-century nickname for what garment?*

a5 Of which country is Nova Scotia a province?

b5 *Of which country is Andalucia a province?*

a6 Which season of the year is known in America as the Fall?

b6 *What does an American mean by gasoline?*

a7 Where is the metatarsal arch?

b7 *Whereabouts in your body is your patella?*

a8 Where, today, would you find a bailliwick?

b8 *In Scotland, what is a claymore?*

a9 Which Italian dictator founded Fascism in 1919?

b9 *Of which country was Konrad Adenauer a statesman?*

a10 In the poem by Edward Lear, what was peculiar about the 'Pobble'?

b10 *In the poem, with whom did Christopher Robin visit Buckingham Palace?*

a11 Which book was first translated into English by John Wycliffe?

b11 *From which book in the Bible comes this quotation: 'The Lord is my shepherd, therefore shall I lack nothing'?*

a12 In which country is the ruined city of Carthage?

b12 *In which country is the site of the ancient city of Troy?*

No. 40 Answers

a1 Anfield (Liverpool)
b1 *Southampton*
a2 Horse
b2 *Retract them*
a3 River Kwai
b3 *Pearl Harbour*
a4 On your feet (*accept*: ankles)
b4 *Men's trousers*
a5 Canada
b5 *Spain*
a6 Autumn
b6 *Petrol*
a7 In your foot
b7 *Knee (kneecap)*
a8 Channel Islands (Jersey, Guernsey) (area governed by a bailiff)
b8 *(Two-edged) sword; broadsword*
a9 (Benito) Mussolini
b9 *West Germany*
a10 It had no toes
b10 *Alice*
a11 The Bible
b11 *Psalms*
a12 Tunisia
b12 *Turkey*

Tie-breaker

Q Mecca is the holy city of the Muslim religion. In which middle eastern country is it situated?
A *Saudi Arabia*

No. 41 Back to School

a1   What do we call a number of loaves of bread?

b1   *What do we often call a number of pearls that have been strung together?*

a2   What is the masculine equivalent of a heifer?

b2   *What is the masculine equivalent of a mare?*

a3   On a map, in which direction are lines of latitude drawn?

b3   *What is the opposite of occidental?*

a4   Which part of speech describes how an action is done?

b4   *In grammar, what function does an adjective perform?*

a5   According to the proverb, what shouldn't call the kettle black?

b5   *According to the proverb, what kind of lane has no turning?*

a6   According to the proverb, what do you need if you're going to sup with the devil?

b6   *According to the proverb, what can't you make without breaking eggs?*

a7   What is the equivalent in degrees fahrenheit of 100 degrees centigrade?

b7   *Approximately, how many litres are there to a gallon?*

a8   Pascal, Cobol, and Basic are all types of what?

b8   *In mathematics, how many different digits or figures are used in the Binary system?*

a9   Colloquially speaking, what do we mean when we talk about a chip off the old block?

b9   *What do we mean when we talk about a dog in the manger?*

a10   Colloquially speaking, what do we mean when we talk about a white elephant?

b10   *What do we mean when we say someone is carrying coals to Newcastle?*

a11   For what do the initials VAT stand?

b11   *For what are the letters TSB an abbreviation?*

a12   What is the first letter of the Greek alphabet?

b12   *What is the second letter of the Greek alphabet?*

No. 41 Answers

a1	Batch
b1	*A rope (accept: string)*
a2	Bullock (young bull)
b2	*Stallion (accept: colt)*
a3	East-west
b3	*Oriental*
a4	Adverb
b4	*Describes a noun*
a5	The pot
b5	*A long lane*
a6	A long spoon
b6	*An omelette*
a7	212
b7	*4½ (4.546) (accept: 4 or 5)*
a8	Computer languages; programming languages
b8	*Two*
a9	A person who is like his or her father or mother
b9	*A person who stops others using what's useless to him*
a10	A gift or object which is more trouble than its worth; something that is of no use
b10	*They're doing an unnecessary job*
a11	Value Added Tax
b11	*Trustee Savings Bank*
a12	Alpha
b12	*Beta*

Tie-breaker

Q As a result of angel faces in Rome, who was sent to England as its first missionary?

A *St Augustine*

94

No. 42 Top of the Class

a1   What collective noun is given to a number of magistrates?

b1   *What do we call a group of company directors?*

a2   What is the wife of a marquis called?

b2   *What is the female equivalent of an earl?*

a3   In this country, in which month is the autumn equinox?

b3   *On a map, which places are joined by a contour?*

a4   What is the plural of the word crisis?

b4   *What is the plural of mongoose?*

a5   According to the proverb, which animal should you not look in the mouth?

b5   *According to the proverb, there's no smoke without — what?*

a6   According to the saying, what is the road to hell paved with?

b6   *According to the proverb, what was not built in a day?*

a7   In yards, how long was a rod, pole, or perch?

b7   *In ancient times what unit of measurement was the distance from your elbow to your fingertips?*

a8   In computing, what is hard copy?

b8   *In the world of computing, what is software?*

a9   Colloquially speaking, what are you doing if you are swinging the lead?

b9   *What do we mean when we talk about a busman's holdiay?*

a10   Colloquially speaking, what do we mean when we say we're sending someone to Coventry?

b10   *What is meant by sticking one's neck out?*

a11   In the Navy, for what is MTB an abbreviation?

b11   *For what do the letters EC stand?*

a12   In printing, what are upper case letters?

b12   *In printing, what is a diphthong?*

No. 42 Answers

a1   A bench
b1   *A board*
a2   Marchioness
b2   *Countess*
a3   September
b3   *Places with the same height*
a4   Crises
b4   *Mongooses*
a5   (Gift) horse
b5   *Fire*
a6   Good intentions
b6   *Rome*
a7   5½
b7   *A cubit*
a8   Information on paper; copy printed out; a print-out
b8   *Programmes, etc., that are fed into a computer*
a9   Malingering, skiving (perhaps by making up a story)
b9   *A holiday where you do the same thing you do at work*
a10   We're not speaking to them
b10   *Asking for trouble; risking saying or doing something*
a11   Motor torpedo boat
b11   *European Community*
a12   Capitals
b12   *Two letters (usually vowels) joined together*

Tie-breaker

Q In which of Dickens' novels does the hero work for a time as a schoolmaster at Dotheboys Hall?
A *Nicholas Nickleby*

No. 43 Abbreviated Forms

a1   Electricity: For what does the abbreviation AC stand?

b1   *In Hi Fi equipment, what is Hi Fi short for?*

a2   For what do the letters PAYE stand?

b2   *For what are the letters PDSA an abbreviation?*

a3   In America, for what do the initials CIA stand?

b3   *In sport, what is the LTA?*

a4   In an advertisement, what is meant by the letters ONO after a price?

b4   *Which charity is known by the initials, SCF?*

a5   After a company's name, for what does the abbreviation Plc stand?

b5   *For what is CBI an abbreviation?*

a6   By what abbreviation is Radio Detection and Ranging equipment widely known? (It came into use during The Second World War.)

b6   *By what abbreviation do we know the Electronic Random Number Indicator Equipment? (It decides who wins premium bond prizes.)*

a7   For what do the initials ICBM stand?

b7   *What is a UXB?*

a8   For what are the initials LSO an abbreviation?

b8   *When referring to a book of hymns, for what do the intials A&M stand?*

a9   What is the OAU?

b9   *For what are the letters WRAC an abbreviation?*

a10   By what abbreviation is the Organization of Petroleum Exporting Countries known?

b10   *On what would you be most likely to see the abbreviation TIR?*

a11   In transport, what did the initials LMS stand for?

b11   *And also in the field of transport, for what do the initials BALPA stand?*

a12   For what are the letters RSC an abbreviation?

b12   *With which army do you associate the abbreviation, SPQR?*

No. 43 Answers

a1	Alternating current
b1	*High Fidelity*
a2	Pay As You Earn
b2	*People's Dispensary for Sick Animals*
a3	Central Intelligence Agency
b3	*Lawn Tennis Association*
a4	'Or nearest offer'
b4	*Save the Children Fund*
a5	Public limited company
b5	*Confederation of British Industry*
a6	RADAR
b6	*ERNIE*
a7	Inter-Continental Ballistic Missile
b7	*Unexploded bomb*
a8	London Symphony Orchestra
b8	*Ancient and Modern*
a9	Organization for African Unity
b9	*Women's Royal Army Corps*
a10	OPEC
b10	*A lorry (Transport International Routier)*
a11	London Midland and Scottish (Railway)
b11	*British Airline Pilots Association*
a12	Royal Shakespeare Company
b12	*Roman (Senatus Populusque Romanus)*

Tie-breaker

Q For what is PVC an abbreviation?
A *Polyvinyl chloride*

No. 44 Definitions, Please

a1   What is or was a Tin Lizzie?
b1   *What is or was an Eton crop?*
a2   What is a fiesta?
b2   *What is a peruke?*
a3   What is an alloy?
b3   *What is an incisor?*
a4   What is a malapropism?
b4   *What is an acronym?*
a5   What is Bombay Duck?
b5   *What is a Portuguese Man-of-War?*
a6   What is a bluestocking?
b6   *What is a Scarlet Runner?*
a7   What was a Messerschmitt?
b7   *What is a Venus fly-trap?*
a8   What are hydroponics?
b8   *What are pyrotechnics?*
a9   What is penury?
b9   *What is pulchritude?*
a10   What is a heliotrope?
a10   *What was a matchlock?*
a11   What is mescalin?
b11   *What is a firkin?*
a12   What is a periwinkle?
b12   *What is a porringer?*

No. 44 Answers

a1   Motor car (Model T Ford)

b1   *Hairstyle*

a2   A festival or holiday

b2   *A wig*

a3   Mixture of two or more metals

b3   *A tooth (a tooth used for cutting)*

a4   Use of a wrong word (as in: 'Faith, hope, and chastity')

b4   *Word or abbreviation made up of initial letters of full names (e.g. NATO, ERNIE)*

a5   Fish

b5   *A jellyfish*

a6   A learned woman or girl (a female student)

b6   *Bean (vegetable)*

a7   German fighter plane (*accept*: bubble car)

b7   *A plant (it eats insects)*

a8   Art of growing plants without soil (i.e. with water)

b8   *Fireworks; a display of fireworks*

a9   Poverty; being very poor

b9   *Beauty (especially in a woman)*

a10   Plant/flower

b10   *Gun (fired by lighting a fuse)*

a11   A drug

b11   *Barrel or small cask (or a measure of liquids)*

a12   Flower or small snail or seafood

b12   *Small basin*

Tie-breaker

Q What is serendipity?

A *The ability to make happy (and unexpected) discoveries by luck or chance*

No. 45 Catch Phrases

a1 Which film comedians are associated with the phrase, 'That's another fine mess you got me in'?

b1 *With which famous detective do you associate the phrase, 'Elementary, my dear Watson'?*

a2 In which TV show did we first hear the phrase, 'Exterminate!'?

b2 *Which sportsman first said, 'I am the greatest'?*

a3 Which comedian was associated with the catch phrase, 'There's no answer to that'?

b3 *With whom do we associate the phrase, 'I wanna tell you a story'?*

a4 With which comedian do you associate the catch phrase, 'It's the way I tell 'em'?

b4 *Which film star is associated with the phrase 'You dirty rat, you'?*

a5 Which entertainer is associated with the phrase, 'Nice to see you, to see you nice'?

b5 *Which comedian's catch phrase was 'You lucky people'?*

a6 Whose catch phrase was 'Wakey, wakey!'?

b6 *Whose catch phrase was 'Hello, playmates'?*

a7 Whose catch phrase was, 'Oo, you are awful, but I like you'?

b7 *Which comedian is famous for opening his act, 'Hello Missus, have you ever been tickled'?*

a8 In which radio programme did we hear the catch phrase: 'Are you sitting comfortably?'

b8 *In which radio programme did we hear the catch phrase: 'He's fallen in the water'?*

a9 With which comedian do you associate the catch phrase, 'Now there's a funny thing!'?

b9 *Who is linked with the phrase, 'Come up and see me sometime'?*

a10 Which entertainer is associated with the phrase, 'Have you ever had any embarrassing moments?'?

b10 *On which TV show did Bob Monkhouse say, 'Bernie, the bolt!'?*

a11 With which comedian do you associate the catch phrase, 'The day war broke out'?

b11 *In which TV show did we first hear the phrase, 'Open the box'?*

a12 Whose catch phrase was 'Can I do you now, Sir'?

b12 *Which comedian had the catch phrase 'Can you hear me, Mother?'?*

No. 45 Answers

a1   Laurel and Hardy
b1   *Sherlock Holmes*
a2   Dr Who
b2   *Muhammed Ali (Cassius Clay)*
a3   Eric Morecambe
b3   *Max Bygraves*
a4   Frank Carson
b4   *James Cagney*
a5   Bruce Forsyth
b5   *Tommy Trinder*
a6   Billy Cotton
b6   *Arthur Askey*
a7   Dick Emery
b7   *Ken Dodd*
a8   'Listen With Mother'
b8   *'The Goon Show'*
a9   Max Wall
b9   *Mae West*
a10   Wilfred Pickles
b10   *'The Golden Shot'*
a11   Robb Wilton
b11   *'Take Your Pick'*
a12   Mrs Mopp (in the radio programme ITMA) (played by Dorothy Summers)
b12   *Sandy Powell*

Tie-breaker

Q   With which comedian was associated the catch phrase, 'I won't take me coat off, I'm not stopping'?
A   *Ken Platt*

No. 46 Classroom Clash!

a1   What is the female equivalent of a tsar?

b1   *What is the male equivalent of a ranee?*

a2   What word do we use to mean a number of arrows?

b2   *What do we call a number of geese?*

a3   Which part of speech can be used to stand instead of a noun?

b3   *Which part of speech is used to link two words or phrases together?*

a4   With which area do we associate the Geordie dialect?

b4   *With which city do we associate the Scouse dialect?*

a5   According to the saying, where do fools rush in?

b5   *According to the proverb, what kind of wind blows no good?*

a6   According to the proverb, what does familiarity breed?

b6   *According to the proverb, if a penny is wise, what is a pound?*

a7   What would you measure in hectares?

b7   *What is measured in British Thermal Units?*

a8   What name is given to the unit of electrical power?

b8   *Into which two elements is water divided by electrolysis?*

a9   In the world of computing, what is a bug?

b9   *Which letter of the alphabet is used as a measure of the size of a computer's memory?*

a10   Colloquially speaking, what do we mean when we talk about a swan song?

b10   *What are crocodile tears?*

a11   For what are the initials DSC an abbreviation?

b11   *For what do the initials ESP stand for?*

a12   What is the third letter of the Greek alphabet?

b12   *The fourth letter of the Greek alphabet is also a geographical term. What is it?*

No. 46 Answers

a1	Tsarina
b1	*Rajah*
a2	A flight (*accept*: quiver)
b2	*A gaggle*
a3	Pronoun
b3	*Conjunction (accept: relative pronoun)*
a4	Tyneside; NE England
b4	*Liverpool*
a5	Where angels fear to tread
b5	*An ill wind*
a6	Contempt
b6	*Foolish (Penny wise, pound foolish)*
a7	Area, (land, ground, fields, etc)
b7	*Heat (accept: 'heat energy') (do not accept 'temperature')*
a8	Watt
b8	*Hydrogen and oxygen*
a9	An error in a program
b9	*K*
a10	Farewell performance or speech
B10	*False tears or false sorrow*
a11	Distinguished Service Corps
b11	*Extra Sensory Perception*
a12	Gamma
b12	*Delta*

Tie-breaker

Q   Which Greek mathematician discovered the principle that the apparent loss of weight of a body immersed in fluid is equal to the weight of the fluid displaced?

A   *Archimedes*

No. 47 The Three Rs

a1   What do we call a number of lions?

b1   *What do we call a herd of whales?*

a2   What is a female sheep called?

b2   *Hart and hind are the male and female of which animal?*

a3   What can travel by conduction, convection, and radiation?

b3   *In chemistry, what do we call a substance which cannot be split into simpler substances?*

a4   What can you do if you are bilingual?

b4   *What is French for the number twenty?*

a5   According to the proverb, at what do drowning men clutch?

b5   *According to the proverb, what happens to a fool and his money?*

a6   According to the proverb, what do you do if you spare the rod?

b6   *According to the proverb, who blames his tools?*

a7   In mathematics, what is an improper fraction?

b7   *In which branch of mathematics would you be working if you were dealing with the sine, cosine, and tangent of angles?*

a8   What do we call a number which cannot be divided by another number (except one) without leaving a remainder?

b8   *What do we call the calculating instrument which consists of two logarithm scales moving alongside each other?*

a9   Colloquially speaking, what is a snake in the grass?

b9   *What do we mean when we talk about a red herring?*

a10   What do we mean if we say something is pukka?

b10   *What is hocus-pocus?*

a11   During the Second World War, what did the letters ARP stand for?

b11   *For what do the initials FRS stand?*

a12   Which letter of the alphabet is used to describe a soft lead pencil?

b12   *How many consonants are there in our alphabet?*

No. 47 Answers

a1 A pride

b1 *A school (Accept: a gam)*

a2 Ewe (or tup)

b2 *Deer (especially red deer)*

a3 Heat

b3 *Element*

a4 Use two languages (fluently)

b4 *Vingt*

a5 Straws

b5 *They're soon parted*

a6 Spoil the child

b6 *A bad workman*

a7 A fraction greater than one, e.g. $\frac{9}{5}$

b7 *Trigonometry*

a8 Prime number

b8 *Slide rule*

a9 A traitor; someone who betrays you

b9 *A false scent, to divert attention*

a10 Of high quality, genuine

b10 *Deception, conjuring, jugglery*

a11 Air Raid Precautions

b11 *Fellow of the Royal Society*

a12 B

b12 *Twenty-one*

Tie-breaker

Q What do we call a substance that aids chemical change in other elements, without being affected itself?

A *Catalyst*

No. 48 Nicknames

a1   Which bird is often known by the nickname Polly?

b1   *Which animal often has the nickname Bruin?*

a2   Which animal is often nicknamed Brock?

b2   *Which animal is often called the King of Beasts?*

a3   What is a copper's nark?

b3   *Who was known as the Lady with the Lamp?*

a4   With which country do you associate the name Springboks?

b4   *What nationality is suggested by the nickname Limey?*

a5   In the last century, who were nicknamed Peelers?

b5   *To an Australian, what is a wool-grower?*

a6   Who was nicknamed the Brown Bomber?

b6   *Which cricketer was known by his initials, WG?*

a7   According to the Germans, who were the Ladies from Hell?

b7   *In World War 2, what was the nickname of the 7th Armoured Division in the Western Desert?*

a8   Which English leader was nicknamed Old Noll?

b8   *Which French king was nicknamed the Sun King?*

a9   Who was known as the Iron Duke?

b9   *Which newspaper was once nicknamed The Thunderer?*

a10   What nickname was given to the unidentified criminal who murdered women in Whitechapel in London in 1888?

b10   *By what name do we remember six Dorset labourers transported 150 years ago, for trying to form a trade union?*

a11   Which comedian was known as the Prime Minister of Mirth?

b11   *Which country is sometimes called the Roof of the World?*

a12   What is Davy Jones's Locker?

b12   *What are Mother Carey's Chickens?*

No. 48 Answers

a1 Parrot
b1 *Bear*
a2 Badger
b2 *Lion*
a3 A spy, an informer
b3 *Florence Nightingale*
a4 South Africa
b4 *Englishman*
a5 Policemen (the force was founded by Sir Robert Peel)
b5 *Sheep farmer*
a6 Joe Louis
b6 *(William Gilbert) Grace*
a7 Highland soldiers, Scottish soldiers, kilted soldiers (World War 1)
b7 *Desert Rats*
a8 Oliver Cromwell
b8 *Louis XIV*
a9 Duke of Wellington
b9 *The Times*
a10 Jack the Ripper
b10 *Tolpuddle Martyrs*
a11 George Robey
b11 *Tibet*
a12 The sea (especially as a grave of drowned sailors)
b12 *Seagulls (or stormpetrels or snowflakes)*

Tie-breaker

Q Which singer was nicknamed the Swedish Nightingale?
A *Jenny Lind*

No. 49 Words from the Past

a1   What is the modern equivalent for the old-fashioned word, betrothal?

b1   *What is the modern equivalent for the old-fashioned word burgher?*

a2   In which country were there originally mandarins?

b2   *What do we now call a phonograph?*

a3   What is a modern equivalent for the word behest?

b3   *What is the modern equivalent for the word benison?*

a4   What was Ethiopia once called?

b4   *What was the former name of Iran?*

a5   By what name is Formosa now known?

b5   *By what name is Siam now known?*

a6   By what name is East Pakistan now known?

b6   *The Asian country of Myanmar was formerly known as what?*

a7   What is the modern equivalent for the old-fashioned word errant (as in 'knight errant')?

b7   *What is the modern equivalent for the old-fashioned word erstwhile?*

a8   What was the ancient Roman name for France?

b8   *What is the modern equivalent for the old-fashioned name Muscovy (as in 'Muscovy duck')?*

a9   What is the modern equivalent for the old fashioned name Hibernia?

b9   *Van Diemen's Land — what is it now called?*

a10 By what name is the ancient city of Byzantium now known?

b10 *What is the modern equivalent for the old fashioned name the Barbary Coast?*

a11 What is a modern word for pecunious?

b11 *For what is kine an old-fashioned name?*

a12 Which country was once called New France?

b12 *What was the African capital city of Harare formerly called?*

No. 49 Answers

a1 Engagement
b1 *Citizen (accept: townsman or woman)*
a2 China
b2 *Gramophone or record player (it often played cylinders rather than discs)*
a3 Order or command
b3 *Blessing*
a4 Abyssinia
b4 *Persia*
a5 Taiwan
b5 *Thailand*
a6 Bangladesh
b6 *Burma*
a7 Wandering
b7 *Formerly, a while ago*
a8 Gaul (Gallia)
b8 *Russian*
a9 Ireland
b9 *Tasmania*
a10 Istanbul
b10 *(North) African Coast*
a11 Wealthy
b11 *Cattle, cows*
a12 Canada
b12 *Salisbury*

Tie-breaker

Q What is the welkin?
A *Sky*

No. 50 The Common Factor

a1   What are humbugs, gobstoppers, and dolly mixtures?

b1   *15, 18, and PG are all classifications of . . . what?*

a2   What have these in common: granny, bowline, sheepshank?

b2   *What do these have in common: Cheshire, Leicester, and Cheddar?*

a3   What have these in common: Charnock Richard, Newport Pagnell, Watford Gap?

b3   *What have these in common: Central, Jubilee, and Bakerloo?*

a4   What have Powys, Gwynedd, and Clwyd in common?

b4   *What do Chester, Chessington, and Whipsnade all have in common?*

a5   Cumulus, stratus, and cirrus are all forms of what?

b5   *Blue, Killer, and Sperm are all types of what?*

a6   Back, Blanket, and Buttonhole are all types of . . . what?

b6   *Sheraton, Hepplewhite and Queen Anne are all types of what?*

a7   What have these in common: Ragged Robin, Lady's Smock, and Old Man's Beard?

b7   *What have the following in common: Effingham, Grenville, Benbow, and Collingwood?*

a8   Clouded yellows, painted ladies, and large whites are all types of what?

b8   *Razor, scallop, and cockle are all types of what?*

a9   What have these in common: Aston, Keele, and Sussex?

b9   *What have Thistle, Brent, and Ninian in common?*

a10   What are Stedman triples, Plain Bob Caters, and Gransire triples?

b10   *What are Sirius, Betelgeuse, and Alpha Centauri?*

a11   What have the following in common: Hastings, New Romney, Hythe, Dover, and Sandwich?

b11   *What have the following in common: Charing Cross, The Middlesex, and Guy's?*

a12   What have the following in common: Wryneck, Wheatear, and Corncrake?

b12   *What have the following in common: ink caps, death caps, and puff balls?*

No. 50 Answers

a1   Sweets

b1   *Films*

a2   They're all knots

b2   *All are cheeses*

a3   They're motorway service stations

b3   *They're London Underground Lines (tubes)*

a4   All are Welsh counties

b4   *They're zoos*

a5   Clouds

b5   *Whale*

a6   Stitches

b6   *(Antique) chairs (accept: furniture)*

a7   All are wild flowers

b7   *British admirals (accept: naval captains/commanders)*

a8   Butterflies

b8   *Shells, or molluscs*

a9   All are universities

b9   *All are (North Sea) oil fields*

a10   Ways of ringing church bells (or changes)

b10   *All are (bright) stars*

a11   Cinque Ports (the original five)

b11   *All are London hospitals or medical schools*

a12   They're birds (summer migrants)

b12   *All are mushrooms*

Tie-breaker

Q   What do these writers have in common: George Sand, Michael Strange, George Eliot?

A   *They're all women*

No. 51

a1   What is a yashmak?

b1   *What kind of clothing is a tam-o'-shanter?*

a2   Which American rodent is famous for building dams and felling trees?

b2   *What kind of mammal is a chamois?*

a3   Which is the main language spoken in Chile?

b3   *In which country is Flemish an official language?*

a4   In which country is Fingal's Cave?

b4   *In which country is the Dordogne?*

a5   In America, of what is the Pentagon the headquarters?

b5   *Which important event happened in Dallas, in November 1963?*

a6   What subject is covered by the magazine *The Lancet*?

b6   *By what abbreviation is an Electrocardiograph often known?*

a7   For what sport is Gordon Pirie remembered?

b7   *In which sport did Duncan Goodhew achieve fame?*

a8   In which Shakespeare play do we meet Shylock?

b8   *In which Shakespeare play do we meet two gravediggers?*

a9   What do we call the Italian city of Firenze? (*say*: Fi-ren-ze)

b9   *By what name is the city of Leningrad once again known?*

a10   Who was king of England from 1413 to 1422?

b10   *Who was king of England from 1135 to 1154?*

a11   In which art did Sir Ralph Richardson achieve fame?

b11   *Which French actor sang 'Louise' and starred in* Gigi?

a12   Which Eastern religion includes the caste system?

b12   *Which religious faith observes Yom Kippur?*

No. 51 Answers

a1 A veil or face covering (worn by Muslim women)
b1 *Hat, bonnet*
a2 Beaver
b2 *Goat*
a3 Spanish
b3 *Belgium*
a4 Scotland
b4 *France*
a5 Department of Defense
b5 *The assassination of President Kennedy*
a6 Medicine (Surgery)
b6 *ECG*
a7 Long-distance running
b7 *Swimming*
a8 'The Merchant of Venice'
b8 *'Hamlet'*
a9 Florence
b9 *St Petersburg*
a10 Henry V
b10 *Stephen*
a11 Acting/theatre
b11 *Maurice Chevalier*
a12 Hindu
b12 *Jewish, Hebrew*

Tie-breaker

Q The towns of Rochester, Chatham, and Gillingham are known collectively by the name of the river on which they stand. What is that river?

A *The Medway*

No. 52

a1 Which animal lives in a drey?

b1 *How does an elephant drink water?*

a2 According to the proverb, what happens when the cat's away?

b2 *According to the proverb, from what do great oaks grow?*

a3 When an American refers to the gas pedal in his car, what is he talking about?

b3 *What does an American mean when he talks of an elevator?*

a4 What is the name of the long robe or dress traditionally worn by Japanese women?

b4 *Which women traditionally wear a sari?*

a5 Which folk singer is primarily associated with the song, 'The Times They are A-Changin''?

b5 *Which pop group took its name from an unemployment benefit card?*

a6 Bavaria, Hanover, and Westphalia are all parts of which country?

b6 *Tuscany, Lombardy, and Sicily are all parts of which country?*

a7 In history, how many queens have ruled France?

b7 *Which country had eleven kings called Ramases?*

a8 What do we call the Chinese system of healing whereby needles are inserted into the body?

b8 *Do your eyes, ears, or knees particularly help you to keep your balance?*

a9 Which sport would you be most likely to see at both Cowdray Park and Hurlingham?

b9 *With which sport do you associate Royal Troon?*

a10 In which town did Jesus grow up?

b10 *In which river was Jesus Christ baptized?*

a11 Who wrote the poem that begins: 'It is an ancient Mariner, And he stoppeth one of three'?

b11 *Who wrote the poem that begins: 'Shall I compare thee to a summer's day'?*

a12 In which African country is the city of Ibadan?

b12 *In which African country is the city of Bulawayo?*

No. 52 Answers

a1	Squirrel
b1	*It uses its trunk to squirt it into its mouth* (accept: *through its mouth*)
a2	The mice will play
b2	*Little acorns*
a3	The accelerator
b3	*A lift*
a4	A kimono
b4	*Hindu* (accept: *Indian*)
a5	Bob Dylan
b5	*UB40*
a6	Germany
b6	*Italy*
a7	None (France has had no sovereign queens)
b7	*Egypt*
a8	Acupuncture
b8	*Ears*
a9	Polo
b9	*Golf*
a10	Nazareth
b10	*The Jordan*
a11	(Samuel Taylor) Coleridge
b11	*Shakespeare*
a12	Nigeria
b12	*Zimbabwe*

Tie-breaker

Q Which English landscape artist painted 'The Haywain' and 'The Cornfield'?

A *(John) Constable*

No. 53

a1   Which people originally wore moccasins?

b1   *Where would you wear a cummerbund?*

a2   What is a natterjack?

b2   *What is a Buff Orpington?*

a3   What is a cassock?

b3   *Who would be most likely to wear a tutu?*

a4   In the Old Testament, which son of David was famous for his wisdom?

b4   *On which mountain was Moses given the ten commandments?*

a5   In cricket, which county plays at home at Edgbaston?

b5   *Which county cricket team plays at home at Old Trafford?*

a6   On which radio programme did we meet Frisby Dyke and Colonel Chinstrap?

b6   *On which radio programme did we meet Major Bloodnok and Henry Crum?*

a7   In which country is the port of Dubrovnik?

b7   *In which country is the spa town, Baden-Baden?*

a8   Who was the last Roman Catholic king of England?

b8   *Which Tudor king came to the throne at the age of ten?*

a9   In which Shakespeare play does a forest move?

b9   *Which of Shakespeare's plays involves a pound of flesh?*

a10   Which American president was assassinated in a theatre?

b10   *Which American president was sometimes called 'Ike'?*

a11   In which art did Lord Olivier achieve fame?

b11   *For what was Isambard Kingdom Brunel famous?*

a12   With which part of the body is orthodontics concerned?

b12   *Which part of the body would be affected by astigmatism?*

No. 53 Answers

a1	American Indians (Red Indians)
b1	*Round the waist*
a2	A toad
b2	*Hen/domestic fowl*
a3	A full length plain coat, worn usually by a priest
b3	*Ballerina*
a4	Solomon
b4	*Mount Sinai*
a5	Warwickshire
b5	*Lancashire*
a6	'ITMA'
b6	*'The Goon Show'*
a7	Croatia
b7	*Germany*
a8	James II
b8	*Edward VI*
a9	*Macbeth* (Birnam Wood 'moves' to Dunsinane Castle)
b9	*'The Merchant of Venice'*
a10	Abraham Lincoln
b10	*(Dwight D.) Eisenhower*
a11	Acting (the theatre)
b11	*Engineer (building bridges, boats, railways, tunnels)*
a12	The teeth (correction of irregularities in position of teeth)
b12	*Eye*

Tie-breaker

Q What is the name of the tiny independent principality which is situated in the Alps and whose capital is the city of Vaduz?

A *Liechtenstein*

No. 54

a1 Of what are clogs traditionally made?

b1 Usually, what colour is a fez?

a2 In which country might you be entertained by geisha girls?

b2 What two-wheeled conveyance was drawn by a Chinese coolie?

a3 Where do mosquitoes lay their eggs?

b3 How does a grasshopper produce its distinctive sound?

a4 In America, what is a greenback?

b4 What do Americans often call a pack of cards?

a5 In dots and dashes, what is the morse code for the letter 'S'?

b5 In dots and dashes, what is the morse code for the letter 'O'?

a6 In which sport was Emil Zatopek famous?

b6 In which sport was Sir Donald Bradman famous?

a7 What is the federal capital of Australia?

b7 In Australia, of which state is Sydney the capital?

a8 Can you name two of the official languages of Switzerland?

b8 Which are the two main languages of Belgium?

a9 Where are your clavicles?

b9 What is the everyday name for your trachea?

a10 Which city is a holy one, for three religions?

b10 For what is Oberammergau famous?

a11 What was the surname of the poet whose first names were Wystan Hugh?

b11 What was the surname of the poet whose first names were Percy Bysshe?

a12 Of which country was Nefertiti once a queen?

b12 Which queen started a nursing service for soldiers?

No. 54 Answers

a1 Wood

b1 *Red*

a2 Japan

b2 *Rickshaw*

a3 In water

b3 *By rubbing its legs against its wings (accept: rubbing its legs together)*

a4 USA bank note; 1-dollar bill

b4 *A deck*

a5 Dot dot dot (...)

b5 *Dash dash dash (---)*

a6 Athletics (running)

b6 *Cricket*

a7 Canberra

b7 *New South Wales*

a8 French, German, Italian, Romansch

b8 *Flemish and French (accept: Dutch and French) (Walloon instead of French)*

a9 At the base of your neck (collar bones)

b9 *Windpipe*

a10 Jerusalem (Christian, Jewish, Muslim)

b10 *Its passion play (held every ten years)*

a11 Auden

b11 *Shelley*

a12 Egypt

b12 *Queen Alexandra*

Tie-breaker

Q In the Old Testament, which leader of the Jews heard a voice coming from a burning bush?

A Moses

No. 55

a1 Which singer first had hits with 'Catch a Falling Star' and 'Magic Moments'?

b1 *Who was known as 'The Old Groaner'?*

a2 Which London football club plays at home at White Hart Lane'?

b2 *Which soccer team is sometimes known as The Pensioners?*

a3 At the entrance to which harbour is the Golden Gate?

b3 *Of which American state is the capital Boston?*

a4 Angora, Chinchilla, and Dutch are types of which pet animal?

b4 *What kind of animals are Galloways, Charolais, and Simmentals?*

a5 Which city is the administrative headquarters of the Strathclyde region?

b5 *Which city is the administrative headquarters of Cumbria?*

a6 In which country would you be most likely to see a woman wearing a mantilla (say: 'man-tee-ya')?

b6 *In Scotland, what style of cloth was illegal from 1745 to 1782?*

a7 Which English king had the nickname the Hammer of the Scots?

b7 *Which English king was nicknamed Rufus?*

a8 Picardy and Brittany are both parts of which country?

b8 *Within which country was Azerbaijan a republic for much of this century?*

a9 What is the main language spoken in Mexico?

b9 *Of which language is Cantonese a dialect?*

a10 In the Bible, who was the Virgin Mary's husband?

b10 *How many Gospels are there in the Bible?*

a11 Whereabouts in your body is your tibia?

b11 *What is the everyday name for your larynx?*

a12 In which Shakespeare play comes the line: 'Ill met by moonlight, proud Titania'?

b12 *According to a famous speech by Shakespeare, how many ages of man are there?*

No. 55 Answers

a1	Perry Como
b1	*Bing Crosby*
a2	Tottenham Hotspur
b2	*Chelsea*
a3	San Francisco
b3	*Massachusetts*
a4	Rabbit
b4	*(Beef) cattle*
a5	Glasgow
b5	*Carlisle*
a6	Spain (veil or shawl)
b6	*Tartan*
a7	Edward I
b7	*William II*
a8	France
b8	*Soviet Union (USSR)*
a9	Spanish
b9	*Chinese*
a10	Joseph
b10	*Four*
a11	Shin
b11	*Voice (box)*
a12	A Midsummer Night's Dream
b12	*Seven*

Tie-breaker

Q If you stood on the Wirral and looked towards Wales, across the mouth of which river would you be looking?

A *The River Dee*

No. 56

a1 In Cockney rhyming slang, what is meant by 'dog and bone'?

b1 *In Cockney rhyming slang, what is meant by 'round the Johnnie Horner'?*

a2 On television, who played the scarecrow Worzel Gummidge?

b2 *Which actor played the manager of the television hotel Fawlty Towers?*

a3 What have the kiwi, emu, and penguin in common?

b3 *Percherons, Shires, and Clydesdales are all types of which animal?*

a4 In cricket, what is a pair, or a pair of spectacles?

b4 *In America, what is a faucet?*

a5 In America, what is a tuxedo?

b5 *Which are the two most famous cricket grounds in London?*

a6 In land area, which is the largest continent?

b6 *In area, which is the world's largest desert?*

a7 Who came to the throne on the death of Henry I?

b7 *Who came to the throne on the death of William IV?*

a8 In medicine, of what is dermatology the study?

b8 *Of what is pathology the study?*

a9 Of which country is Hanoi the capital?

b9 *Of which country is Lima the capital?*

a10 What was a farthingale?

b10 *What was a doublet?*

a11 Which season in the Christian Calendar comes just before Christmas?

b11 *In the Christian faith, which festival immediately follows Lent?*

a12 Who wrote *Paradise Lost*?

b12 *In a poem, which animal did Blake describe as 'burning bright'?*

No. 56 Answers

a1 Telephone

b1 *Round the corner*

a2 Jon Pertwee

b2 *John Cleese*

a3 All are birds that cannot fly

b3 *Horses*

a4 Scoring nought in both innings; scoring a duck in both innings of a match

b4 *A tap*

a5 Dinner jacket

b5 *Lords and the Oval*

a6 Asia

b6 *Sahara*

a7 Stephen

b7 *Victoria*

a8 The skin, *or* skin diseases

b8 *Diseases*

a9 Vietnam

b9 *Peru*

a10 A hooped under-skirt

b10 *A man's close-fitting jacket, usually waisted*

a11 Advent

b11 *Easter*

a12 John Milton

b12 *Tiger*

Tie-breaker

Q A British landscape artist, he became famous in later life for his paintings of sea and sky, including pictures such as 'Rain, Steam and Speed' and 'Snow Storm'. Who was he?

A *(Joseph Mallord William) Turner*

No. 57

a1   What are large whites and saddlebacks?

b1   *What kind of animal is a Suffolk Punch?*

a2   Which singer made famous the song 'Puppet on a String'?

b2   *In the pop song, what colour was the itsy bitsy teeny weeny polkadot bikini?*

a3   Which people speak Yiddish?

b3   *In which country is Afrikaans an official language?*

a4   Traditionally, who would wear a cap and bells?

b4   *Nowadays, who might wear a wimple?*

a5   Of which country is Jutland a part?

b5   *In which country is the Giant's Causeway?*

a6   Which king was responsible for building the Tower of London?

b6   *Can you name a battle in which an English king was killed?*

a7   In which American state is Long Beach?

b7   *In which American state is the city of Memphis?*

a8   With which sport do you associate Rosemary Casals?

b8   *With which sport do you associate Henry Cotton?*

a9   Where in your body is your frontal bone?

b9   *Whereabouts in the body is the thyroid gland?*

a10   Who wrote *The Compleat Angler*?

b10   *Who wrote* A History of the English-Speaking Peoples?

a11   In the Bible, Abraham was asked to sacrifice his son. Name his son.

b11   *In the Book of Genesis, a group of men built a tower. What was it called?*

a12   Which city was once called Sarum?

b12   *What was the city of Volgograd once called?*

No. 57 Answers

a1 Pigs
b1 *A horse*
a2 Sandie Shaw
b2 *Yellow*
a3 The Jews (*accept*: Slavonic people)
b3 *South Africa (accept: Namibia)*
a4 A jester (*accept*: a fool)
b4 *A nun*
a5 Denmark
b5 *Northern Ireland*
a6 William I (the Conqueror)
b6 *Battle of Hastings (Harold) or Battle of Bosworth (Richard III)*
a7 California
b7 *Tennessee*
a8 Tennis
b8 *Golf*
a9 Forehead
b9 *In the neck*
a10 (Izaak) Walton
b10 *(Sir Winston) Churchill*
a11 Issac
b11 *Tower of Babel (accept: Tower of Babylon)*
a12 Salisbury
b12 *Stalingrad (also once called Tsaritsyn)*

Tie-breaker

Q What was the name of the company founded in 1600, which later in effect became the ruler of a large part of India, until the Indian Mutiny?

A *East India Company*

No. 58

a1 Cob and Pen are the male and female of which bird?

b1 *In natural history, what do we call a male pea-fowl?*

a2 Which common garden bird is jet black, but has a yellow bill?

b2 *What sort of bird is a Cinnamon Norwich?*

a3 In Canada, of which province is Winnipeg the capital?

b3 *In Canada, of which province is Toronto the capital?*

a4 What were Oxford bags?

b4 *In the tropics, why are white clothes preferred to black ones?*

a5 In what kind of theatre did Vesta Tilley become famous?

b5 *If you drove from Portugal to France, which one intervening country must you cross?*

a6 Which country lies immediately south of Estonia?

b6 *In which American city is there a famous road called Pennslyvania Avenue?*

a7 In which city is a famous street called Wall Street?

b7 *In which sport is the US Masters a major competition?*

a8 In golf, what is a birdie?

b8 *In which of Bernard Shaw's plays did Eliza say, 'Not bloody likely'?*

a9 Who came to the throne on the death of Elizabeth I?

b9 *Who came to the throne on the death of James I?*

a10 What do your olfactory organs help you do?

b10 *Of what is obstetrics the study?*

a11 For how many days was Jesus tempted in the wilderness?

b11 *On which day does the Church celebrate the entry of Jesus into Jerusalem?*

a12 What is blank verse?

b12 *In a book, what is a frontispiece?*

No. 58 Answers

a1   Swan

b1   *Peacock*

a2   (Male) blackbird

b2   *Canary*

a3   Manitoba

b3   *Ontario*

a4   (Very wide) trousers

b4   *White reflects heat rays, black absorbs heat*

a5   Music hall

b5   *Spain*

a6   Latvia

b6   *Washington*

a7   New York

b7   *Golf*

a8   A hole done in one stroke under 'par' or 'bogey'

b8   Pygmalion

a9   James I

b9   *Charles I*

a10   To smell

b10   *Childbirth*

a11   Forty

b11   *Palm Sunday*

a12   Verse that doesn't rhyme (usually iambic pentameter)

b12   *A photograph or other illustration, usually facing the title page* (accept: *picture at the beginning*)

Tie-breaker

Q   In 1832 an American portrait painter set about inventing an electrically-based signalling system and later invented a code for sending messages? What was his name?

A   *(Samuel) Morse*

No. 59

a1 What do we call a large group of locusts?

b1 What do we call a large number of angels?

a2 In which city is the Parthenon?

b2 In which city is Sacré Coeur?

a3 In America, what was sold by a bootlegger?

b3 What is the American word for pavement or footpath?

a4 Fleetwood Mac had a hit with a tune named after a bird. What was it?

b4 Which pop group had hits with 'Let it Be' and 'Strawberry Fields Forever'?

a5 In which country are kiwis found?

b5 Which Australian bird is famous for laughing?

a6 If you left London on the M4, in which direction would you be going?

b6 If you were driving at 50 mph, at how many kilometres per hour would you be going (approximately)?

a7 In geography, what is a cataract?

b7 What is a tarn?

a8 Of which country was Mrs Bandaranaike Prime Minister?

b8 Of which country was Aldo Moro formerly Prime Minister?

a9 In which Shakespeare play does a character say 'Out damned spot'?

b9 In Shakespeare, who was prepared to give up his kingdom for a horse?

a10 Which soccer team plays at home at Carrow Road?

b10 Which soccer team plays at home at Ninian Park?

a11 What name is given to the area over which a bishop is in charge?

b11 Before a marriage in the Church of England, how many times must the banns be called?

a12 What is anthrax?

b12 What medical condition is caused by a lack of insulin?

No. 59 Answers

a1 A plague *or* swarm
b1 *A host*
a2 Athens
b2 *Paris*
a3 (Illegal) alcohol
b3 *Sidewalk*
a4 Albatross
b4 *The Beatles*
a5 New Zealand
b5 *Kookaburra*
a6 West (to Bristol, South Wales)
b6 *80 kph*
a7 Waterfall, downpour of rain, rush of water
b7 *Small mountain lake*
a8 Ceylon (now Sri Lanka)
b8 *Italy*
a9 *Macbeth (Lady Macbeth while sleep-walking)*
b9 *Richard III (Richard Crookback, Richard of Gloucester)*
a10 Norwich City
b10 *Cardiff City*
a11 Diocese *or* See
b11 *Three*
a12 A disease (often spread by cattle and horses)
b12 *Diabetes*

Tie-breaker

Q In which year was the kingship abolished and the reigning monarch beheaded?

A *1649*

130

No. 60

a1   On which animal would you normally use a curry-comb?

b1   *With which animal do you associate the word feline?*

a2   According to the proverb, if speech is silver, what is golden?

b2   *According to the proverb, which vessels make the most sound?*

a3   What is the background colour of a motorway sign?

b3   *According to the highway code, what does a double white line down the centre of the road mean?*

a4   In which city is the ship HMS *Victory*?

b4   *In which city is Topkapi?*

a5   In the Wild West, for what was Annie Oakley famous?

b5   *Which American folk-hero was 'King of the Wild Frontier'?*

a6   Who wrote the shows *The Dancing Years* and *King's Rhapsody*?

b6   *Who wrote the shows* Bitter Sweet *and* Private Lives?

a7   Which soccer team plays at home at Bramall Lane?

b7   *Which English soccer team plays at home at Molyneux?*

a8   Of which country is Manitoba a province?

b8   *Which province of Canada has a large French-speaking population?*

a9   Which English king died at the age of fifteen?

b9   *For how long did Lady Jane Grey reign?*

a10   In 1859, who wrote *On the Origin of Species*?

b10   *Who wrote* Mein Kampf?

a11   Which people would fast during Ramadan?

b11   *Which religious group wear their hair in 'dreadlocks' and use reggae music to express their beliefs?*

a12   What is the normal pulse-rate of a grown man?

b12   *What is the generally accepted normal human blood temperature?*

No. 60 Answers

a1	Horse
b1	*Cat*
a2	Silence
b2	*Empty vessels*
a3	Blue
b3	*No crossing of the white line*
a4	Portsmouth
b4	*Istanbul*
a5	Shooting: markswoman (she often used a playing card as a target)
b5	*Davy Crockett*
a6	Ivor Novello
b6	*Noel Coward*
a7	Sheffield United
b7	*Wolves (Wolverhampton Wanderers)*
a8	Canada
b8	*Quebec*
a9	Edward VI
b9	*Nine days*
a10	Charles Darwin
b10	*Adolf Hitler*
a11	Muslims (*accept*: Mohammedans, but qualify)
b11	*Rastafarians (accept: Rastas)*
a12	72 beats per minute (*accept*: 65–80)
b12	*98.4°F, 36.9°C (accept: 37°C)*

Tie-breaker

Q Which novelist created the characters, Michael Henchard, Tess, and 'Jude the Obscure'?

A (Thomas) Hardy

No. 61

a1 In which town does the annual Veteran Car Run end each year?

b1 *What make of car was the 1906 Silver Ghost?*

a2 Which is the southernmost point of South America?

b2 *In which continent is the Kalahari desert?*

a3 From which plant did the Egyptians make the first paper?

b3 *From the fibres of which plant is linen made?*

a4 In America, what is Airforce One?

b4 *What is the official national anthem of the United States of America?*

a5 Until his death in 1969, of which pop group was Brian Jones a member?

b5 *Which pop group has had hits with 'Shang-a-lang' and 'Summerlove Sensation'?*

a6 If you went to Wentworth, which sport would you be most likely to be going to watch?

b6 *In cricket, which county has played at home at Bramall Lane?*

a7 In Australia, of which state is Perth the capital?

b7 *In Australia, of which state is Melbourne the capital?*

a8 When Jesus was crucified, who was the Roman Governor of Jerusalem?

b8 *In the Bible, who was paid thirty pieces of silver?*

a9 Which word is used to denote a number of quails?

b9 *What is the collective noun used to describe a number of nightingales?*

a10 Over which country did the Ptolemies once rule?

b10 *Which Chinese leader was famous for his 'little red book'?*

a11 In which Shakespeare play do we meet Rosencrantz and Guildenstern?

b11 *In which Shakespeare play is Pistol forced to eat a leek?*

a12 With which profession is the Hippocratic Oath associated?

b12 *Of what is the Red Crescent the Muslim equivalent?*

No. 61 Answers

a1	Brighton
b1	*Rolls Royce*
a2	Cape Horn
b2	*Africa*
a3	Papyrus (*accept*: reeds)
b3	*Flax*
a4	The President's plane
b4	*'The Star-Spangled Banner'*
a5	The Rolling Stones
b5	*Bay City Rollers*
a6	Golf
b6	*Yorkshire*
a7	Western Australia
b7	*Victoria*
a8	(Pontius) Pilate
b8	*Judas Iscariot*
a9	A bevy
b9	*A watch*
a10	Egypt
b10	*Chairman Mao; Mao Tse-tung*
a11	'Hamlet'
b11	*'Henry V'*
a12	Medical (doctors)
b12	*The Red Cross*

Tie-breaker

Q Which European country was ruled by a military group called 'The Colonels' from 1967 to 1974?

A *Greece*

No. 62

a1 What kind of bird is a peregrine?

b1 *What kind of bird is an eider?*

a2 What is irrigation?

b2 *What name is given to the heavy summer rains in Asia?*

a3 What does or did a schoolchild mean if he or she said 'Fains'?

b3 *What do we mean if we describe someone as a pocket Hercules?*

a4 In which European country is the seaport of Malmö?

b4 *In which country is the port of Genoa?*

a5 Which English king was known as the Unready?

b5 *Which English king was known as Longshanks?*

a6 In the play *Pygmalion*, who was Eliza Doolittle's teacher?

b6 *On which children's book is A.A. Milne's play* Toad of Toad Hall *based?*

a7 Which is, or was, the home state of President Jimmy Carter?

b7 *Which American State was founded by the Quaker William Penn in 1682?*

a8 With which sport do you associate David Wilkie?

b8 *With which sport do you associate Jo Durie?*

a9 What is alopecia?

b9 *What kind of drug is an amphetamine?*

a10 With which holy city do we associate the name Zion?

b10 *With which musical instrument is David associated?*

a11 Who wrote *Das Kapital*?

b11 *Which Greek poet wrote* The Iliad?

a12 From which London station would you leave if you were travelling to Bournemouth?

b12 *From which London railway station would you leave if you were travelling to Norwich?*

No. 62 Answers

a1   Falcon (*accept*: bird of prey)

b1   *Duck*

a2   A system of watering land, crops

b2   *Monsoon*

a3   'Not I'; 'Bags not I'

b3   *He's small but strong*

a4   Sweden

b4   *Italy*

a5   Ethelred

b5   *Edward I*

a6   (Professor Henry) Higgins

b6   *'The Wind in the Willows' (by Kenneth Grahame)*

a7   Georgia

b7   *Pennsylvania*

a8   Swimming

b8   *Tennis*

a9   Baldness

b9   *Pep pill; stimulant; induces 'well-being'*

a10   Jerusalem

b10   *The harp (or lyre)*

a11   Karl Marx

b11   *Homer*

a12   Waterloo

b12   *Liverpool Street*

Tie-breaker

Q   The ceiling of the Sistine Chapel, the *Last Judgement*, and *David* are all famous works of which Italian artist?

A   *Michelangelo*

No. 63

a1 Which Scandinavian animals are famous for running over cliff tops?

b1 *What sort of animal is a cony?*

a2 In which city would you be if you were walking along Sauchiehall Street?

b2 *In population, which is Scotland's largest city?*

a3 What does an American mean when he talks of a sedan?

b3 *What does an American mean when he talks of a zip code?*

a4 Who was the lead singer of the group, The Who?

b4 *Who sang the title tune 'Bright Eyes' from the film Watership Down?*

a5 What is the capital of Malta?

b5 *What is the capital of the Falkland Islands?*

a6 What is meant by 'playing gooseberry'?

b6 *What would be the state of a person said to be in 'Carey Street'?*

a7 Of which country was Haile Selassie once emperor?

b7 *Of which country was John George Diefenbaker prime minister?*

a8 How many teeth should an adult have?

b8 *How many ribs do you have?*

a9 In which country does the Bengali language originate?

b9 *Swahili, Hausa, and Bantu are all native languages in which continent?*

a10 In which Shakespeare play do we hear about Yorrick?

b10 *In which play do Brutus and Cassius kill a noble Roman?*

a11 Horse racing: name two of the 'Classic' races.

b11 *Goodwood is famous for racing; where is Goodwood?*

a12 If you hope to get to Nirvana, what faith do you follow?

b12 *Of which religion is Zen a form or sect?*

No. 63 Answers

a1	Lemmings
b1	*Rabbit (usually an adult one)*
a2	Glasgow
b2	*Glasgow*
a3	A (saloon) car
b3	*Post code*
a4	Roger Daltrey
b4	*Art Garfunkel*
a5	Valletta
b5	*Port Stanley*
a6	Being a chaperone
b6	*Bankrupt*
a7	Ethiopia (Abyssinia)
b7	*Canada*
a8	32
b8	*24 (12 pairs)*
a9	Bangladesh (E. Pakistan)
b9	*Africa*
a10	'Hamlet'
b10	*'Julius Caesar'*
a11	Oaks, St Ledger, Derby, Two Thousand Guineas, One Thousand Guineas
b11	*Sussex (West Sussex, near Chichester)*
a12	Buddhism
b12	*Buddhism*

Tie-breaker

Q The novels *The Trumpet Major*, *Under the Greenwood Tree*, and *The Return of the Native* are all set in Wessex. Who is their author?

A *(Thomas) Hardy*

No. 64

a1   Which bird can hold up to three gallons of water in a pouch below its beak?

b1   *Which bird hammers holes in trees to extract insects from the wood?*

a2   In Cockney rhyming slang, what is meant by 'North and South'?

b2   *In Cockney rhyming slang, what is meant by 'plates of meat'?*

a3   Of which country is Freetown the capital?

b3   *Of which country is Kuala Lumpur the capital?*

a4   Which soccer team plays at home at Turf Moor?

b4   *Which football team plays at home at Stamford Bridge?*

a5   Of which American state is Honolulu the capital?

b5   *Of which American state is Phoenix the capital?*

a6   On what date do Burns Night celebrations take place each year?

b6   *If you go over the sea to Skye, to which group of islands are you sailing?*

a7   In which language did Aristophanes write his plays?

b7   *In which country did Noh plays originate?*

a8   From which London railway station would you leave if you were travelling to York?

b8   *From which London station should you leave if you were travelling to Carlisle?*

a9   What do we call the book that records a ship's progress at sea?

b9   *What does the reference book* Crockfords *list?*

a10   In which town or village did Jesus turn water into wine?

b10   *Before he became a disciple of Jesus, what was Matthew's job?*

a11   What is the name of the bone in your thigh?

b11   *Where is your epiglottis?*

a12   Whom did Edward VII marry?

b12   *Who was the first member of the House of Hanover to rule this country?*

No. 64 Answers

a1   Pelican
b1   Woodpecker
a2   Your mouth
b2   Feet
a3   Sierra Leone
b3   Malaysia
a4   Burnley
b4   Chelsea
a5   Hawaii
b5   Arizona
a6   January 25th
b6   (Inner) Hebrides
a7   Greek
b7   Japan
a8   King's Cross
b8   Euston
a9   The log
b9   The clergy of the Church of England
a10   Cana (in Galilee)
b10   Tax-collector
a11   Femur
b11   Back of your tongue (accept: throat)
a12   Princess Alexandra of Denmark
b12   George I

Tie-breaker

Q Who was the American patriot whose famous ride to warn the towns
of Lexington and Concord of the approach of British troops in 1775,
was later commemorated in a poem?

A *Paul Revere* (Paul Revere's Ride *by Longfellow*)

No. 65

a1   By what name are cavies often known?

b1   When a cow stands up, which legs does it get up on first?

a2   Which Indian city had an infamous Black Hole?

b2   Within which city is the Forbidden City?

a3   What do we call a group of partridges?

b3   What do we call a group of bishops?

a4   What is the background colour of road signs showing directions on primary roads (or A roads)?

b4   What is signified by a road sign which is a white capital letter 'R' on a green background?

a5   Can you name two seas which are named after colours?

b5   In area, which is the largest ocean?

a6   Of which country was Frederick the Great a king?

b6   Of which country was Archbishop Makarios prime minister?

a7   Which famous American Black Rights leader was assassinated in 1968?

b7   What do Americans celebrate on the 4th of July?

a8   For which county did Geoff Boycott play cricket?

b8   Which country was represented in the Olympics by the gymnast Olga Korbut?

a9   In your body, what do arteries do?

b9   Where does the alimentary canal begin?

a10   In the Old Testament, from which town did King David come?

b10   Which book in the New Testament describes the journeys of St Paul?

a11   Who wrote the play *Under Milk Wood*?

b11   Who wrote the play Androcles and the Lion?

a12   In Shakespeare, what is the name of the fat old knight who is a friend to Prince Hal?

b12   In a Shakespeare play, who kills Desdemona?

No. 65 Answers

a1	Guinea pigs
b1	*Back (hind)*
a2	Calcutta
b2	*Peking (also Lhasa, in Tibet)*
a3	A covey
b3	A bench
a4	Green
b4	*Ring road*
a5	Red, Black, White, Yellow
b5	*Pacific*
a6	Prussia
b6	*Cyprus*
a7	Martin Luther King
b7	*Independence*
a8	Yorkshire
b8	*Soviet Union (USSR)*
a9	Carry blood *from* the heart
b9	*At the mouth (passage through the body, through which food travels)*
a10	Bethlehem
b10	*Acts (of the Apostles)*
a11	Dylan Thomas
b11	*Bernard Shaw*
a12	(Sir John) Falstaff
b12	*Othello*

Tie-breaker

Q In science, what do we call the smallest possible unit of any substance, composed of a central nucleus surrounded by electrons?

A *Atom*

No. 66

a1 What was the occupation of the legendary 'Casey' Jones?

b1 *With which early American innovation do you connect Henry Wells and William Fargo?*

a2 Which football team plays at home at the Victoria ground?

b2 *Which soccer team plays at home at Portman Road?*

a3 In which film did Judy Garland sing 'Over the Rainbow'?

b3 *Who sang 'On the good ship Lollipop'?*

a4 Besides Venice, which European city is built on canals?

b4 *Which city was built on seven hills?*

a5 Which country does a car come from if it carries the International Registration letter 'L'?

b5 *Which country does a car come from if it carries the International registration letters 'CDN'?*

a6 What is the common name for the Crane Fly?

b6 *Which bird is often nicknamed 'Jenny'?*

a7 Where in the body is the humerus?

b7 *Whereabouts in your body is the bone known as the sternum?*

a8 Who is second in line to the throne?

b8 *Who was known as the Black Prince?*

a9 By what name is the Paris underground railway system known?

b9 *On a railway, why might you decide to travel in a wagon-lit?*

a10 On which sea is Venice situated?

b10 *In which ocean are the Azores?*

a11 Who wrote *A History of the Decline and Fall of the Roman Empire*?

b11 *Boswell wrote the biography of another famous writer. Who?*

a12 In the Bible, who said 'I find no fault in this man'?

b12 *What is the name of the hill where Jesus Christ was crucified?*

No. 66 Answers

a1	Railroad Engineer (*accept:* Engine driver)
b1	*Wells Fargo Express*
a2	Stoke City
b2	*Ipswich Town*
a3	'The Wizard of Oz'
b3	*Shirley Temple (Black)*
a4	Amsterdam
b4	*Rome*
a5	Luxembourg
b5	*Canada*
a6	Daddy Long Legs
b6	*Wren*
a7	Upper arm
b7	*Centre of the chest*
a8	Prince William
b8	*Edward Prince of Wales (Son of Edward III)*
a9	The Metro
b9	*Because you wanted to go to sleep; it's a sleeping car*
a10	Adriatic
b10	*Atlantic*
a11	(Edward) Gibbon
b11	*(Dr Samuel) Johnson*
a12	Pontius Pilate
b12	*Calvary (or Golgotha)*

Tie-breaker

Q Which French artist painted the famous picture, 'At the Moulin Rouge'?
A *(Henri) Toulouse-Lautrec*

No. 67

a1   What cargo did the ship, the *Cutty Sark*, carry?

b1   *In 1787, on what ship did Fletcher Christian lead a mutiny?*

a2   What is a black widow?

b2   *In the world of insects, what is a Painted Lady?*

a3   From which musical comes the song
'Supercalifragilisticexpialidocius'?

b3   *Who played the title role in the film* Mary Poppins*?*

a4   According to the proverb, what is the mother of invention?

b4   *According to the proverb, what is the better part of valour?*

a5   On a car, what does a tachometer show?

b5   *What do we call the part of the car which mixes air with petrol to
form an explosive mixture?*

a6   Of which country was Golda Meir once prime minister?

b6   *In 1946, which country's emperor was made to renounce his
supposed divinity?*

a7   In which Shakespeare play do two housewives make a fool of
Falstaff?

b7   *In which Shakespeare play do we meet Ophelia?*

a8   Of which American state is Little Rock the capital?

b8   *Of which American state is Salt Lake City the capital?*

a9   What part of your body would be affected if you were suffering from
myopia?

b9   *What do we call the coloured part of the eye?*

a10 Of which country is Dynamo Zagreb an association football team?

b10 *Of which country is Ajax a famous football team?*

a11 What happens at an ordination ceremony?

b11 *What do Roman Catholics call the state or place where souls are
purified after death?*

a12 In which country is the city of Jakarta?

b12 *In which country is Casablanca?*

No. 67 Answers

a1 Tea

b1 *HMS* Bounty

a2 Spider (it is *not* an insect)

b2 *Butterfly*

a3 'Mary Poppins'

b3 *Julie Andrews*

a4 Necessity

b4 *Discretion*

a5 Engine speed; number of engine revolutions per minute

b5 *Carburettor*

a6 Israel

b6 *Japan's (Hirohito)*

a7 'The Merry Wives of Windsor'

b7 *'Hamlet'*

a8 Arkansas

b8 *Utah*

a9 Eyes (short sighted)

b9 *Iris*

a10 Yugoslavia

b10 *Holland (the Netherlands)*

a11 A person is made a priest (or clergyman, etc.); admitted to holy orders

b11 *Purgatory*

a12 Indonesia

b12 *Morocco*

Tie-breaker

Q Who was born in Hull in 1759, spent much of his life fighting slavery, and lived to see the slave trade abolished in 1806?

A *(William) Wilberforce*

No. 68

a1 Blue, Great, Coal, and Long-tailed are all types of which kind of bird?

b1 *Iceland, Herring, and Blackheaded are all types of which bird?*

a2 In which city would you find the Doge's Palace?

b2 *Which famous tower opened in 1889?*

a3 When you're driving a car in Britain, what is the hand signal for turning left?

b3 *What is the road sign meaning 'No Entry'?*

a4 What is an ebb tide?

b4 *What do we call an area of water separated from the open sea by a coral reef?*

a5 In the 1920s, which American city was dominated by Al Capone?

b5 *In which month do Americans hold Thanksgiving Day?*

a6 Whereabouts in your leg is your fibula?

b6 *Which part of the body is described by the word labial?*

a7 Which British king reigned from 1820 to 1830?

b7 *Who was the mother of the first Queen Elizabeth?*

a8 To what does the adjective crepuscular refer?

b8 *If you're lachrymose, what do you tend to do?*

a9 In the theatre, for what is Marcel Marceau famous?

b9 *As what did Grimaldi achieve fame?*

a10 What sort of book was compiled by Moody and Sankey?

b10 *In* A Midsummer Night's Dream, *what happens to Bottom's head?*

a11 Which biblical king had to preside over a law case in which two women both wanted the same baby?

b11 *Which bird did Noah first send out of the Ark?*

a12 In which sport would you be taking part if you wore the 'yellow jersey' or *le maillot jaune?*

b12 *Which sport can take place on ice, sand, or water?*

No. 68 Answers

a1   Tit

b1   *Gull*

a2   Venice (there is another in Genoa)

b2   *Eiffel Tower*

a3   Turning your right arm in a circle

b3   *Red disc, with white bar*

a4   Falling tide, sea going out

b4   *Lagoon*

a5   Chicago

b5   *November (fourth Thursday)*

a6   Lower leg, shin, below the knee

b6   *The lips; of the lips*

a7   George IV

b7   *Anne Boleyn*

a8   Evening

b8   *Cry a lot*

a9   Mime

b9   *Clown (pantomime)*

a10   Hymn book

b10   *It is turned into an ass's head*

a11   Solomon

b11   *Raven*

a12   Cycle races (especially Tour de France or Milk Race)

b12   *Yachting (sailing)*

Tie-breaker

Q   Which novelist wrote the books *Howard's End* and *Where Angels Fear to Tread?*

A   *E. M. Forster*

No. 69

a1 In which London square were nightingales supposed to sing?

b1 In which capital city can you walk along Princes Street and the Royal Mile?

a2 In a rattlesnake, where is its rattle?

b2 Which is Britain's only poisonous snake?

a3 In cricket, how many balls are there usually in an over?

b3 Which wood is traditionally used to make cricket bats?

a4 Which river flows through the famous Grand Canyon in America?

b4 Of which American State is Long Island a part?

a5 What disease afflicts deep-sea divers who rise to the surface too quickly?

b5 By what other name is the disease rubella often known?

a6 Of which country is the Murray River the chief river?

b6 On which river is the Aswan Dam?

a7 In which West Country city is there a railway station called St David's?

b7 In which American city is Grand Central Station?

a8 Who co-starred with Celia Johnson in the film *Brief Encounter*?

b8 Who was Vivien Leigh's co-star in the film Gone with the Wind?

a9 Which soccer team plays at home at Ibrox Park?

b9 Which team has its ground at Highbury?

a10 Which empire was ruled by Titus?

b10 In the fifth century, who was the famous king of the Huns who laid waste much of Europe?

a11 What is a dumb waiter?

b11 In Australia, what is a jumbuck?

a12 Which Irish saint founded a monastery on the island of Iona?

b12 Which Welsh saint has given his name to a tiny cathedral city in north Wales?

No. 69 Answers

a1	Berkeley Square
b1	*Edinburgh*
a2	In its tail (horny pieces that vibrate)
b2	*Adder (or viper)*
a3	Six
b3	*Willow*
a4	Colorado River
b4	*New York*
a5	The bends (Caisson disease)
b5	*German measles*
a6	Australia
b6	*Nile*
a7	Exeter
b7	*New York*
a8	Trevor Howard
b8	*Clark Gable*
a9	Glasgow Rangers
b9	*Arsenal*
a10	Roman
b10	*Attila*
a11	A lift (for food in a restaurant) *or* (a small table that turns ona fixed base)
b11	*Sheep*
a12	St Columba
b12	*St Asaph*

Tie-breaker

Q In the English Civil War, which side was victorious in the Battle of Marston Moor and in the final Battle of Naseby?

A *Parliamentarians (accept: Cromwell, Puritans, Roundheads, Ironsides)*

No. 70

a1   On the edge of which desert is the city of Timbuctoo?

b1   Which wall is about 1,500 miles long?

a2   What kind of animal is a Friesian?

b2   What kind of creature is a gecko?

a3   What is the name of the famous active volcano on the island of Sicily?

b3   What do we call the molten rocks that pour out of volcanoes?

a4   In the London theatre, which is the longest running play ever?

b4   Which bird is also the name of a play by Chekhov?

a5   If a farmer leaves a field to lie fallow, what does he not do to it?

b5   If a person is garrotted, how are they killed?

a6   Which British city has a station called Temple Meads?

b6   From which London railway station do you normally travel to Bristol?

a7   Which young king of Egypt's tomb was discovered at Luxor in 1922?

b7   Of which ancient empire was Nebuchadnezzar king?

a8   Who is meant by the Fourth Estate?

b8   What is or was an Iron Horse?

a9   For which country did Franz Beckenbauer play?

b9   For which country did Denis Law play soccer?

a10   In the Bible, to which city was the traveller journeying in the parable of the Good Samaritan?

b10   To which town was Paul travelling when he was converted?

a11   If (in America) you were travelling by 'Am-Track', how would you be travelling?

b11   If in America you travelled by 'Greyhound', how would you be travelling?

a12   Which nation gave the Statue of Liberty to the United States?

b12   Where do the United States keep their gold reserves?

No. 70 Answers

a1   Sahara

b1   *Great Wall of China*

a2   Cow; a kind of cattle

b2   *Lizard (accept: reptile)*

a3   Etna (highest volcano in Europe)

b3   *Lava*

a4   *The Mousetrap*

b4   The Seagull

a5   Doesn't sow it; leaves it without a crop growing in it

b5   *Strangled (by a noose; originally by a metal collar)*

a6   Bristol

b6   *Paddington*

a7   Tutankhamen

b7   *Babylonian (accept: Sumerian or Chaldean)*

a8   Journalists; the press

b8   *Steam locomotive*

a9   West Germany

b9   *Scotland*

a10   Jericho

b10   *Damascus*

a11   Railway *(accept:* train, railroad)

b11   *By bus (long-distance coach)*

a12   France

b12   *Fort Knox (in Kentucky)*

Tie-breaker

Q   Which chemical element emits a greenish glow in air, and unless kept in water, burns of its own accord?

A   *(White) phosphorus*

No. 71

a1   Which city has or had the nickname of Auld Reekie?

b1   In which city is the famous Little Mermaid?

a2   In America, what was the Pony Express?

b2   Who made a famous 'last stand' at Little Big Horn in 1876?

a3   What kind of plant is Stink Horn?

b3   What kind of plant is maidenhair?

a4   What is the capital of New Zealand?

b4   Of which country is La Paz the capital?

a5   In which film did we first hear the Harry Lime theme?

b5   In the film Genevieve, what was Genevieve?

a6   Of which people is Romany the language?

b6   Which is the main language spoken in Hungary?

a7   Which British king reigned from 1830 to 1837?

b7   What was the name of the wife of Prince William of Orange, who became William III of England?

a8   In which English city are there railway stations called Oxford Road, Piccadilly, and Victoria?

b8   Which English city's main railway station is called New Street?

a9   What is a dramatis personae?

b9   What is meant by the phrase, bona fide?

a10   In which art has Barbara Hepworth become famous?

b10   In which art did Sir Henry Irving become famous?

a11   What sport would you practise if you were a toxophilite?

b11   In which sport might you win the Curtis Cup?

a12   In the Bible, who was the son of Elizabeth and Zacharias?

b12   Who asked for the head of John the Baptist?

No. 71 Answers

a1 Edinburgh
b1 *Copenhagen*
a2 A government mail system (before the days of railways and telegraphs)
b2 *General Custer*
a3 Fungus (*not* mushroom)
b3 *Fern (accept: grass)*
a4 Wellington
b4 *Bolivia*
a5 *The Third Man*
b5 *A veteran car (1904 Darracq)*
a6 Gypsies (travelling people, Romanies)
b6 *Magyar*
a7 William IV
b7 *Mary*
a8 Manchester
b8 *Birmingham*
a9 The list of characters in a play
b9 *Genuine; in good faith*
a10 Sculpture
b10 *Acting, theatre (also a theatre manager)*
a11 Archery
b11 *Golf (women's)*
a12 John (the Baptist)
b12 *Salome (accept: Herodias, her mother)*

Tie-breaker

Q On Richard Nixon's resignation in 1974, who succeeded him as President of the United States of America?
A Gerald Ford

a1   If you were suffering from *mal de mer*, from what would you be suffering?

b1   What is meant by jeunesse dorée?

a2   Which English city is famous for steel and cutlery?

b2   What was the name of the South American city of gold, which many explorers sought in vain?

a3   Which woman became Prime Minister of India in 1966?

b3   In 1979, who became leader of Iran?

a4   What is the official language of Mexico?

b4   In its own language, which country is called Cymru?

a5   Whereabouts on a horse are its withers?

b5   Whereabouts on a whale are its flukes?

a6   For what is Delft in Holland famous?

b6   In the world of antiques, for what has Dresden been famous since the eighteenth century?

a7   Who wrote the play *A Man for All Seasons*?

b7   Who wrote the plays Death of a Salesman *and* View from the Bridge?

a8   On a London underground map, what colour is the Northern line?

b8   On a London underground map, what colour is the Piccadilly line?

a9   Which American city is named after a British Prime Minister?

b9   Which American President's wife was known as 'Ladybird'?

a10 In astronomy, what are falling stars properly called?

b10 When the sun is at its zenith, where is it?

a11 Who was the first athlete to run the mile in less than four minutes?

b11 In ancient times, what was awarded to winning athletes in the Olympic Games?

a12 In the theatre, what colour costume is usually worn by a pierrot?

b12 In the theatre, what is vaudeville?

No. 72 Answers

a1 Sea sickness

b1 *Young people who are rich and/or fashionable (literally: gilded youth)*

a2 Sheffield

b2 *Eldorado*

a3 Mrs (Indira) Gandhi

b3 *Ayatollah Khomeini*

a4 Spanish

b4 *Wales*

a5 Shoulders (just above its shoulders)

b5 *On its tail*

a6 Pottery (blue and white)

b6 *China, porcelain*

a7 Robert Bolt

b7 *Arthur Miller*

a8 Black

b8 *(Dark) blue*

a9 Pittsburgh

b9 *(Lyndon) Johnson*

a10 Meteors

b10 *Directly overhead; at its highest point in the sky*

a11 Roger Bannister

b11 *A (laurel) wreath (sometimes an olive wreath)*

a12 White (with black pompoms)

b12 *Light entertainment (sequence of songs and sketches originally French music hall)*

Tie-breaker

Q In 1950, Ramadhin and Valentine took 59 test wickets when playing against England. For which test team did these two bowlers play?

A *West Indies*

No. 73

a1 Which creature's 'tears' are said to be a sign of insincere grief?

b1 Where does the primrose path traditionally lead?

a2 According to the proverb, what is the sincerest form of flattery?

b2 According to the proverb, what makes the heart grow fonder?

a3 From which animal do we get astrakhan?

b3 From which animal do we get ermine?

a4 What have the following in common: Hawes, Crummock, and Ullswater?

b4 What have the following in common: Hickling, Barton, and Breydon Water?

a5 Of which American state is Denver the capital?

b5 Until 1963, as what was Alcatraz famous?

a6 What have vertebrates got that invertebrates haven't?

b6 In the animal kingdom, what do herbivores eat?

a7 The Olivier, the Lyttleton, and the Cottesloe are all part of which famous building?

b7 Where is the Royal Shakespeare Company's London home?

a8 In which country is Havana?

b8 In which country is the city of Salzburg?

a9 In a car, what is the device called that secures electrical ignition?

b9 Where would you find a Dead Man's Handle?

a10 In politics, what other title is held by whoever is the First Lord of the Treasury?

b10 What is the popular name for the speech in which the Chancellor of the Exchequer introduces the Finance Bill?

a11 On which date each year does grouse shooting begin?

b11 In which season of the year is baseball played in North America?

a12 In which art did Diaghilev achieve fame?

b12 As what did Casanova become famous?

No. 73 Answers

a1 Crocodile
b1 *The everlasting bonfire (Macbeth) (accept: hell)*
a2 Imitation
b2 *Absence*
a3 Sheep (it's lamb skin)
b3 *Stoat*
a4 Lakes (in the Lake District)
b4 *Norfolk Broads*
a5 Colorado
b5 *Prison (island fortress)*
a6 A backbone (or spinal column)
b6 *Grass, plants*
a7 Royal National Theatre
b7 *The Barbican*
a8 Cuba
b8 *Austria*
a9 Sparking plug
b9 *In an electric train/tube train*
a10 Prime Minister
b10 *The Budget (speech)*
a11 August 12th
b11 *Summer (April–October)*
a12 Ballet (dance)
b12 *As a lover*

Tie-breaker

Q Who was the first woman MP to take her seat in the House of Commons?
A *Nancy Astor*

No. 74

a1 Before it is boiled, what colour is a lobster?

b1 *Usually, what two colours is a piebald horse?*

a2 Which important ship canal was built by Ferdinand de Lesseps?

b2 *Whose country home is Chequers?*

a3 From what do we get real pearls?

b3 *From what do we get saccharine?*

a4 What kind of animal is a merino?

b4 *What kind of animal is a predator?*

a5 What would a misogynist hate?

b5 *If you practise nepotism, who do you favour?*

a6 Which country does a car come from if it carries the International Registration letter 'D'?

b6 *Which country does a car come from if it carries the International Registration letters 'CH'?*

a7 By population, which is the largest city in the United States of America?

b7 *In 1906, which American city suffered a disastrous earthquake?*

a8 What is the name of the royal yacht?

b8 *Which American President had the first names John Fitzgerald?*

a9 What do you do if you take a siesta?

b9 *What is meant by the German word* kaput?

a10 In which sport does the Harlequin Club compete?

b10 *In which sport is the Waterloo Cup an important race?*

a11 What nationality was the playwright Ibsen?

b11 *Which Russian dramatist wrote the play* The Cherry Orchard?

a12 In the Bible, who turned into a pillar of salt?

b12 *Which Old Testament book is all about the sufferings of one man?*

No. 74 Answers

a1   Bluish-black
b1   *Black and white*
a2   Suez Canal
b2   *The prime minister's*
a3   Oysters (*accept*: clams, mussels)
b3   *Coal, coal tar*
a4   Sheep
b4   *One that preys on other animals*
a5   Women
b5   *A relative*
a6   Germany
b6   *Switzerland*
a7   New York
b7   *San Francisco*
a8   Britannia
b8   *Kennedy*
a9   Take a nap, a sleep, (at midday)
b9   *Done for; broken; finished*
a10   Rugby Union
b10   *Coursing*
a11   Norwegian
b11   *Chekhov*
a12   Lot's wife
b12   *Job*

Tie-breaker

Q   Which Austrian musician, while composing the opera *Don Giovanni* found time also to write *Eine Kleine Nachtmusik* (or 'A Little Night Music')?
A   *Mozart (Wolfgang Amadeus)*

No. 75

a1   Hybrid tea, floribunda, and musk are all types of which flower?

b1   *Broad, dwarf, and runner are all types of which vegetable?*

a2   Over a short distance, which is generally said to be the fastest land animal?

b2   *Nowadays, which is the largest land animal in the world?*

a3   What is meant by the Italian phrase *Che* (say: 'Kay') *sarà sarà?*

b3   *What is meant by the French phrase* Faux pas *(say: 'Foh pa')?*

a4   Which brothers starred in the films *Horse Feathers* and *Duck Soup?*

b4   *Which actress starred with Bing Crosby and Bob Hope in the 'Road' films?*

a5   In which country is the sea port of Alexandria?

b5   *Is the Horn of Africa in the north, south, east or west of the continent?*

a6   For what achievement is Valentina Tereshkova famous?

b6   *In what way did a Russian dog called Laika achieve fame?*

a7   On which river does swan-upping take place?

b7   *Which range of mountains is known as the Backbone of England?*

a8   Which British city has stations called Haymarket and Waverley?

b8   *In which city are there stations called Central, Moor Street, and Lime Street?*

a9   Which prime minister received a promise of 'peace in our time' in 1938?

b9   *Which prime minister made famous the phrase, 'You've never had it so good'?*

a10   In 1966, which team did England beat to win the Final of the World Cup?

b10   *What do we call the lightest weight in boxing?*

a11   Which country's ruler has a retreat called Camp David?

b11   *In America, who or what was Senator McCarthy hunting in his so-called witch-hunts?*

a12   In area, which is the largest railway station in Britain?

b12   *In which town or city would you be if you were driving along the Via Appia?*

No. 75 Answers

a1 Rose
b1 *Bean*
a2 Cheetah
b2 *Elephant*
a3 'Whatever will be, will be'
b3 *False step, mistake, clumsy behaviour*
a4 The Marx Brothers
b4 *Dorothy Lamour*
a5 Egypt (*or* United Arab Republic)
b5 *East*
a6 She was the first woman in space
b6 *The world's first space traveller (1957)*
a7 The Thames
b7 *The Pennines*
a8 Edinburgh
b8 *Liverpool*
a9 (Neville) Chamberlain
b9 *(Harold) Macmillan*
a10 West Germany
b10 *Flyweight (under 8 stones)*
a11 USA; America
b11 *Communists*
a12 Clapham Junction
b12 *Rome*

Tie-breaker

Q Which near contemporary of Shakespeare wrote the plays, *Tamburlaine* and *The Jew of Malta*?

A *(Christopher) Marlowe*

No. 76

a1 What is *joie de vivre?*

b1 *What is* carte blanche?

a2 What does an American mean when he talks of a diaper?

b2 *What does an American mean when he talks of a check, in a restaurant?*

a3 If you were using a spinnaker, what would you be doing?

b3 *In tennis, what is a let?*

a4 Westerns: what was the name of Gene Autry's horse?

b4 *Marion Morrison was the real name of which American film star?*

a5 How do marsupial animals carry their young?

b5 *What part of a creature is its mandible?*

a6 Roughly, where does the M5 go to and from?

b6 *In which direction from London would you travel to reach the North Downs?*

a7 If you flew in a straight line from Pakistan to Afghanistan, which one intervening country would you cross?

b7 *Which country lies immediately east of Iraq?*

a8 Of which country is the prime minister known as the Taoiseach (*say:* Tee-shock)?

b8 *Of which West European country is the Lower House of Parliament known as the Bundestag?*

a9 Which star is sometimes called the Lode Star?

b9 *Which planet is sometimes called the Red Planet?*

a10 For which parliament were direct elections first held in 1979?

b10 *In 1980, in which country did the Solidarity movement start?*

a11 In the Bible, who said, 'The serpent beguiled me and I did eat'?

b11 *In the Bible, at whose feast did writing appear on the wall?*

a12 For what did Augustus John become famous?

b12 *For what did Bela Bartok achieve fame?*

No. 76 Answers

a1 Joy of living

b1 A free hand; blank paper; scope to do what you like

a2 A baby's nappy

b2 The bill

a3 Sailing/yachting

b3 When a serve touches the net, but lands fairly ('Let' balls do not count)

a4 Champion

b4 John Wayne

a5 In a pouch

b5 Jaw (accept: mouth, beak, claw of a crab)

a6 The Midlands to the South-West (Birmingham to Bristol and Devon)

b6 South (south-east)

a7 India

b7 Iran

a8 Eire, Republic of Ireland

b8 Germany

a9 Pole Star, North Star

b9 Mars

a10 European Parliament

b10 Poland

a11 Eve

b11 Belshazzar's Feast

a12 Painter/artist

b12 Composer (musician)

Tie-breaker

Q Who was the son of an Ipswich butcher who became Archbishop of York, Lord Chancellor, and a cardinal?

A *(Thomas) Wolsey*

No. 77

a1   In the popular song, how many lovely black eyes were there?

b1   *According to the song, which road do I have to take to get to Scotland 'afore ye'?*

a2   According to legend, what are you meant to find at the end of a rainbow?

b2   *Which legendary bird rose from its own ashes?*

a3   What does a botanist study?

b3   *Whom might you expect to see working in a dig?*

a4   In 1871 which two explorers met at Ujiji, in Africa?

b4   *Which archbishop was murdered in the year 1170?*

a5   On what date is St George's Day each year?

b5   *What date is St Swithin's Day?*

a6   According to the proverb, what is better than no bread?

b6   *According to the proverb, what sweep clean?*

a7   For what does the abbreviation E and OE stand?

b7   *For what are the letters OM an abbreviation?*

a8   Which London building is nicknamed 'Ally Pally'?

b8   *Which London palace was destroyed by fire in 1936?*

a9   What do we call an angle of less than 90 degrees?

b9   *What do we call an eight-sided polygon?*

a10   What is shepherd's purse?

b10   *What is a corncrake?*

a11   In a children's story, what kind of creature is Baloo?

b11   *In a children's book, what kind of animal is Eeyore?*

a12   Who was commander of the Allied forces in Europe from 1943 to 1945?

b12   *Who was the victorious commander at the Battle of El Alamein?*

No. 77 Answers

a1 Two
b1 *The low road*
a2 Pot of gold
b2 *Phoenix*
a3 Plant life
b3 *An archaeologist*
a4 Stanley and Livingstone
b4 *Thomas à Becket (Archbishop of Canterbury)*
a5 23 April
b5 *15 July*
a6 Half a loaf
b6 *New brooms*
a7 Errors and Omissions Excepted
b7 *Order of Merit*
a8 Alexandra Palace
b8 *Crystal Palace*
a9 Acute
b9 *Octagon*
a10 Wild flower (*accept*: weed)
b10 *Bird (rail family) (also known as a Landrail)*
a11 Bear (Kipling's *Jungle Book*)
b11 *Donkey (Winnie the Pooh by A. A. Milne)*
a12 Eisenhower (General Dwight)
b12 *Montgomery*

Tie-breaker

Q What was the nickname of the English-speaking broadcaster from Germany in the Second World War who was hanged for treason at the end of the war?

A *Lord Haw-Haw*

No. 78

a1   From which country do we get Parmesan cheese?

b1   From which country does Gouda cheese come?

a2   Who wrote *Animal Farm*?

b2   Who wrote Cider with Rosie?

a3   Who usually lives at No. 11 Downing Street?

b3   Whose official residence is the Mansion House in London?

a4   Which musician is particularly associated with the tune 'Stranger on the Shore'?

b4   According to the song, how many trombones led the big parade?

a5   In olden times, what did you have to do at a turnpike gate?

b5   In history, what was jousting?

a6   What kind of animal is a Persian Blue?

b6   What kind of mammal is an Aberdeen Angus?

a7   Which day of the week is the Jewish Sabbath?

b7   Which day of the week is the Muslim holy day?

a8   Who first spoke of 'Government of the people, by the people, for the people'?

b8   Who claimed that 'History is Bunk'?

a9   If a ship runs up a plain yellow flag, what does it mean?

b9   At night, what colour light is shown on the starboard side of ship?

a10   Of which Second World War action was 'Operation Overlord' the code name?

b10   What killed over 70,000 people on 6 August 1945?

a11   In mythology, whose face launched a thousand ships?

b11   In mythology, who were the Amazons?

a12   Scientists: what did Galileo chiefly study?

b12   What does a meteorologist study?

No. 78 Answers

a1 Italy
b1 *Holland*
a2 George Orwell
b2 *Laurie Lee*
a3 The Chancellor of the Exchequer
b3 *Lord Mayor of London*
a4 Acker Bilk
b4 *76*
a5 Pay a toll
b5 *Mock battle on horseback*
a6 Cat
b6 *Bull/cow*
a7 Saturday
b7 *Friday*
a8 Abraham Lincoln
b8 *Henry Ford*
a9 There is no disease aboard; and it requires clearance
b9 *Green*
a10 D-Day; Allied Invasion of Normandy
b10 *The atomic bomb at Hiroshima*
a11 Helen (of Troy)
b11 *Strong, warrior women*
a12 Astronomy (*accept*: physics, telescopes)
b12 *The atmosphere* (accept: *the weather*)

Tie-breaker

Q For what did the German brothers Jakob Ludwig and Wilhelm Karl Grimm become famous?

A Grimm's Fairy Tales (accept: *Grimm's Law*)

No. 79

a1   When did a judge used to wear a black cap?

b1   *If libel is a written defamation, what do we call a spoken defamation?*

a2   According to the proverb, what is there 'twixt cup and lip'?

b2   *What will help pounds to look after themselves?*

a3   What does a cook mean by a *vol au vent*?

b3   *In cooking, what is meant by* bouquet garni?

a4   In the First World War, for what was Baron von Richthofen famous?

b4   *In which country was the Battle of the Somme fought?*

a5   Which is the tallest existing mammal?

b5   *Which is the smallest bird?*

a6   Who wrote the novels *The Spy Who Came in From the Cold* and *Tinker, Tailor, Soldier, Spy*?

b6   *Who wrote the book* The Cruel Sea?

a7   Which south coast seaside resort is famous for its Royal Pavilion?

b7   *In which English city is there a cathedral known as 'Paddy's Wigwam'?*

a8   Who composed the opera *Carmen*?

b8   *Who composed the opera* The Tales of Hoffman?

a9   Which year was the Battle of Waterloo?

b9   *In which year did the Battle of Trafalgar take place?*

a10   In mythology, of what were the Pipes of Pan made?

b10   *In mythology, what happened to anything that was touched by King Midas?*

a11   In a hospital, what is the job of an almoner?

b11   *Who uses a mahlstick (or maulstick) in their work?*

a12   Name four planets that move round the Sun.

b12   *Name four of the letters used in the Roman system of numbering.*

No. 79 Answers

a1   When sentencing someone to death

b1   *Slander*

a2   Many a slip

b2   *Looking after the pence*

a3   Light case of puff pastry, pastry case (usually filled with meat/fish/poultry in a creamed sauce)

b3   *Herbs, mixed herbs, sweet herbs*

a4   He was a fighter pilot

b4   *France*

a5   Giraffe

b5   *Humming bird (Helena's humming bird)*

a6   John le Carré

b6   *Nicholas Monsarrat*

a7   Brighton

b7   *Liverpool*

a8   Bizet

b8   *Offenbach*

a9   1815

b9   *1805*

a10   Reeds

b10   *It turned to gold*

a11   Social worker, medico-social worker

b11   *Painter (sign writer)*

a12   4 of: Mercury, Earth, Jupiter, Mars, Uranus, Pluto, Venus, Saturn, Neptune

b12   *I V X L C D M*

Tie-breaker

Q   Who was the Russian composer, (famous for a number of ballets, including *The Sleeping Beauty*) who died a few days after the first performance of his symphony the *Pathétique*?

A   *(Peter) Tchaikovsky*

No. 80

a1   What kind of food are *crêpes Suzettes*?

b1   *What are pretzels?*

a2   In olden times, for what was Tyburn famous?

b2   *Originally, who or what were camp-followers?*

a3   With which musical instrument is the name Bechstein usually associated?

b3   *Which pianist had hits with 'Side Saddle', 'Roulette', and 'Trampoline'?*

a4   On which date is St Patrick's Day?

b4   *Which saint's day falls on 30 November?*

a5   On a ship or boat, what is a painter?

b5   *On board ship, what is meant by the term bulkhead?*

a6   In Roman numerals, what is the answer to L minus XX?

b6   *In Roman numerals, what is L taken away from C?*

a7   Which monkey possesses a blood factor otherwise found only in humans?

b7   *Which bird has a brilliant blue-green plumage and dives for fish in a river?*

a8   From which port was the bulk of the British Expeditionary Force evacuated in 1940?

b8   *In 1942, which island was awarded the George Cross?*

a9   Who first said, 'Anybody who hates children and dogs can't be all bad'?

b9   *Who first sang, 'Like Webster's Dictionary, we're Morocco bound'?*

a10   In London, for what has Newgate been chiefly famous?

b10   *In which lane in the East End of London is there a famous street market?*

a11   In legend, who was the poet or magician at the court of King Arthur?

b11   *Whose wife was Guinevere?*

a12   In children's fiction, which bear came from Peru?

b12   *Who wrote about Tigger, Piglet, and Eeyore?*

No. 80 Answers

a1	Pancakes (usually with cointreau)
b1	*Savoury snacks; savouries*
a2	(Public) executions (*accept:* hangings)
b2	*People who followed armies (washer women, pedlars, prostitutes, etc)*
a3	Piano
b3	*Russ Conway*
a4	17 March
b4	*St Andrew's*
a5	Rope
b5	*Partition (wall)*
a6	XXX (30)
b6	*L (50)*
a7	Rhesus
b7	*Kingfisher*
a8	Dunkirk
b8	*Malta*
a9	W. C. Fields
b9	*Bing Crosby and Bob Hope*
a10	Prison, gaol
b10	*Petticoat Lane*
a11	Merlin
b11	*King Arthur's*
a12	Paddington
b12	*A. A. Milne*

Tie-breaker

Q Which British musician composed a number of operas including *The Perfect Fool* and an orchestral suite called *The Planets*?

A (Gustav) Holst

No. 81

a1   With which famous battle do we associate Biggin Hill?

b1   *Which part of the British Isles was occupied by the Germans during the Second World War?*

a2   According to the proverb, what is as good as a feast?

b2   *And also according to a proverb, what will fine words not butter?*

a3   What kind of food is gazpacho?

b3   *From which country does mousaka come?*

a4   What is the main diet of a koala bear?

b4   *Which mammal's survival would be threatened if there was a bamboo shortage?*

a5   In which country was there a group of warriors known as the Samurai?

b5   *What name was given to the medieval warlike expeditions to the Holy Land?*

a6   On which island is Queen Victoria's former home, Osborne House?

b6   *Which gorge is crossed by the Clifton Suspension Bridge?*

a7   In fiction, who lived in the stables at Birtwick Hall?

b7   *In* A Christmas Carol, *what is Scrooge's first name?*

a8   For what did Edith Piaf achieve fame?

b8   *And for what is Frank Lloyd Wright famous?*

a9   What would a subpoena normally require you to do (say: su-pee-na)?

b9   *If you have committed patricide, what have you done?*

a10   In our solar system, which planet takes the least time to orbit the sun?

b10   *Name a planet in our solar system which is surrounded by rings*

a11   What would an amanuensis do for you?

b11   *Where does a purser normally work?*

a12   In Greek mythology, of what was Eros the god?

b12   *What was the Roman name for Eros?*

No. 81 Answers

a1	Battle of Britain
b1	*Channel Islands*
a2	Enough
b2	*Parsnips*
a3	Soup (cold; tomato and onion)
b3	*Greece (accept: Turkey, the Middle East)*
a4	Eucalyptus leaves
b4	*The panda*
a5	Japan
b5	*The Crusades*
a6	Isle of Wight
b6	*The Avon Gorge*
a7	Black Beauty
b7	*Ebenezer*
a8	Her singing
b8	*Architecture*
a9	To appear in court
b9	*You have killed your father*
a10	Mercury
b10	*Saturn or Uranus*
a11	Write things down for you; copy written documents
b11	*On board ship*
a12	Love
b12	*Cupid*

Tie-breaker

Q Which fictional character composed a monograph on the ashes of 140 different varieties of pipe, cigar, and cigarette tobacco?
A *Sherlock Holmes*

No. 82

a1   What is a quail?

b1   What is a black mamba?

a2   What is a gavotte?

b2   What is a spinet?

a3   Of which political party were the Black Shirts a uniform?

b3   Of which political party were the Brown Shirts a private army?

a4   From which country does Camembert cheese come?

b4   From which country does Gruyère cheese come?

a5   Where in London is there a statue of Peter Pan?

b5   In which London building are most of the Promenade Concerts held?

a6   In legend, for what was Don Juan famous?

b6   Who was Oberon?

a7   What is the name of the cathedral in Venice?

b7   In Canada, of which province is St John's the capital?

a8   Who wrote *Gulliver's Travels*?

b8   Who wrote a famous novel about Kenilworth in Warwickshire?

a9   For what would you normally use the chemical DDT?

b9   What is EPNS?

a10   Which part of the United Kingdom has a bank holiday to commemorate the Battle of the Boyne?

b10   21 October commemorates a famous naval battle — which one?

a11   In which year was the first manned space flight?

b11   In which year did men first land on the moon?

a12   On board ship, what is meant by the term belay?

b12   On a ship, what is the manifest?

No. 82 Answers

a1   Bird (type of pheasant)

b1   *Snake (African)*

a2   A stately minuet (a dance)

b2   *Musical instrument (keyboard) (smaller than a harpsichord)*

a3   Fascist (especially Mussolini's Italian Fascists)

b3   *(German) Nazi party*

a4   France (Normandy)

b4   *Switzerland*

a5   Kensington Gardens

b5   *Albert Hall*

a6   Famous lover, seducer

b6   *King of the Fairies (especially* A Midsummer Night's Dream*)*

a7   St Mark's

b7   *Newfoundland*

a8   Swift (Jonathan)

b8   *Sir Walter Scott*

a9   To kill insects

b9   *Electro-plated nickel silver (actually there's no silver in it) (accept: Electro-plate)*

a10   Northern Ireland

b10   *Trafalgar*

a11   1961 (Yuri Gagarin)

b11   *1969*

a12   Make fast a rope

b12   *A (detailed) list of the cargo*

Tie-breaker

Q   In which of Dickens' novels do we read about Peggotty, Betsy Trotwood, and Uriah Heep?

A   *David Copperfield*

No. 83

a1   According to the proverb, when must you not count your chickens?

b1   According to the proverb, what might you as well be hanged for?

a2   What were Grants, Shermans, and Cromwells?

b2   What is an IRBM?

a3   What is meant by the Latin phrase *Quo vadis*?

b3   What is meant by the phrase tempus fugit?

a4   In Roman numerals, what is the answer to L plus L?

b4   Which month of the year was originally the tenth month of the Roman calendar?

a5   Name two types of weather that can be described as 'precipitation'?

b5   Can you name a hydrocarbon fuel?

a6   In which great mutiny was the Siege of Lucknow?

b6   In which city was General Gordon put to death?

a7   Which famous palace was built by Cardinal Wolsey and later given to Henry VIII?

b7   In 1969, which castle was the scene of the Investiture of the Prince of Wales?

a8   Whose cave inspired Mendelssohn to compose his Hebrides overture?

b8   Whose Piano Sonata No. 14 is known as the Moonlight Sonata?

a9   What kind of food is borscht?

b9   What kind of food is saveloy?

a10   What might you learn by the Pitman Method?

b10   With what would you be concerned if you were a member of the Howard League?

a11   Who wrote the novel *Bulldog Drummond*?

b11   Who wrote the novel My Friend Maigret?

a12   Which animal's name means 'river horse'

b12   Which animal's name means, literally, 'earth pig'?

No. 83 Answers

a1	Before they're hatched
b1	*A sheep as a lamb*
a2	Tanks
b2	*(Intermediate Range Ballistic) Missile*
a3	'Where are you going'?
b3	*'Time flies'*
a4	C (100)
b4	*December*
a5	Rain, sleet, snow, hail
b5	*Coal, gas, oil*
a6	Indian Mutiny (1857)
b6	*Khartoum*
a7	Hampton Court Palace
b7	*Caernarvon*
a8	Fingal's
b8	*Beethoven*
a9	(Russian) soup (beetroot, vegetables, etc)
b9	*Sausage (dry, cooked)*
a10	Shorthand/typing
b10	*Prison reform, penal reform*
a11	Sapper (Herman Cyril McNeile)
b11	*Simenon*
a12	Hippopotamus
b12	*Aardvark*

Tie-breaker

Q Besides being a very useful batsman, why did the cricketer Godfrey Evans win a place on the England team from 1946 to 1959?

A *He was a wicket keeper*

No. 84

a1   In a suit of armour, what is protected by the visor?

b1   What did a press gang do?

a2   Who is reputed to have said 'I really do not see the signal', while putting a telescope to his blind eye?

b2   Who first said 'I have nothing to offer but blood, toil, tears and sweat'?

a3   What is meant by the phrase *hors de combat*?

b3   What is a nom de plume?

a4   In law, what does a testator make?

b4   In court, who is the defendant?

a5   What was the name of Francis Drake's ship which sailed round the world?

b5   What was the name of the ship in which Captain Cook sailed to Australia?

a6   What kind of plants are basil, lovage, and sage?

b6   What kind of animal is a pipistrelle?

a7   In cookery, what is meant by coddling?

b7   What does the term sauté mean in cooking?

a8   Who wrote the Waverley novels?

b8   Who wrote the Barchester novels?

a9   Which Gilbert and Sullivan opera is set in Venice?

b9   In which Gilbert and Sullivan opera is there a 'Lord High Everything Else'?

a10   What is an equilateral triangle?

b10   In geometry, what is meant by concentric?

a11   Mount Ararat is the traditional resting place of which ship or boat?

b11   What sign did God give Noah that the Earth would not be flooded again?

a12   Of the Seven Wonders of the World, where were the Hanging Gardens?

b12   Of the Seven Wonders of the World, where was the Colossus?

No. 84 Answers

a1 Your eyes (*accept*: face — *not* head)

b1 *Kidnapped men to make them serve in the navy; recruited sailors*

a2 Lord Nelson

b2 *Sir Winston Churchill*

a3 Out of the battle/fight

b3 *Pen name, pseudonym*

a4 A will

b4 *The accused*

a5 *Golden Hind* (*accept*: *Pelican*; it was renamed the Golden Hind)

b5 *Endeavour*

a6 Herbs

b6 *A bat*

a7 Simmering for a short while (e.g. eggs)

b7 *Toss (in hot fat)*

a8 (Sir Walter) Scott

b8 *(Anthony) Trollope*

a9 *The Gondoliers*

b9 The Mikado

a10 One with all three sides of equal length (*accept*: one with three equal angles)

b10 *Having the same centre*

a11 Noah's Ark

b11 *A rainbow*

a12 Babylon

b12 *Rhodes*

Tie-breaker

Q One port on mainland France remained under British rule until it was taken by the French in the reign of Mary. Which port was it?

A *Calais*

No. 85

a1 In which town, in 1914, was an archduke assassinated?

b1 *In 1915, which British liner was sunk by a German submarine?*

a2 The word fauna is used to describe animal life. Which word describes plant life?

b2 *Which disease or virus was used to limit the number of wild rabbits?*

a3 What was a Sopwith Camel?

b3 *Whose aircraft was named 'Spirit of St Louis'?*

a4 Food: of which animal is a flitch a part?

b4 *What kind of meat is properly used to make Wiener Schnitzel?*

a5 What is a prima donna?

b5 *What is the beau monde?*

a6 According to the proverb, what do little pitchers have?

b6 *According to the proverb, which fruit tastes sweetest?*

a7 In which London park is Rotten Row?

b7 *In which London park is Birdcage Walk?*

a8 What was the trade of the famous Russian Fabergé?

b8 *Which trade is especially likely to use an awl?*

a9 By what name is Mid-Lent Sunday popularly known?

b9 *Traditionally, each harvest, what is made out of the last sheaf of corn?*

a10 Which famous wooden puppet was first written about by Carlo Collodi?

b10 *In a book, which shipwrecked sailor dreamed of toasted cheese?*

a11 In which year was the Franco-Prussian War?

b11 *Which war was fought in Southern Africa from 1899 to 1902?*

a12 Who composed Finlandia?

b12 *Who composed the oratorio Messiah?*

No. 85 Answers

a1   Sarajevo
b1   *Lusitania*
a2   Flora
b2   *Myxomatosis*
a3   Aeroplane (First World War)
b3   *(Charles) Lindbergh*
a4   Pig (side of a pig, bacon)
b4   *Veal*
a5   The principal singer in an opera; leading lady
b5   *World of fashion; 'society'*
a6   Long ears
b6   *Forbidden fruit*
a7   Hyde Park
b7   *St James's Park*
a8   Goldsmith (decorating gold eggs)
b8   *Leatherworker* or *shoemaker*
a9   Mothering Sunday (*accept*: Mother's Day)
b9   *Corn Dolly*
a10   Pinocchio
b10   *Ben Gunn (in* Treasure Island *by Robert Louis Stevenson)*
a11   1870
b11   *Boer War*
a12   Sibelius
b12   *Handel*

Tie-breaker

Q In which city were the 1972 Olympic Games held, during which eleven Israeli competitors were killed by terrorists?
A *Munich*

No. 86

a1   What would you keep in a menagerie?

b1   What is an amphibian mammal?

a2   To what might someone add a codicil?

b2   What is the legal term for telling lies under oath?

a3   On a ship, what is meant by abaft?

b3   On a ship, what is a block?

a4   What kind of alcoholic drink is Manzanilla?

b4   Which alcoholic drink is flavoured with juniper?

a5   Who discovered penicillin?

b5   What was pioneered by the Austrian physician Dr Mesmer?

a6   In which far eastern country was there war from 1957 to 1973?

b6   What tragedy occurred at Skopje in 1963?

a7   Who wrote the words, 'The workers have nothing to lose but their chains'?

b7   Who wrote 'I shall tell you a tale of four little rabbits whose names were Flopsy, Mopsy, Cottontail, and Peter'?

a8   What was the name for the ancient Egyptian good luck charm in the shape of a beetle?

b8   In the Bible, which rich queen made a famous visit to Solomon?

a9   With which musical instrument is Stephane Grapelli principally associated?

b9   With which musical instrument do we associate James Galway?

a10   In which of Dickens' novels do we read about Bill Sikes?

b10   In which of Dickens' novels do we read about Sam Weller?

a11   In South America, what kind of building is a hacienda?

b11   For what kind of building is Rievaulx in North Yorkshire famous?

a12   In the Second World War, in which country was the Anzio Landing?

b12   In which country was the Battle of Arnhem fought?

No. 86 Answers

a1	Animals
b1	*One at home on land or water*
a2	A will
b2	*Perjury*
a3	Astern
b3	*A pulley*
a4	Sherry
b4	*Gin*
a5	(Sir Alexander) Fleming
b5	*Hypnotism, mesmerism*
a6	Vietnam
b6	*Earthquake*
a7	Karl Marx
b7	*Beatrix Potter*
a8	The scarab
b8	*The Queen of Sheba*
a9	Violin
b9	*Flute*
a10	*Oliver Twist*
b10	The Pickwick Papers
a11	(Large) estate/farm house
b11	*Abbey*
a12	Italy
b12	*Holland*

Tie-breaker

Q In the sixteenth century, which Spanish soldier captured and then ruled Mexico?

A (Hernando) Cortes

No. 87

a1   In which month of the year does Father's Day occur?

b1   *In which part of the year is an Indian Summer?*

a2   According to the proverb, what does the early bird catch?

b2   *What can't you make out of a sow's ear?*

a3   Besides sugar, what is the principal ingredient of marzipan?

b3   *When made as a European dish, what are two of the main ingredients of a kedgeree?*

a4   Are sea-urchins animal, vegetable, or mineral?

b4   *Is an 'okapi' animal, vegetable, or mineral?*

a5   According to the song, during the war, on what were we going to hang out the washing?

b5   *Which wartime singer was nicknamed the Forces Sweetheart?*

a6   What is meant by *Répondez, s'il vous plaît* (say: 'Ray-pon-day see voo play')?

b6   *What is meant by the phrase* coup de grâce*?*

a7   What job is done by a horologist?

b7   *What does a lexicographer write or make?*

a8   What is anthracite?

b8   *What is chlorophyll?*

a9   Who wrote the three novels, *Lord of the Rings*?

b9   *Which writer created the character, Bertie Wooster?*

a10   At the end of what famous road in London is Buckingham Palace?

b10   *In London, on to which famous thoroughfare does Downing Street lead?*

a11   Which country won the battle of Poitiers?

b11   *Which country won the battle of Flodden?*

a12   If a violinist was playing *pizzicato*, what would he be doing?

b12   *In music, what is meant by* pianissimo*?*

No. 87 Answers

a1	June
b1	*Autumn*
a2	The worm
b2	*Silk purse*
a3	Almonds
b3	*Two of: fish, rice, eggs (as an Indian dish, kedgeree also has onions, meat, lentils)*
a4	Animal
b4	*Animal*
a5	The Siegfried Line
b5	*Vera Lynn*
a6	Reply, please (Reply, if you please)
b6	*Finishing stroke; mercy blow*
a7	He makes or repairs clocks (or watches)
b7	*Dictionaries*
a8	A kind of coal (burns slowly without smoke)
b8	*The green colouring matter in plants*
a9	(J. R. R.) Tolkien
b9	*P. G. Wodehouse*
a10	The Mall
b10	*Whitehall*
a11	England
b11	*England*
a12	Plucking the strings
b12	*Very softly*

Tie-breaker

Q Which English novelist wrote *Eyeless in Gaza*, *Crome Yellow*, and also the famous satire *Brave New World*?

A *Aldous Huxley*

No. 88

a1 Who was the first major criminal to be arrested as a result of the use of radio?

b1 *Which infamous series of murders occurred in London in 1888?*

a2 What 'Yellow dogs' are regarded as serious pests in Australia?

b2 *Which breed of dog is sometimes nicknamed Spotted Dick or Plum Pudding?*

a3 How did witches use wax models of people to cause illness or death to occur?

b3 *Which priests were associated with mistletoe, the oak tree, and ancient Britain?*

a4 In which city was there formerly a parliament building called the Reichstag?

b4 *By what name is the world famous mausoleum at Agra in India generally known?*

a5 What is a farl?

b5 *What is a filbert?*

a6 In which year did Winston Churchill die?

b6 *Which great French leader died in 1970?*

a7 Who said 'Father, I cannot tell a lie'?

b7 *With which film do we associate the line 'Frankly, my dear, I don't give a damn.'?*

a8 Which strait links the Black Sea and the Sea of Marmara?

b8 *The Bering Sea separates Russia from which American state?*

a9 After taking a magic drink, which American legendary character fell asleep for twenty years?

b9 *In a fairy story, a queen had to guess the name of a little man, or lose her baby. What was his name?*

a10 What was the middle name of William S. Gilbert (of Gilbert and Sullivan fame)?

b10 *Which German composer (whose name has been borrowed by a singer) composed the opera* Hansel and Gretel?

a11 Who wrote the novel *Lucky Jim*?

b11 *Who wrote the novel* Tropic of Cancer?

a12 Approximately, how many million miles is the sun from the Earth?

b12 *How many days does it take the moon to travel round the earth?*

No. 88 Answers

a1   'Dr' Crippen
b1   *Jack the Ripper murders*
a2   Dingoes
b2   *Dalmation*
a3   They stuck pins in them, or melted them
b3   *Druids*
a4   Berlin
b4   *Taj Mahal*
a5   Loaf (or oatcake; quadrant-shaped)
b5   *A nut (hazel-nut) (accept: Hazel-nut tree)*
a6   1965
b6   *Charles de Gaulle*
a7   George Washington
b7   *Gone with the Wind*
a8   The Bosphorous (or Bosporus)
b8   *Alaska*
a9   Rip Van Winkle
b9   *Rumpelstiltskin*
a10   Schwenck
b10   *Engelbert Humperdinck*
a11   Kingsley Amis
b11   *Henry Miller*
a12   91–93 million (it varies: average distance: 92,955,829 miles)
b12   *27⅓ days (accept: 27 or 28)*

Tie-breaker

Q   For which English county did the cricketer Herbert Sutcliffe play?
A   *Yorkshire*

No. 89

a1   According to the proverb, which animal should you take by the horns?

b1   According to the proverb what makes Jack a dull boy?

a2   Which long-legged bird often builds its nest on a roof-top?

b2   Which black and white bird has a reputation for stealing?

a3   Which seafood is sometimes served in the Thermidor manner?

b3   What kind of seafood are moules à la marinière?

a4   In which year did America enter the Second World War?

b4   In which year was the heroic evacuation of Dunkirk?

a5   If you were a member of Equity, what would be your job?

b5   What job would you probably have if you were a member of the NFU?

a6   Where in London is the Chamber of Horrors?

b6   In which London building is the Whispering Gallery?

a7   In which book did William the First record a survey of England?

b7   Which Scottish king murdered King Duncan?

a8   What does an anemometer measure?

b8   What instrument is used by a surveyor to measure angles?

a9   What name do we often call nitrous oxide?

b9   Which chemical is sometimes called quicksilver?

a10   Which dance is usually performed to Offenbach's *Orpheus in the Underworld*?

b10   In which ballet suite is there a Sugar Plum fairy?

a11   What is the name of the marmalade cat created by Kathleen Hale?

b11   In which book would you find 'Mrs Do-as-you-would-be-done-by'?

a12   On which country's stamps would you find the word 'Helvetia'?

b12   On which country's stamps would you find the words 'Magyar Posta'?

No. 89 Answers

a1   Bull
b1   *All work and no play*
a2   Stork
b2   *Magpie*
a3   Lobster
b3   *Mussels*
a4   1941
b4   *1940*
a5   Actor/actress
b5   *Farmer (accept: farm worker) (National Farmers' Union)*
a6   Madame Tussaud's (Baker Street)
b6   *St Paul's Cathedral*
a7   Domesday Book
b7   Macbeth
a8   Wind speed
b8   *Theodolyte*
a9   Laughing gas
b9   *Mercury*
a10   Can-can
b10   *The Nutcracker*
a11   Orlando
b11   The Water Babies *(by Charles Kingsley)*
a12   Switzerland
b12   *Hungary*

Tie-breaker

Q   Between the years 1095 and 1270, there were eight expeditions or wars, in which European nations attempted to win the Holy Land from control by Turks and Muslims. What name is given to these expeditions?

A   *The Crusades*

No. 90

a1 What kind of animal is a Kerry Blue?

b1 *Of which flower is the Ox-eye a type?*

a2 In which sort of building would you expect to see a safety curtain?

b2 *On what type of building would you be most likely to see crenellation?*

a3 What is meant by the phrase *ad infinitum*?

b3 *What is meant by the phrase* de rigueur?

a4 What colourless gas (discovered in 1898) is used to illuminate signs and advertisements?

b4 *What is the poisonous gas emitted from a car exhaust?*

a5 On what does an army march, according to Napoleon?

b5 *Who first said, 'We shall fight on the beaches, we shall fight on the landing grounds'?*

a6 For what is the Medoc area of France famous?

b6 *What kind of alcoholic drink is Amontillado?*

a7 In Europe, which war was fought from 1936 to 1939?

b7 *Which war was fought in the Far East from 1950 to 1953?*

a8 What was the name of the naval hero Sir Richard Greville's famous ship?

b8 *In which famous ship did the Pilgrim Fathers set sail for America?*

a9 700 years ago, which town on the River Weser was supposed to be plagued by rats?

b9 *In German fable, who sold his soul to Mephistopheles?*

a10 Who composed the 'Thunder and Lightning' polka?

b10 *Who composed the famous 'Pomp and Circumstance' marches?*

a11 Louisa M. Alcott — what did the 'M' stand for?

b11 *What was the surname of the writer whose first names were William Makepeace?*

a12 In Britain, which is the ultimate court of appeal?

b12 *What is special about a stipendiary magistrate?*

No. 90 Answers

a1   Dog (terrier)
b1   *Daisy*
a2   Theatre
b2   *Castle (accept: tower, fortress, walls)*
a3   For ever, to infinity
b3   *Necessary, compulsory*
a4   Neon
b4   *Carbon monoxide*
a5   Its stomach
b5   *Winston Churchill*
a6   Wines (Bordeaux)
b6   *Sherry*
a7   Spanish Civil War
b7   *Korean War*
a8   *The Revenge*
b8   The Mayflower
a9   Hamelin (Hameln) (1284)
b9   *Faust*
a10   (Johann) Strauss (the younger)
b10   *(Edward) Elgar*
a11   May
b11   *Thackeray*
a12   House of Lords
b12   *Is full-time, paid*

Tie-breaker

Q   Who is the Roman equivalent of Zeus, the King of the gods?
A   *Jupiter*

No. 91 Take Your Partners

a1   Pig is to sty, as horse is to . . . what?

b1   *Tear is to sorrow, as smile is to . . . what?*

a2   Can you complete this: 'flotsam and . . .'?

b2   *Can you complete this: 'pestle and . . .'?*

a3   With which festival do we associate mistletoe?

b3   *With which ceremony do we associate orange blossom?*

a4   With what is Savile Row associated?

b4   *With what is Harley Street associated?*

a5   Tortoiseshells, Fritillaries, and Red Admirals are all types of what?

b5   *Golden Shower, Wendy Cussons, and Dorothy Perkins are all types of which flower?*

a6   What have the Hayward, the National, and the Tate in common?

b6   *What have the Bluebell, the Watercress, and the Severn Valley all in common?*

a7   Suspension, Bailey, Pontoon are all constructions of what kind?

b7   *Bridgewater, Grand Trunk, and Grand Union are all . . . what?*

a8   What are Cheshire, Gouda, and Gorgonzola?

b8   *What are granaries, baps, and bloomers?*

a9   What are Rhum, Eigg, and Muck?

b9   *What are drivers, mashies, and niblicks?*

a10   Cornice, Bon Chretin, and Conference are all types of which fruit?

b10   *Short, choux, and puff are all types of what food?*

a11   Anne Ziegler and . . . Who was her partner?

b11   *Can you complete this pair of famous film stars and comedians: 'Abbot and . . . who?*

a12   What do Trog, Low, and Giles have in common?

b12   *Dag Hammarskjöld, U Thant, and Kurt Waldheim have all held which office?*

No. 91 Answers

a1   Stable
b1   *Happiness (or joy)*
a2   Jetsam
b2   *Mortar*
a3   Christmas
b3   *Weddings*
a4   Tailoring
b4   *Doctors*
a5   Butterflies
b5   *Rose*
a6   All are (London) art galleries
b6   *(Preserved) railways*
a7   Bridges
b7   *Canals*
a8   Cheeses
b8   *Bread (loaves)*
a9   (Scottish) Islands
b9   *Golf clubs*
a10   Pears
b10   *Pastry*
a11   Webster Booth
b11   *(Lou) Costello*
a12   They are all (newspaper) cartoonists
b12   *Secretary-general, United Nations*

Tie-breaker

Q   Long trotting, laying on, and legering are all tactics in which sport or hobby?
A   *Angling*

No. 92 What's the Word?

a1   What name is given to the rope cowboys use to catch horses?

b1   *What do we call a Red Indian's war axe?*

a2   What word is used for the dormant condition of some animals in winter?

b2   *Some birds move north or south during the winter. Which word describes this movement?*

a3   What one word means a period of ten years?

b3   *What do we call the two days of the year when night and day are of equal length?*

a4   What do we call the oven in which a potter fires his pots?

b4   *What do we call a man who makes barrels?*

a5   What name is given to the salary paid to a clergyman?

b5   *What do we call a list of subjects that are to be discussed at a meeting?*

a6   What do we call the study of birds?

b6   *What name is given to the annual marking of the swans on the River Thames?*

a7   What name was given to an airship that could be steered?

b7   *What one word means an aircraft with two sets of wings?*

a8   What do we call the making of patterns by inlaying different coloured pieces of wood?

b8   *Which word describes architecture and furniture dating from the time of James I?*

a9   Which Spanish word is used to address a young or unmarried lady?

b9   *What word describes a person who can speak several languages?*

a10   What name is given to the heavy summer rains in Asia?

b10   *What do we call the wearing away of land and rocks by the sea and the wind?*

a11   What word describes two straight lines that are always the same distance apart?

b11   *What is the medical name for a fear of open spaces?*

a12   What do we call the minimum number of members of a committee who must be present in order for it to reach valid decisions?

b12   *Nowadays a nickelodeon is a juke box. Originally, what was it?*

No. 92 Answers

a1 Lasso, lariat (larriot)
b1 *Tomahawk*
a2 Hibernation/hibernates
b2 *Migration*
a3 Decade
b3 *Equinoxes*
a4 Kiln
b4 *A cooper*
a5 Stipend
b5 *Agenda*
a6 Ornithology
b6 *Swan-upping*
a7 Dirigible
b7 *Bi-plane*
a8 Marquetry
b8 *Jacobean*
a9 Señorita
b9 *Polygot (accept: multi-lingual)*
a10 Monsoon
b10 *Erosion*
a11 Parallel
b11 *Agoraphobia*
a12 A quorum
b12 *(Early) cinema (you paid a nickel)*

Tie-breaker

Q In everyday usage, what do we call a cloud that comes down to ground level (and reduces visibility to less than a kilometre)?

A *Fog*

No. 93 Who's Who?

a1   Which Music Hall comedian was known as the Cheeky Chappie?

b1   *For what is Salvador Dali remembered?*

a2   As what has Delia Smith become famous?

b2   *For what was Anna Pavlova famous?*

a3   Sir Robert Walpole is generally said to have been the first person to have held which high office?

b3   *To which parliamentary party did Anthony Eden belong?*

a4   In which industry was Lord Nuffield a pioneer?

b4   *Of which country was Bulganin once prime minister?*

a5   As what has Aaron Copland achieved fame?

b5   *For what is Billy Graham famous?*

a6   What was Hitler's original nationality?

b6   *What nationality was the writer Voltaire?*

a7   Of which country was Sir Robert Menzies a prime minister?

b7   *Of which country was Sir Roy Welensky a former statesman?*

a8   As what did Inigo Jones become famous?

b8   *As what did Shostakovitch achieve fame?*

a9   As what did Henry Purcell achieve fame?

b9   *As what did Beau Brummel achieve fame?*

a10   As what did Sir Malcolm Campbell achieve fame?

b10   *For which art was Caruso famous?*

a11   In which art did John and Ethel Barrymore achieve fame?

b11   *As what did Francisco Goya achieve fame?*

a12   As what did Antonio Stradivari achieve fame?

b12   *As what did Confucius achieve fame?*

No. 93 Answers

a1 Max Miller
b1 *(Surreal) paintings (and sculpture)*
a2 Cookery writer/cook
b2 *Ballet*
a3 Prime minister
b3 *Conservative*
a4 Motor-car manufacturing
b4 *Russia*
a5 Composer *(accept:* conductor)
b5 *Evangelism, preaching*
a6 Austrian
b6 *French*
a7 Australia
b7 *Rhodesia (accept: Zimbabwe)*
a8 Architect
b8 *Composer*
a9 Composer
b9 *Fashion-leader (clothes)*
a10 Racing driver, speed boat pilot, speed record holder
b10 *(Italian) Opera*
a11 Acting (theatre and films)
b11 *Artist*
a12 Violin maker
b12 *Philosopher, teacher*

Tie-breaker

Q As what did Hieronymous Bosch achieve fame?
A *Artist*

No. 94 Mainly Mathematical

a1   If a can of coke costs 17p, how many can you get for £1, *and* how much change do you get?

b1   *If a particular type of pen costs 88p, how many can you get with a £5 note and what change do you get?*

a2   Can you describe the sign used in mathematics to mean 'therefore'?

b2   *And can you describe the sign meaning 'greater than'?*

a3   What is ¾ + ⅕?

b3   *And what is ⅔ + ¼?*

a4   If VAT is 15 per cent what is the VAT on a cassette costing 80p?

b4   *And what is the VAT on a video cassette costing £4.20?*

a5   If you buy something costing £1.37, what change should you get from a £5 note?

b5   *And if you buy something costing £7.62, what change should you get from a £10 note?*

a6   What is .25 of 336?

b6   *And what is one seventh of 343?*

a7   To one place of decimals, how many centimetres equal one inch?

b7   *And to one place of decimals, how many litres equal one gallon (one UK gallon, that is)?*

a8   In trigonometry, what does the ratio 'opposite side over hypotenuse' equal?

b8   *And the ratio 'opposite side over adjacent side' equals . . .?*

a9   What is 15 per cent of £60?

b9   *If an article costs £1.35, how much will 200 cost?*

a10   Which branch of calculus is concerned with rates and speeds?

b10   *What is measured by the SI unit, the kelvin?*

a11   Which country used to have a coin called a bawbee?

b11   *What new denomination of coin was issued in the United Kingdom in 1983?*

a12   What is the unit of currency in Iran?

b12   *Of which country is the zloty the unit of currency?*

No. 94 Answers

a1	Five; 15p
b1	*Five; 60p*
a2	∴
b2	*> (arrow head pointing to the smaller number)*
a3	$^{19}/_{20}$
b3	$^{11}/_{12}$
a4	12p
b4	*63p*
a5	£3.63
b5	*£2.38*
a6	84
b6	*49*
a7	2.5
b7	*4.5*
a8	The sine of an angle
b8	*The tangent of an angle*
a9	£9
b9	*£270*
a10	Differential
b11	*Temperature (SI = Système Internationale)*
a11	Scotland (originally = 6 Scottish pennies; now slang = 1 English halfpenny)
b11	*£1*
a12	The rial
b12	*Poland*

Tie-breaker

Q How many acres are there in a square mile?
A 640

No. 95 Places of Interest

a1 With which country do we associate pizzas?

b1 *With which country do we associate haggis?*

a2 With which country do we associate 'sweet and sour'?

b2 *With which country do we associate pappadoms and chapattis?*

a3 With which country do we associate paella?

b3 *With which country do we associate mousaka?*

a4 Which novel, set in Yorkshire, is all about a young boy called Billy Casper who trains a hawk?

b4 *Where in Yorkshire is test cricket played?*

a5 On which Yorkshire race course is the St Leger run?

b5 *Which novel, set in Yorshire, features Heathcliff and Catherine Earnshaw?*

a6 On which Yorkshire moor was a battle fought on July 2nd 1644?

b6 *Which city was once known as Eboracum?*

a7 Pickering and Grosmont are connected by a famous form of transport. What is it?

b7 *Which motorway crosses the Pennines?*

a8 By what name do most English people know the mountain Yr Wyddfa?

b8 *In which county are the Brecon Beacons?*

a9 In 1404, which Welsh hero partially destroyed Cardiff Castle?

b9 *By what Welsh name is the Welsh Nationalist Party known?*

a10 In an American school, what is a grade?

b10 *And what do we call the game checkers?*

a11 Across the Atlantic, what part of a car is its hood?

b11 *And what is the piece of clothing they call suspenders?*

a12 What do we call a thumb tack?

b12 *And finally, what is a casket?*

a1	Italy
b1	*Scotland*
a2	China
b2	*India*
a3	Spain
b3	*Greece*
a4	*Kestrel for a Knave* by Barry Hines (also titled *Kes*)
b4	*Headingley (Leeds)*
a5	Doncaster
b5	Wuthering Heights *(Emily Brontë)*
a6	Marston Moor
b6	*York*
a7	Preserved steam railway (North Yorkshire Moors Railway)
b7	*M62*
a8	Snowdon
b8	*Powys*
a9	Owain Glyndwr (Owen Glendower)
b9	*Plaid Cymru*
a10	Class, form, year (e.g. 'fourth grade')
b10	*Draughts*
a11	Bonnet
b11	*Braces*
a12	Drawing pin
b12	*Coffin*

Tie-breaker

Q In which country is Timbuctoo?
A *Mali*

No. 96 Word Power

In this round we begin by looking for a number of 'imps'; that is words all beginning I-M-P... for example, the imp that you can't get by is 'impassable'.

a1   Which imp is 'getting better'?

b1   *Which imp can't you achieve, or can't happen?*

a2   Which imp is unlikely?

b2   *Which imp imitates someone else?*

a3   On which imp might you have to pay customs duty?

b3   *Which imp is urgent or commanding?*

a4   Which imp is a handicap or difficulty?

b4   *And which imp does not take sides?*

Next, a group about prefixes. (A prefix is a group of letters places at the beginning of a word which qualifies its meaning.) What are the meanings of the following prefixes?

a5   'Bio' as in biography and biology?

b5   *'Geo' as in geography and geology?*

a6   'Hydro' as in hydrofoil and hydroelectrics?

b6   *'Mono' as in monocle and monotonous?*

a7   'Thermo' as in thermometer and thermostat?

b7   *'Photo' as is photosensitive and photograph?*

a8   'Poly' as in polygon and polymers?

b8   *'Tele' as in television and telecommunications?*

Finally, a number of malapropisms. (That's when someone uses the wrong word for what they mean but a word that sounds quite like the correct one.) In each of the following sentences, which word is the malapropism and what should it have been?

a9   In winter, many species of birds gyrate southwards.

b9   *Hedgehogs moderate during cold weather.*

a10   The doctor told his patient to take a fixative.

b10   *The priest went to the pulpit, carrying a small black missile.*

a11   There are many carnivorous forests in Norway.

b11   *She admired the weightlifter's magnificent forceps.*

a12   In 1665, London was hit by bucolic plague.

b12   *And one from the character Dogberry in Shakespeare's* Much Ado About Nothing *where he objects that 'Comparisons are odorous'.*

No. 96 Answers

a1	Improving
b1	*Impossible*
a2	Improbable
b2	*Impersonate(s)/Impersonation*
a3	Import
b3	*Imperative*
a4	Impediment
b4	*Impartial*
a5	Life, to do with life
b5	*Earth, to do with earth*
a6	Water, to do with water
b6	*Single*
a7	Warm, heat, to do with heat
b7	*Light, to do with light*
a8	Many
b8	*Far, at or over a distance*
a9	Gyrate/migrate
b9	*Moderate/hibernate*
a10	Fixative/laxative
b10	*Missile/missal (prayer- or service-book)*
a11	Carnivorous (flesh-eating)/coniferous (cone-bearing trees)
b11	*Forceps/biceps*
a12	Bucolic (to do with the country)/bubonic
b12	*Odorous/odious*

Tie-breaker

Q All three sides are equal in an equatorial triangle
A *Equatorial/Equilateral*

No. 97 Spot the Join!

a1 Which pop star is linked forever with blue suede shoes?

b1 *Which dancing partner do you principally associate with Fred Astaire?*

a2 With what was Fleet Street formerly associated?

b2 *With what is Threadneedle Street associated?*

a3 With what is the name Wedgwood associated?

b3 *What insect do you connect with both Miss Muffet and Robert the Bruce?*

a4 Dr Jekyll and Mr Hyde — of these two, which was the unpleasant character?

b4 *In the Second World War, which two leaders had a famous meeting in the Brenner Pass?*

a5 Which is the odd one out of these: cod, pike, carp, roach?

b5 *Queens, workers, and drones are all kinds of which creature?*

a6 King Edward, Golden Wonder, Majestic: what have these in common?

b6 *Forties, Ninian, Frigg, and Ekofisk are all what?*

a7 Which sport do Hobbs, Bradman, and Compton have in common?

b7 *Monet, Manet, and Renoir have what in common?*

a8 Tom Thumb, Tennis Ball, and Winter Density are all types of what?

b8 *Tagliatelle, ravioli, and lasagne are all types of which kind of food?*

a9 In carpentry, what completes a mortise joint?

b9 *Where would you find treads and risers close together?*

a10 What are goby, pollack, and bream?

b10 *What are vichyssoise, consommé, and minestrone?*

a11 In London, the Cambridge, the Lyric and Adelphi are all what?

b11 *For what product are Honiton, Nottingham, and Brussels all famous?*

a12 Which famous British film company is associated with the symbol of a man striking a gong?

b12 *Which flower is particularly associated with Mary, the Madonna?*

No. 97 Answers

a1	Elvis Presley (or Carl Perkins)
b1	*Ginger Rogers*
a2	Newspapers
b2	*Bank of England*
a3	Pottery (and China)
b3	*A spider*
a4	Mr Hyde
b4	*Hitler and Mussolini (it's in the Alps)*
a5	Cod (salt water fish; the others are freshwater fish)
b5	*Bees*
a6	All are types of potato
b6	*North sea oil rigs*
a7	Cricket
b7	*All are artists (French Impressionists)*
a8	Lettuce
b8	*Pasta*
a9	Tenon (mortise = socket)
b9	*On a staircase (treads — the flat parts; risers — the vertical parts)*
a10	All are fish
b10	*Soups*
a11	Theatres
b11	*Lace*
a12	The Rank Organization
b12	*Lilies*

Tie-breaker

Q Can you explain which great leader links the islands of Corsica, Elba and St Helena — and why?

A *Napoleon. He was born on Corsica; imprisoned on Elba, and died on St Helena*

No. 98 Hall of Fame

a1   For what is Constance Spry best known?

b1   *For what did Dame Nellie Melba achieve fame?*

a2   In which art has Beryl Grey achieved fame?

b2   *For what did Ronald Colman achieve fame?*

a3   Where is Lord Nelson buried?

b3   *What nationality was the playwright August Strindberg?*

a4   As what did Henri Fabre achieve fame?

b4   *As what has Dietrick Fischer-Dieskau become famous?*

a5   Who was Edith Cavell?

b5   *For what discovery is Marie Curie famous?*

a6   Which famous Saxon hero held out against the Normans, in the Fens?

b6   *During the Second World War, for what did Dame Myra Hess become widely known?*

a7   Which English statesman had the first names William Ewart?

b7   *Winston S. Churchill — what did the 'S' stand for?*

a8   In which art has Joan Sutherland achieved fame?

b8   *In which art did Nijinsky achieve fame?*

a9   In which industry was Sir Richard Arkwright a pioneer?

b9   *Of which country was Field-Marshall Smuts a statesman?*

a10   For what is Sigmund Freud remembered?

b10   *As what did Sibelius achieve fame?*

a11   Which world-famous Indian leader was assassinated on his way to a prayer meeting?

b11   *What is the name of the holy city which was the birthplace of the prophet Mohammed?*

a12   As what did Aeschylus achieve fame?

b12   *As what did Euclid achieve fame?*

No. 98 Answers

a1	Flower arranging
b1	*Singing*
a2	Ballet (dance)
b2	*Acting (or charm, looks, voice!)*
a3	St Paul's Cathedral
b3	*Swedish*
a4	Naturalist, entomologist
b4	*Singer (opera)*
a5	English nurse executed by the Germans in 1915
b5	*Radium (accept: Polonium)*
a6	Hereward the Wake
b6	*Piano recitals*
a7	Gladstone
b7	*Spencer*
a8	Opera, singing
b8	*Ballet*
a9	Cotton
b9	*South Africa*
a10	Developed psychoanalysis; studying the sub-conscious
b10	*Composer (musician)*
a11	(Mahatma) Gandhi
b11	*Mecca (in Saudi Arabia)*
a12	Playwright (Greek)
b12	*Mathematician (he laid the foundations of geometry)*

Tie-breaker

Q What was the surname of the mother and daughters who did much for the 'Votes-for-Women' movement?

A *Pankhurst*

No. 99 Where is Home?

a1   What do we call the home of a hare?

b1   *What do we call the home of an eagle?*

a2   What do we call the home of a fox?

b2   *Who or what live in a holt?*

a3   In which continent would you find a coyote in the wild?

b3   *Of which continent is the tiger a native?*

a4   What do we call the home of a beaver?

b4   *What creature live in a formicary?*

a5   Who lives in a kraal?

b5   *Who lives in a manse?*

a6   Whose official residence is Lambeth Palace?

b6   *Which statesman's country home was Chartwell in Kent (and is now a memorial to him)?*

a7   Which continent was the original home of the Hottentots?

b7   *Which is the homeland of the famous troops, the Gurkhas?*

a8   Who is generally said to be the most famous person born at Alloway in Ayrshire?

b8   *Which naturalist lived at Selbourne in Hampshire?*

a9   Which city is the home of the National Railway Museum?

b9   *Which city is the home of the Hallé Orchestra?*

a10   Which novelist is especially associated with Eastwood and Nottingham?

b10   *Which religious writer was born in Elstow, near Bedford?*

a11   Amritsar is a holy city for which followers of which religion?

b11   *For followers of which religion is the River Ganges a holy place?*

a12   Belmont is the home of Portia in which Shakesperian play?

b12   *Which Shakesperian play takes place in Illyria?*

No. 99 Answers

a1	Form
b1	*Eyrie*
a2	Earth (*or* lair)
b2	*Otters*
a3	(North) America (prairie wolf)
b3	*Asia (Indian sub-continent)*
a4	Lodge
b4	*Ants*
a5	A Zulu
b5	*A minister (Methodist, Church of Scotland or Free Church) (accept Clergyman)*
a6	The Archbishop of Canterbury's
b6	*Sir Winston Churchill*
a7	Africa
b7	*Nepal*
a8	Robert Burns
b8	*Gilbert White*
a9	York
b9	*Manchester (Free Trade Hall)*
a10	D. H. Lawrence
b10	*John Bunyan*
a11	Sikhism; the Sikh religion
b11	*Hinduism*
a12	The Merchant of Venice
b12	Twelfth Night

Tie-breaker

Q In ancient Greece, in what is the philosopher Diogenes said to have lived?

A A tub or barrel

No. 100 Can You Spell?

a1 Can you spell 'February'?
b1 *Spell the word 'stationary' when it means 'standing still'?*
a2 Spell 'humorous'
b1 *Spell 'embarrassed'*
a3 Can you spell the word 'correspondence'?
b3 *How do you spell 'desiccated'?*
a4 Can you spell 'apparent'?
b4 *Spell 'allegiance'*
a5 Spell 'Psalmist' (as in the Bible)
b5 *Spell 'questionnaire'*
a6 How do you spell 'permanent'?
b6 *Spell 'reminiscence'*
a7 Spell 'irresistible'
b7 *Spell 'surreptitious'*
a8 Can you spell 'susceptible'?
b8 *Spell 'unnecessary'*
a9 Can you spell 'antirrhinum'?
b9 *Can you spell 'rhododendron'?*
a10 Can you spell 'Caribbean'?
b10 *Spell 'Mediterranean'*
a11 Spell 'physicist'
b11 *Spell 'physiotherapist'*
a12 Spell 'schizophrenia'
b12 *Spell 'resuscitation'*

No. 100 Answers

a1 February
b1 Stationary
a2 Humorous
b2 Embarrassed
a3 Correspondence
b3 Desiccated
a4 Apparent
b4 Allegiance
a5 Psalmist
b5 Questionnaire
a6 Permanent
b6 Reminiscence
a7 Irresistible
b7 Surreptitious
a8 Susceptible
b8 Unnecessary
a9 Antirrhinum
b9 Rhododendron
a10 Caribbean
b10 Mediterranean
a11 Physicist
b11 Physiotherapist
a12 Schizophrenia
b12 Resuscitation

Tie-breaker

Q How do you spell Anti-disestablishmentarianism?
A *Anti-dis-establish-ment-arian-ism*

No. 101

a1   What colour is angelica?

b1   *What colour is cochineal?*

a2   According to the proverb, how many wrongs don't make a right?

b2   *If two are company, how many make a crowd?*

a3   What is sold by a costermonger?

b3   *In what trade would you find a compositor?*

a4   Aneroid and mercury are both types of which kind of instrument?

b4   *What are woofers and tweeters?*

a5   What is meant by the phrase *savoir-faire*?

b5   *What is meant by the phrase* tête-à-tête?

a6   In which Libyan seaport did Australians end a siege in the Second World War?

b6   *Which German battle ship was involved in the Battle of the River Plate in 1939?*

a7   In London, for what is Hatton Garden famous?

b7   *What is Lombard Street associated with?*

a8   Perry Mason was the creation of which writer?

b8   *Which writer created 'The Saint'?*

a9   In which year was the Gunpowder Plot?

b9   *In which year was Magna Carta sealed?*

a10   Which is the largest bird in the world?

b10   *Which animal is generally said to live the longest?*

a11   In music, what is meant by the instruction *fortissimo*?

b11   *What is meant in music by the term* diminuendo?

a12   In geometry, what does the formula $2\pi r$* help you to calculate? (*two-pi-r)

b12   *In geometry, how many degrees are there in a complete circle?*

213

No. 101 Answers

a1	Green
b1	*Red*
a2	Two
b2	*Three*
a3	Fruit and/or vegetables
b3	*Printing*
a4	Barometer
b4	*Loudspeakers (types of)*
a5	Know-how, tact, knowing what to do
b5	*Privately, one to another*
a6	Tobruk
b6	*Graf Spee*
a7	Jewellery, diamonds
b7	*Banking, finance*
a8	Erle Stanley Gardner
b8	*Leslie Charteris (Leslie Charles Yin)*
a9	1605
b9	*1215*
a10	Ostrich
b10	*Tortoise (Marion's tortoise)*
a11	Play it very loudly
b11	*Getting softer/quieter*
a12	The circumference of a circle
b12	*360*

Tie-breaker

Q Antonio, Bassanio and Portia are all characters in the same play by Shakespeare. Which play is that?

A *The Merchant of Venice*

No. 102

a1   What colour are the flowers of oil seed rape?

b1   Carmine is a shade of what colour?

a2   For what would you use an abacus?

b2   Why might you use a plumb line?

a3   Which pink bird, common on some African lakes, sleeps on one leg?

b3   Which bird is celebrated for its song while soaring high in the sky?

a4   On board a sailing ship, what are the sheets?

b4   Whereabouts on a ship is the fo'c'sle?

a5   What food is Melton Mowbray famous for?

b5   Which biscuit is named after a nineteenth-century Italian soldier?

a6   What was a hobgoblin?

b6   Who is (or was) Beelzebub?

a7   What is the common name for solidified carbon dioxide?

b7   By what name is magnesium sulphate commonly known?

a8   Which Irish author wrote Ulysses and Finnegan's Wake?

b8   Who wrote the novels Sons and Lovers and The Rainbow?

a9   In which wars were Mafeking and Ladysmith relieved?

b9   Which Italian dictator invaded Ethiopia in 1935?

a10   Who composed the opera Porgy and Bess?

b10   Who composed the operas Otello and Falstaff?

a11   In which kind of building would you find a transept?

b11   In what sort of building would you be most likely to find a portcullis?

a12   Of which organization is the kite-mark its sign of approval?

b12   Where would you see a Plimsoll line?

No. 102 Answers

a1 Yellow
b1 *Red*
a2 Counting, calculating
b2 *To check if a wall is vertical; to measure depth of water*
a3 Flamingo
b3 *Skylark/lark*
a4 Ropes
b4 *Front, in the bows (it's the raised part of the deck)*
a5 Pork pies (accept: Stilton cheese)
b5 *Garibaldi*
a6 Imp; 'bogy'
b6 *The devil (literally: the Lord of the Flies)*
a7 Dry ice
b7 *Epsom salts*
a8 (James) Joyce
b8 *D. H. Lawrence*
a9 Boer Wars (South African Wars)
b9 *Mussolini*
a10 George Gershwin
b10 *Verdi*
a11 Church (or cathedral)
b11 *Castle (accept: keep)*
a12 British Standards Institute
b12 *On the side of a ship (the ship may be safely loaded until that line is just awash)*

Tie-breaker

Q Who was the rag-time composer and pianist whose music was featured prominently on the soundtrack of the film *The Sting*?
A *Scott Joplin*

No. 103

a1   What job is done by a chandler?

b1   What job is done by a drover?

a2   Which part of the United Kingdom's flag shows a St Andrew's cross on a blue background?

b2   What musical instrument is on the British Royal Standard?

a3   According to the proverb, where does charity begin?

b3   What should people who live in glass houses not do?

a4   What is meant by the phrase *mea culpa*?

b4   What is meant by sotto voce?

a5   What colour is lapis lazuli?

b5   What colour is malachite?

a6   If you landed at Ringway Airport in which city would you be?

b6   Which city is served by Kennedy Airport?

a7   Which musical instrument do we associate with the comedian Jack Benny?

b7   With which instrument do we associate the musician Artur Rubinstein?

a8   In 1860, which Italian soldier conquered Sicily and Naples, and helped to unite Italy?

b8   Which state came into being in 1948 under the leadership of David Ben-Gurion?

a9   Under Hitler, who was the Nazi Minister of Propaganda?

b9   Which German general was nicknamed the Desert Fox?

a10   In London, which road runs from Marble Arch to Tottenham Court Road?

b10   In London, which road runs from Charing Cross to Fleet Street?

a11   Which bird has the greatest wing span?

b11   Nowadays, which is the largest British bird?

a12   Who wrote the novel *The Naked Lunch*?

b12   Who wrote the novel Cakes and Ale?

No. 103 Answers

a1   Deals in (or makes) candles (oil/soap/paint/groceries) (Ship's chandler deals in rope and canvas)

b1   *He drives sheep or cattle (usually to market)*

a2   Scotland

b2   *A harp*

a3   At home

b3   *Throw stones*

a4   'My fault'; 'I'm to blame'

b4   *'In a low voice'; 'under your breath'*

a5   Blue

b5   *Green*

a6   Manchester

b6   *New York*

a7   Violin

b7   *Piano*

a8   (Guiseppe) Garibaldi

b8   *Israel*

a9   Goebbels

b9   *Rommel*

a10   Oxford Street

b10   *The Strand*

a11   Albatross

b11   *Mute swan*

a12   William Burroughs

b12   *Somerset Maugham*

Tie-breaker

Q   In which sport has Alwin Schockemöhle achieved a remarkable number of successess?

A   *Show jumping (accept: equestrianism)*

No. 104

a1   What do you particularly need to play the card game Canasta?

b1   *With what do you play cribbage?*

a2   What was invented by Richard Gatling?

b2   *During the last war, which vegetable did the Ministry of Food encourage people to eat, to help them see in the dark?*

a3   In which ocean is the Sargasso Sea?

b3   *In which country is the Kiel Canal?*

a4   What does a Frenchman mean when he says *Quel dommage?*

b4   *What does an Italian mean when he says,* Prego?

a5   Oxford and Cambridge in Britain are to Harvard and which other university in America?

b5   *King's, Bedford, and Birkbeck are all colleges of which university?*

a6   What kind of soup is *bouillabaisse?*

b6   *What flavour is* crème de menthe?

a7   What kind of bird is a widgeon?

b7   *What species of bird is a condor?*

a8   Which writer created the detective Commander Adam Dalgliesh?

b8   *Who was the pilot of the future who starred on the front page of the comic* The Eagle?

a9   Which alloy of tin and lead is often used for making tankards and mugs?

b9   *Which metal do we make from bauxite?*

a10   On what date in 44 BC was Julius Caesar murdered?

b10   *In AD 63 and AD 79, which town was destroyed by Vesuvius?*

a11   Which famous Suffolk composer established the Aldeburgh Festival?

b11   *With which composer is the German town of Bayreuth associated?*

a12   Which Egyptian monument has the head of a human on a lion's body?

b12   *In their buildings, for what did Romans use a hypocaust system?*

No. 104 Answers

a1 Two packs of cards
b1 *Playing cards (matchsticks are often used for scoring, but not actually for playing the game)*
a2 (Machine) gun, type of gun
b2 *Carrots*
a3 (North) Atlantic
b3 *Germany*
a4 'What a pity'
b4 *'Not at all, don't mention it'*
a5 Yale
b5 *London*
a6 Fish (from Provence)
b6 *Peppermint*
a7 Duck
b7 *Vulture (accept: eagle)*
a8 P. D. James
b8 *Dan Dare*
a9 Pewter
b9 *Aluminium*
a10 Ides of March (15 March)
b10 *Pompeii (and/or Herculaneum)*
a11 Benjamin Britten
b11 *Wagner*
a12 The Sphinx
b12 *Heating (underfloor)*

Tie-breaker

Q The Knight, the Pardoner, and the Nun's Priest all appear in which literary work?
A *(Chaucer's)* Canterbury Tales

No 105

a1 In a song, with which fair in Devon is Tom Pearce associated?

b1 *On which feast day did King Wenceslas look out?*

a2 What is or was sold by an apothecary?

b2 *What are made by wainwrights?*

a3 Which country's flag is white, with a red disc on it?

b3 *Which country has a single cedar tree on its flag?*

a4 For what is the inventor Samuel Colt remembered?

b4 *Who invented a system of printed dots enabling the blind to read by touch?*

a5 What colour is jade?

b5 *What colour is an amethyst?*

a6 What fraction is a tithe?

b6 *021 is the dialling code for which English city?*

a7 In 1916, in which city was the Easter Rising?

b7 *In 1965, which country declared UDI?*

a8 Who wrote the 'Merry Widow' waltz?

b8 *Who wrote the 'Blue Danube' waltz?*

a9 In the reign of Queen Elizabeth I what sort of events took place in The Globe?

b9 *What Egyptian obelisk stands on the Thames Embankment?*

a10 Collared, Turtle, and Ring are all types of which bird?

b10 *Black, Whooper, and Bewick are all types of which bird?*

a11 In which city is Heriot-Watt university?

b11 *Which university is situated at Uxbridge in Middlesex?*

a12 In which novel is John Ridd the central male character?

b12 *In fiction, who fell asleep in the Catskill Mountains for twenty years?*

No. 105 Answers

a1	Widecombe
b1	*The feast of Stephen (26 December)*
a2	Medicines, drugs
b2	*Waggons, carts*
a3	Japan
b3	*Lebanon*
a4	Inventing the six-shot revolver; guns
b4	*Louis Braille*
a5	Green (*accept*: white)
b5	*Purple/Violet*
a6	One-tenth
b6	*Birmingham*
a7	Dublin
b7	*(Southern) Rhodesia (now Zimbabwe)*
a8	Franz Lehar
b8	*Johann Strauss*
a9	Plays were performed
b9	*Cleopatra's Needle*
a10	Dove
b10	*Swan*
a11	Edinburgh
b11	*Brunel University*
a12	*Lorna Doone* (by R. D. Blackmore)
b12	*Rip Van Winkle*

Tie-breaker

Q The painting 'The Creation of Adam', in which God's finger is almost touching Adam's, is used in the opening sequence of television's 'South Bank Show'. Who painted the original picture?

A Michelangelo

No. 106

a1   On what will you find the Juggler, the Female Pope, and the Hanged Man?

b1   *In 1886, where did Joseph Hobson Jagger break the bank?*

a2   Which American state is known as the Golden State?

b2   *What is a golden hello?*

a3   What kind of beans are made into baked beans?

b3   *Of which product is Meaux (say: 'Mo') a type?*

a4   Why would it be dangerous to put a hot test-tube into cold water to cool it?

b4   *What colour light is made by all the colours of the spectrum together?*

a5   Which is the highest voice of these: bass, tenor, baritone?

b5   *Which is the highest female voice?*

a6   How many wings has a bee?

b6   *How many legs has a spider?*

a7   When was the Eiffel Tower built?

b7   *What is the name of the great palace built by Louis XIV, south-west of Paris?*

a8   How is the time displayed on an analogue clock or watch?

b8   *What are recorded on a seismograph?*

a9   For which series of children's books is Richmal Crompton famous?

b9   *Which writer created the character Biggles?*

a10   At which Scottish school were Prince Phillip and Prince Charles both educated?

b10   *If someone is an Old Wykehamist, to which school did they go?*

a11   Who became King of the Huns in AD 434?

b11   *Who was Rasputin?*

a12   Which sea lies to the north of Turkey?

b12   *Which country almost surrounds the White Sea?*

No. 106 Answers

a1	Tarot cards
b1	*Monte Carlo*
a2	California
b2	*An enticement to join a company*
a3	Haricot beans
b3	*Mustard*
a4	It would crack (due to rapid change in temperature)
b4	*White*
a5	Tenor
b5	*Soprano*
a6	Four
b6	*Eight*
a7	1889 (started in 1888)
b7	*Versailles*
a8	By two (or three) hands (It's an ordinary, non-digital watch)
b8	*Earthquakes*
a9	William
b9	*Captain W. E. Johns*
a10	Gordonstoun
b10	*Winchester (College)*
a11	Attila
b11	*Russian monk; key figure in the Tsar's court*
a12	Black Sea
b12	*Russia (Russian Federation)*

Tie-breaker

Q What do we call the sum of money demanded by a court to obtain temporary release of a prisoner not yet brought to trial?

A *Bail*

No. 107

a1 What is a poinsettia?

b1 What is cuckoo-spit?

a2 What three colours appear on the Italian flag?

b2 What three colours appear on the German flag?

a3 Traditionally, which bird do sailors say it is unlucky to kill?

b3 Which animal was usually said to be a witch's familiar?

a4 What colour are the flowers of jasmine?

b4 What colour was the ancient dye called woad?

a5 Of which country is Olympic Airways a national airline?

b5 Which country's airline is called Aeroflot?

a6 With which part of your body is a trichologist concerned?

b6 What does an anthropologist study?

a7 In 1759, which British general captured Quebec?

b7 In 1649, which English king was executed?

a8 Which musical instrument is especially associated with Segovia?

b8 Which musical instrument was played by Fritz Kreisler?

a9 On what machine is weaving done?

b9 What kind of material is cheesecloth?

a10 Who wrote the novel *Brideshead Revisited*?

b10 Who wrote The Secret Life of Walter Mitty?

a11 Of which famous school was Thomas Arnold headmaster?

b11 Which university is based in Milton Keynes?

a12 Which modern theatre near Waterloo Station was designed by Denys Lasdun?

b12 In London, which is the tallest office block?

No. 107 Answers

a1	Flower, flowering shrub
b1	*Froth given out by the larvae of some insects*
a2	Green, white, and red
b2	*Black, red, and yellow*
a3	Albatross
b3	*Cat*
a4	Yellow or white
b4	*Blue*
a5	Greece
b5	*Russia (Russian Federation) (accept: Commonwealth of Independent States or CIS)*
a6	Your hair
b6	*He studies Man (his physiology, social, religious, and cultural habits)*
a7	(General James) Wolfe
b7	*Charles I*
a8	Guitar
b8	*Violin*
a9	A loom
b9	*Muslin (cotton)*
a10	Evelyn Waugh
b10	*James Thurber*
a11	Rugby
b11	*Open University*
a12	(Royal) National Theatre
b12	*National Westminster Bank, Bishopsgate (600 feet)*

Tie-breaker

Q In the *Odyssey*, Odysseus has to sail between a sea monster and a whirlpool. The monster was called Scylla. What was the name of the whirlpool?

A *Charybdis*

No. 108

a1   To see which sport would you be most likely to travel to Chepstow?

b1   To see which sport would you be most likely to go to Oulton Park?

a2   What is the principal ingredient of a fondue?

b2   What is bubble and squeak made from?

a3   What is the common name for the larvae of the Furniture Beetle?

b3   Which plant do Colorado beetles most often threaten?

a4   If there was a cross on a house door in 1665, what did it mean?

b4   In what sort of shop is the Great Fire of London said to have started?

a5   What is a maelstrom?

b5   What is an archipelago?

a6   What kind of creature was Rikki-Tikki-Tavi?

b6   In the novel by Henry Williamson, what kind of animal was Tarka?

a7   Which sea lies between Sweden and Poland?

b7   Across which ocean does the Gulf Stream flow?

a8   What is manufactured from silicates of lime, soda, and potash?

b8   For what do we use the gas, acetylene?

a9   Where is Southwark Cathedral?

b9   In which city is the Rockefeller Centre?

a10   Who composed the opera *The Barber of Seville*?

b10   Who composed the opera Die Walküre?

a11   Which university is situated at Guildford?

b11   What happens to a student if he is rusticated?

a12   In mythology, which animal was half lion, half eagle?

b12   Which legendary beast was half man, half horse?

No. 108 Answers

a1 Racing

b1 *Motor racing*

a2 Cheese (plus wine, bread)

b2 *Cold meat (corned beef) fried with vegetables or cold potatoes fried with green vegetables*

a3 Woodworm

b3 *Potato*

a4 Someone in there had the plague

b4 *A baker's shop (in Pudding Lane)*

a5 Whirlpool (*accept*: series of events leading to destruction)

b5 *Collection of islands*

a6 Mongoose (in the story by Rudyard Kipling)

b6 *An otter (Tarka the Otter)*

a7 Baltic Sea

b7 *(North) Atlantic*

a8 Glass

b8 *Giving heat or light/cutting metal, when it is burnt*

a9 In London (south London, near London Bridge)

b9 *New York*

a10 Rossini

b10 *Wagner*

a11 University of Surrey

b11 *Sent away from university or college (as a punishment) (literally: 'sent to the country')*

a12 Griffin

b12 *Centaur*

Tie-breaker

Q Mary Ann Evans was a successful Victorian novelist. Under what pseudonym did she publish her books?

A *George Eliot*

No.109

a1   Properly, in which game is there a Grand Slam?

b1   In which game do you pass 'Go' and collect £200?

a2   What kind of insect is a cockchafer?

b2   On which kind of bird might someone use a jess?

a3   What tradesman uses a goose to finish off what he makes?

b3   In what occupation do you have to beware of firedamp?

a4   What colour and value was the first postage stamp?

b4   In the song 'D'ye ken John Peel', what colour was John Peel's coat?

a5   What is a mandate?

b5   What is a mandrake?

a6   In geometry, what do we call an angle of more than 90 but less than 180 degrees?

b6   What do we call a line which bisects a circle?

a7   Who wrote the book *The Innocence of Father Brown*?

b7   Who wrote the book Three Men in a Boat*?*

a8   Before the Spanish conquests, which empire flourished in Peru?

b8   Which great conqueror had a horse called Bucephalus?

a9   What nationality was the composer Franz Liszt?

b9   What nationality was the composer Antonin Dvorák? (say: Vor-jhak)

a10   Which city owes its beginning to Leofric and his wife, Godiva?

b10   Which city is famous for lace and its Goose Fair?

a11   Which bird is a national emblem of France?

b11   The beaver is sometimes used as the emblem of which country?

a12   On what would a fresco be painted?

b12   In painting, what are the three primary colours?

No. 109 Answers

a1 Bridge
b1 *Monopoly*
a2 Beetle
b2 *Hawk, falcon*
a3 A tailor (it's a smoothing iron)
b3 *Coalmining*
a4 Penny black (*accept*: twopenny blue)
b4 *Grey*
a5 An order, command
b5 *Plant (from which a sleep inducing drug can be made) with two roots, which look like a man's legs*
a6 Obtuse
b6 *Diameter*
a7 G. K. Chesterton
b7 *Jerome K. Jerome*
a8 Incas
b8 *Alexander the Great*
a9 Hungarian
b9 *Czech (accept: Bohemian)*
a10 Coventry
b10 *Nottingham*
a11 Cockerel
b11 *Canada*
a12 A wall *or* a ceiling (it is painted before the plaster is dry)
b12 *Red, yellow, blue*

Tie-breaker

Q Which county cricket club has been captained in post-war years by Norman Yardley, Brian Close, and Chris Old?
A *Yorkshire*

No. 110

a1 What does a cardiologist study?

b1 *In First Aid, what is the purpose of a tourniquet?*

a2 What three colours appear on the Dutch flag?

b2 *What three colours appear on the Belgian flag?*

a3 In which country is the Algarve Coast?

b3 *Of which country is Sardinia a part?*

a4 Why does a snake not close its eyes when it sleeps?

b4 *Which snake is Cleopatra said to have used to poison herself?*

a5 Which musical begins with 'Oh, What A Beautiful Morning'?

b5 *Which famous musical was based on a book called* Anna and the King of Siam?

a6 Which sea do the French call *La Manche*?

b6 *Which sea would you cross if you sailed from Suez to Aden?*

a7 In 1903, which brothers made the first manned, powered aeroplane flight?

b7 *Who was the famous woman aviator who flew from England to Australia in 1930?*

a8 What kind of food is lobscouse?

b8 *When would you eat tiffin?*

a9 Who wrote the novels known as *The Forsyte Saga*?

b9 *Who wrote the novel* A Passage to India?

a10 Which London church is particularly associated with the RAF?

b10 *Where in London was the British Empire Exhibition held in 1924?*

a11 Who composed the *Eroica* and *Pastoral* symphonies?

b11 *Who composed* Music for the Royal Fireworks *and the* Water Music?

a12 In which year did Britain go over to decimal currency?

b12 *In which year did Britain join the Common Market?*

No. 110 Answers

a1   The heart
b1   *To stop bleeding*
a2   Red, white, and blue
b2   *Black, yellow, and red*
a3   Portugal
b3   *Italy*
a4   Because it has no eyelids
b4   *Asp*
a5   *Oklahoma*
b5   The King and I
a6   The English Channel
b6   *Red Sea*
a7   The Wright Brothers
b7   *Amy Johnson*
a8   Stew (*accept*: thick soup)
b8   *Mid-morning or lunch time (light snack)*
a9   John Galsworthy
b9   *E. M. Forster*
a10   St Clement Dane's
b10   *Wembley*
a11   Beethoven
b11   *Handel*
a12   1971 (February)
b12   *1973*

Tie-breaker

Q What is the name of the towers built around the south and east coast for protection during the Napoleonic wars?
A *Martello Towers*

No. 111

a1 Of which country is the chipmunk a native?

b1 *From what is chipboard made?*

a2 What colour are gorse flowers?

b2 *What colour are Aylesbury ducks?*

a3 On which river does the City of Cambridge stand?

b3 *In Oxford, what is the Bodleian?*

a4 From which musical do the numbers 'Anything You Can Do', 'Doin' What Comes Naturally', and 'The Girl That I Marry' come?

b4 *From which musical comes the song 'Don't Cry for Me, Argentina'?*

a5 On which race course is the St Leger run?

b5 *On which race course are the Chair, Canal Turn, and Beecher's Brook?*

a6 What idea is sometimes represented by a statue of a blindfolded woman holding a pair of scales?

b6 *Which flower do you associate with the Earl Haig Fund?*

a7 With what is an actuary concerned?

b7 *What does a philatelist collect?*

a8 What is hard water?

b8 *What is cordite?*

a9 Who wrote the lines, 'Should auld acquaintance be forgot/And never brought to mind'?

b9 *According to the carol, on Christmas Day in the morning, how many ships came sailing by?*

a10 Who hid in an oak tree after the Battle of Worcester?

b10 *Whose troops were known as Ironsides?*

a11 What is a siskin?

b11 *What is a basilisk?*

a12 In a novel by Richard Adams, what sort of animal is Hazel?

b12 *Whose monster was created by the novelist Mary Shelley?*

No. 111 Answers

a1   Canada or USA
b1   *Waste (or small) pieces of wood*
a2   Yellow
b2   *White*
a3   Cam
b3   *Library*
a4   *Annie Get Your Gun*
b4   Evita
a5   Doncaster
b5   *Aintree*
a6   Justice
b6   *Poppies*
a7   Statistics, numbers, insurance
b7   *Postage stamps*
a8   Water which does not lather easily with soap or water; which contains lime or other chemicals
b8   *An explosive (smokeless)*
a9   (Robert) Burns
b9   *Three*
a10   Charles the Second
b10   *Cromwell (Oliver) (not Thomas)*
a11   A bird (a type of finch)
b11   *A reptile or lizard (supposed to be able to blind by its stare)*
a12   A rabbit (in *Watership Down*)
b12   *Frankenstein's*

Tie-breaker

Q Which English poet, born in America, wrote the poems *The Waste Land* and *Four Quartets*, and a series of poems about 'Practical Cats' which now form the basis of the new musical *Cats?*

A *T. S. Eliot*

No. 112

a1 What is a male sheep called?

b1 *What is a male goose called?*

a2 What two colours are there on the Austrian flag?

b2 *What two colours appear on the Greek flag?*

a3 For which flower is larkspur another name?

b3 *Which early spring flower, grown from bulbs, may be purple, white, or yellow?*

a4 On which island is the seaport of Famagusta?

b4 *Off the coast of which county are the Goodwin Sands?*

a5 Which food was not rationed during the war but *was* rationed from 1946?

b5 *After the last war, in which of these years did food rationing end: 1947, 1950, 1954?*

a6 Which two countries fought each other at Flodden in 1513?

b6 *Which two countries fought each other at Poitiers in 1356?*

a7 In London, where is the ceremony of the keys performed each night?

b7 *In Westminster Abbey, where is the Stone of Scone to be found?*

a8 What is special about the chameleon lizard?

b8 *What is distinctive about a crustacean?*

a9 If fusion is the joining of particles, what is fission?

b9 *In olden times, what did alchemists try to do to ordinary metals?*

a10 Which English soccer team plays at home at the Baseball Ground?

b10 *Which soccer team plays at home at Maine Road?*

a11 Which one word indicates that a piece of music is to be played in an abrupt, sharply detached manner?

b11 *If a musical note is raised by a sharp, what lowers it?*

a12 Who wrote the novel *Madame Bovary*?

b12 *What nationality were the writers Goethe and Schiller?*

No. 112 Answers

a1   Ram (*or* wether)
b1   *Gander*
a2   Red and white
b2   *Blue and white*
a3   Delphinium
b3   *Crocus*
a4   Cyprus
b4   *Kent*
a5   Bread
b5   *1954*
a6   England, Scotland
b6   *England, France*
a7   Tower of London
b7   *Beneath the Coronation Chair*
a8   It can change its colour (*accept*: also it can go for a long time without food)
b8   *They have a hard shell (and two pairs of feelers) (e.g. crabs, lobsters)*
a9   The splitting (of atoms)
b9   *Turn them into gold*
a10 Derby (County)
b10 *Manchester City*
a11 Staccato
b11 *A flat*
a12 (Gustave) Flaubert
b12 *German*

Tie-breaker

Q   Which legendary king of Thebes killed his father without knowing and then married his mother?
A   *Oedipus*

No. 113

a1 What is a greenhorn?

b1 *Who would wait in a green room?*

a2 What colour is indigo?

b2 *What colour is ormolu?*

a3 What is (or was) a gentleman's gentleman?

b3 *What does a builder use to check if something is level?*

a4 When we spoke of the motor car, the Morris 8, what did the 8 indicate?

b4 *Which country does a car come from if it carries the International Registration letters GBJ?*

a5 How many degrees in a right angle?

b5 *How many faces has a triangular based pyramid?*

a6 Which English county is often known as 'Constable Country'?

b6 *In which county is Windsor Castle?*

a7 What nationality was the composer Gustav Holst?

b7 *What nationality was the composer Rimsky-Korsakov?*

a8 *In which year did the General Strike take place?*

b8 *In which year did men first climb Everest?*

a9 Peter May, Ray Illingworth, and Ted Dexter have all captained the England team in the same sport. What sport is that?

b9 *In which sport is the Thomas Cup played for?*

a10 From which fish does caviar traditionally come?

b10 *Through what stage does a butterfly go, between being an egg and a chrysalis?*

a11 In the famous hymn, what line comes after 'Onward Christian Soldiers'?

b11 *The hymn beginning, 'And did those feet . . .' is known by the name of which city?*

a12 In a book, 'All for one and one for all' is the motto of what group?

b12 *Which author set many of his novels in the Five Towns?*

No. 113 Answers

a1 Someone who is ignorant, naïve

b1 *Actors, performers (a rest room or room used for socializing or eating, backstage in a theatre)*

a2 Deep blue (blue/violet)

b2 *Gold or bronze*

a3 A manservant, a valet

b3 *Spirit-level*

a4 Its horse power

b4 *Jersey*

a5 Ninety

b5 *Four*

a6 Suffolk

b6 *Berkshire*

a7 English (Swedish descent)

b7 *Russian*

a8 1926

b8 *1953*

a9 Cricket

b9 *Badminton*

a10 Sturgeon

b10 *Caterpillar (or larva)*

a11 'Marching as to war'

b11 Jerusalem

a12 The Three Musketeers

b12 *Arnold Bennett*

Tie-breaker

Q Which legend is the basis of an opera by Gounod, a play by Goethe, and a symphony by Liszt?

A *Faust*

No. 114

a1 Which people go hunting in kayaks?

b1 *What was strange about the ship the* Marie Celeste *when it was found in the Atlantic in 1872?*

a2 What is meant in cookery by the term devilled?

b2 *What is meant by basting?*

a3 How many carats is chemically pure gold?

b3 *For which chemical element is K the symbol?*

a4 Which historical figure was known as the Young Pretender?

b4 *Traditionally, what was Nell Gwyn's job when Charles II first saw her?*

a5 In which sport would you use a foil or an épée?

b5 *In which game in 1978 did Anatoly Karpov battle it out against Viktor Korchnoi?*

a6 With which bird is the island of Lundy traditionally associated?

b6 *When the dove is a symbol of peace, what is it often shown holding in its mouth?*

a7 Who wrote the novel The Old Curiosity Shop?

b7 *Who wrote* Black Beauty?

a8 For what festival is Colchester particularly noted?

b8 *On the day before Good Friday, what does the Queen distribute each year?*

a9 In London, what does the Monument commemorate?

b9 *Which London square was laid out to commemorate a famous naval battle of 1805?*

a10 In grammar, what is the difference between a phrase and a clause?

b10 *What is a euphemism?*

a11 Who composed the opera Il Trovatore?

b11 *Who composed the opera* The Marriage of Figaro?

a12 Of what two main colours is the flag of the city of London?

b12 *What are the two main colours on the Vatican flag?*

No. 114 Answers

a1 Eskimos (kayaks = sealskin boats)
b1 *No one on it, everything else normal*
a2 Grilled or mixed with a hot sauce (e.g. curry, mustard, chilli)
b2 *Pouring hot fat (or other liquid) over meat while it is cooking*
a3 Twenty-four
b3 *Potassium (Kalium)*
a4 Bonnie Prince Charlie (Charles Edward Stuart)
b4 *Orange-seller*
a5 Fencing
b5 *Chess (world championship)*
a6 Puffin
b6 *Olive branch, sprig of olive*
a7 Charles Dickens
b7 *Anna Sewell*
a8 Oyster festival (Oyster Feast)
b8 *Maundy Money*
a9 The (start of the) Great Fire of London (in 1666)
b9 *Trafalgar Square*
a10 A clause has a (finite) verb in it
b10 *A polite or 'nice' way of saying something unpleasant*
a11 Verdi
b11 *Mozart*
a12 Red and white
b12 *Yellow and white*

Tie-breaker

Q Which dramatist wrote the plays *Jumpers*, *Dirty Linen*, and *Travesties*?
A *Tom Stoppard*

No. 115

a1   In slang, what is a fence?
b1   In which activity are 'Yoicks and 'Tally ho' traditionally shouted?
a2   In heraldry, what colour is 'or'?
b2   Sepia is a shade of what colour?
a3   What are young pilchards called?
b3   What kind of fish is a finnan?
a4   With which country is sangria particularly associated?
b4   Of which country is Juventus an association football team?
a5   In the game of chess, which piece must be protected at all costs?
b5   In chess, how does a bishop move?
a6   For what is Cranwell in Lincolnshire famous?
b6   For which city is Le Bourget an airport?
a7   Which is the longest river in France?
b7   On which African river are the Victoria Falls?
a8   Between 73 and 71 BC, who led a revolt of slaves and gladiators against the Romans?
b8   Who is said to have brought up Romulus and Remus?
a9   Besides being a racehorse, who or what was Nijinsky?
b9   Which popular singer died in 1977, after playing a round of golf?
a10   Who was the author of *Ivanhoe*?
b10   Which famous writer set his novels in 'Wessex'?
a11   Which English county is traditionally the centre of the cotton industry?
b11   For what has Glyndebourne in Sussex become famous?
a12   Who composed the *Nutcracker* ballet suite?
b12   Who composed the opera Götterdämmerung?

No. 115 Answers

a1   A receiver of stolen goods
b1   *Hunting*
a2   Gold
b2   *Brown*
a3   Sardines
b3   *Haddock (cured)*
a4   Spain
b4   *Italy*
a5   King
b5   *Diagonally*
a6   RAF (Training establishment)
b6   *Paris*
a7   Loire
b7   *Zambezi*
a8   Spartacus
b8   *A wolf*
a9   Ballet dancer
b9   *Bing Crosby*
a10   Sir Walter Scott
b10   *Thomas Hardy*
a11   Lancashire
b11   *Opera*
a12   Tchaikovsky
b12   *Wagner*

Tie-breaker

Q   When the Danes invaded England King Ethelred paid them money
to keep away. By what name was that money known?
A   *Danegeld*

No. 116

a1 Complete the following proverb: 'One man's meat . . .'
b1 *Complete the following proverb: 'One swallow . . .'*
a2 What kind of fruit is a calabash?
b2 *What kind of fruit is a nectarine?*
a3 Which British prime minister was forced to resign in 1940?
b3 *Which was the first Labour Government in this country to have an outright majority in the Commons?*
a4 Whereabouts does a fish have its dorsal fin?
b4 *How many wings have butterflies and moths?*
a5 Which is the highest mountain in the Alps?
b5 *Which is the smallest of the four main Channel Islands?*
a6 If silver is your 25th wedding anniversary, what metal denotes your tenth?
b6 *How long have you been married if you are celebrating your wooden anniversary?*
a7 Of which geometrical figure can you find the area by using the formula ½×width×height?
b7 *In geometry, which word describes a line that is at right angles to the horizontal?*
a8 The Campbells massacred the Macdonalds in a Scottish valley in 1692. Name the valley.
b8 *Name the village or town near Hastings where the famous battle was fought in 1066.*
a9 Who composed the *New World Symphony*?
b9 *Which composer is famous for his* Rhapsody in Blue?
a10 What is the name of the island in the Thames where Magna Carta was sealed by King John?
b10 *What do we call the large sandbanks off the east coast of Kent?*
a11 Which country lies immediately west of Algeria?
b11 *Which country lies immediately south of Mongolia?*
a12 Who wrote the novel *The Hunchback of Notre Dame*?
b12 *Who wrote the novel* Saturday Night and Sunday Morning?

No. 116 Answers

a1   '. . . is another man's poison'
b1   *'doesn't make a summer'*
a2   Gourd (*accept*: Melon)
b2   *Type of peach*
a3   (Neville) Chamberlain
b3   *Attlee's (in 1945)*
a4   On its back (or its top)
b4   *Four*
a5   Mont Blanc
b5   *Sark*
a6   Tin
b6   *Five years*
a7   Triangle
b7   *Perpendicular*
a8   Glencoe
b8   *Battle*
a9   (Antonin) Dvorák
b9   *George Gershwin*
a10   Runnymede
b10   *Goodwin Sands (Goodwins)*
a11   Morocco
b11   *China*
a12   Victor Hugo
b12   *Alan Sillitoe*

Tie-breaker

Q   Which English composer's works include the operas *Peter Grimes* and *Billy Budd*, the ballet *Death in Venice* and also *The Young Person's Guide to the Orchestra*?
A   *Benjamin Britten*

No. 117

a1 According to the proverb, what happens to a fool and his money?

b1 *According to the proverb, who laughs loudest?*

a2 Into which ocean does the River Amazon flow?

b2 *Into which sea does the River Mississippi flow?*

a3 What article of furnishing do you associate with the town of Kidderminster?

b3 *What famous dance takes place in Helston each year?*

a4 Is a sea-horse a fish, a mammal, or a reptile?

b4 *What kind of creature is a salamander?*

a5 Which Queen of France was executed in 1793?

b5 *Which fortress was stormed at the beginning of the French Revolution?*

a6 Which famous keeper of a diary wrote, 'And so to bed'?

b6 *Which queen said of Gladstone, 'He speaks to me as though I was a public meeting'?*

a7 What form of entertainment requires a libretto?

b7 *Which Gilbert and Sullivan opera takes place on board an English warship?*

a8 In which county is the market town Bakewell?

b8 *In which county is the Isle of Ely?*

a9 Who painted the ceiling of the Sistine Chapel?

b9 *Which artist painted* The Yellow Chair, Sunflowers *and* The Sower?

a10 In which of Dickens' books do we meet Smike and Wackford Squeers?

b10 *In which of Dickens' novels do we read about Mr Micawber?*

a11 In Great Britain, in which month of the year does the flat racing season traditionally start?

b11 *In the 1974 World Cup, of which international team was the footballer Johan Cruyff the captain?*

a12 In science, what do we call the asexual reproduction of a genetic carbon copy of an animal or plant?

b12 *In space, 'zero G' is another term for . . . what?*

No. 117 Answers

a1   They're soon parted
b1   *He who laughs last*
a2   (South) Atlantic
b2   *Gulf of Mexico (accept: Atlantic Ocean)*
a3   Carpets
b3   *Floral Dance (or Furry Dance)*
a4   Fish
b4   *Reptile (lizard/amphibian)*
a5   Marie Antoinette
b5   *Bastille*
a6   Samuel Pepys
b6   *Queen Victoria*
a7   Opera or oratoria (*accept*: operetta, cantata)
b7   HMS Pinafore
a8   Derbyshire
b8   *Cambridgeshire*
a9   Michelangelo
b9   *Vincent Van Gogh*
a10   *Nicholas Nickleby*
b10   David Copperfield
a11   March
b11   *Holland*
a12   Clone
b12   *Weightlessness*

Tie-breaker

Q In Greek mythology, what was the job of Ganymede?
A *Cup-bearer (to Zeus)*

No. 118

a1   What do we call a female fox?

b1   *What was the Bunny Hug?*

a2   What is the colour of ripe bilberries?

b2   *Which fruit is a cross between a blackberry and a raspberry?*

a3   Which Scottish king defeated the English at the Battle of Bannockburn?

b3   *Which Scottish outlaw gave his name to a book by Walter Scott?*

a4   In which radio programme did we regularly hear the question 'Are you sitting comfortably'?

b4   *In which radio serial did we meet Dick, Jock, and Snowy?*

a5   Which creature is said to have the most legs?

b5   *How many legs has a Bombay Duck?*

a6   Which king ruled in England from 1087 to 1100?

b6   *Which queen said, 'I have the body of a weak and feeble woman'?*

a7   What is the name of the tiny republic situated on the Italian peninsula not far from the resort of Rimini?

b7   *What is the name of the tiny principality high in the Pyrenees, between Spain and France?*

a8   Who wrote the novel *Round the World in Eighty Days*?

b8   *Who wrote the novel* The Invisible Man?

a9   What is the equivalent in degrees fahrenheit of 100 degrees centigrade?

b9   *Light changes direction when entering a substance like glass or water from the air. What do we call this?*

a10   Close to which island are the rocks known as the Needles?

b10   *What is the name of the chief town on the island of Guernsey?*

a11   What is meant by the musical term *allegro*?

b11   *In music what is meant by the term* forte?

a12   In a lunar month, how many phases of the moon are there?

b12   *How many sheets of writing paper make a quire?*

No. 118 Answers

a1   Vixen
b1   *Dance*
a2   Dark blue (*accept* but qualify, purple)
b2   *Loganberry*
a3   Robert the Bruce
b3   *Rob Roy*
a4   *Listen with Mother*
b4   Dick Barton
a5   Millipede
b5   *None (it's a fish)*
a6   William II
b6   *Elizabeth I*
a7   San Marino
b7   *Andorra*
a8   Jules Verne
b8   *H. G. Wells*
a9   212
b9   *Refraction*
a10   Isle of Wight
b10   *St Peter Port*
a11   Fairly fast; lively; briskly
b11   *Strongly; loudly*
a12   Four
b12   *Twenty-four*

Tie-breaker

Q   By what name is the medical condition hypertension more commonly known?

A   *High blood pressure*

No. 119

a1   In cookery, what is meant by *au gratin*?

b1   What would be sold in the patisserie department of a supermarket?

a2   What is the radius of a circle?

b2   What is the plural of the word radius?

a3   For what kind of paintings did Sir Joshua Reynolds become famous?

b3   Which animal was George Stubbs famous for painting?

a4   Which two countries form the bulk of the Iberian Peninsula?

b4   Which two countries are separated by the Rio Grande?

a5   In which war was the Battle of Edge Hill?

b5   In which war did the battle of Inkerman take place?

a6   What noise is the bittern famous for making?

b6   Whereabouts does a fish have its pelvic fin?

a7   What nationality was the composer Henry Purcell?

b7   What nationality was the composer Mozart?

a8   Of which metropolitan county is Gateshead a borough?

b8   In which new county is the Clifton Suspension Bridge?

a9   In a novel, on which island were Jack, Ralph, and Peterkin shipwrecked?

b9   In the novel by John Buchan, how many steps were there?

a10   In grammar, what function does an adjective perform?

b10   In English, which word has the name 'definite article'?

a11   In which Welsh county is Cardiff?

b11   In which town are the administrative headquarters of the Orkney Islands?

a12   By what name are members of the Unification Church often known?

b12   What religious cult or system was founded by Mary Baker Eddy?

No. 119 Answers

a1   Covered with cheese or breadcrumbs; with a crust

b1   Cakes

a2   Distance from the centre to the circumference

b2   Radii

a3   Portraits

b3   The horse

a4   Spain and Portugal

b4   USA and Mexico

a5   The English Civil War (1642)

b5   Crimean

a6   Booming

b6   Underneath it; on its belly

a7   English/British

b7   Austrian

a8   Tyne and Wear

b8   Avon

a9   Coral Island

b9   Thirty-nine

a10   Describes a noun

b10   The

a11   *South* Glamorgan

b11   Kirkwall

a12   Moonies

b12   Christian Science

Tie-breaker

Q Which English novelist wrote a number of satirical and comic novels, including *Scoop*, *Put Out More Flags*, and *Vile Bodies*?

A *Evelyn Waugh*

No. 120

a1 By what abbreviated name was wartime spiced ham known?

b1 *For what would you use cyclamate?*

a2 For what does the abbreviation anon. stand?

b2 *For what word is pram an abbreviation?*

a3 Which young man from Gloucestershire became a rich merchant and was three times Lord Mayor of London?

b3 *From 1861 to 1865, in which country was there a civil war, between the northern and southern states?*

a4 What colour is the fruit of an aubergine?

b4 *What kind of fruit is a cantaloup?*

a5 Into which sea does the River Rhone flow?

b5 *Into which sea does the River Jordan flow?*

a6 In England, where is the Weald?

b6 *In which county is Bodmin Moor?*

a7 In printing, what is an asterisk?

b7 *In printing, what sign is called an ampersand?*

a8 In natural history, what kind of creature is an osprey?

b8 *What is a barracuda?*

a9 Who wrote the novel *The Great Gatsby*?

b9 *Who wrote the novel* Barnaby Rudge?

a10 Which mountains are called the backbone of Wales?

b10 *Of which canal or waterway does Loch Ness form a part?*

a11 If you're celebrating your crystal wedding anniversary, how many years have you been married?

b11 *How long have you been married if you are celebrating your china wedding?*

a12 Who composed the music of the religious song, 'Jesu, Joy of Man's Desiring'?

b12 *Which composer is famous for his* Eine Kleine Nacht Musik?

No. 120 Answers

a1 Spam
b1 *To sweeten food or drink (non-fattening)*
a2 Anonymous (*accept*: without a name)
b2 *Perambulator*
a3 (Sir Richard or Dick) Whittington
b3 *United States of America*
a4 Purple
b4 *Melon*
a5 Mediterranean Sea
b5 *Dead Sea*
a6 Kent (and parts of Surrey and Sussex) (*accept*: South East England)
b6 *Cornwall*
a7 Star (*)
b7 *The sign for 'and' (&)*
a8 Bird (sea-eagle; sea-hawk)
b8 *A fish (like a large pike)*
a9 F. Scott Fitzgerald
b9 *Charles Dickens*
a10 Cambrian Mountains
b10 *Caledonian Canal*
a11 Fifteen
b11 *Twenty years*
a12 J. S. Bach
b12 *Mozart*

Tie-breaker

Q IN 1976, within a period of fifty days, who won the Olympic, World, and European men's figure skating titles?
A *John Curry*

No. 121

a1 Where are Britain's Royal Botanic Gardens?

b1 *Which tree or flower was named after a royal gardener called William Forsyth?*

a2 What is the opposite of a spring tide?

b2 *Which compass point is directly opposite south-south-east?*

a3 In 1917, in which country was there an October Revolution?

b3 *In 1812, who led the retreat from Moscow?*

a4 For what achievement did Louis Bleriot become famous in 1909?

b4 *What device was introduced by Leslie Hore-Belisha while he was Minister of Transport?*

a5 In which two countries is Lake Geneva?

b5 *Which two countries border Lake Superior?*

a6 Which French artist is famous for painting ballet dancers?

b6 *With which Italian city was Canaletto associated?*

a7 Who composed the opera *Rigoletto*?

b7 *Who composed the opera* The Magic Flute?

a8 In which English county is the new town of Telford?

b8 *In which English county is the town of Boston?*

a9 By what abbreviation is the Supreme Headquarters Allied Powers Europe known?

b9 *In the army, what is a WO?*

a10 In astrology, can you name two of the earth signs?

b10 *In astrology, can you name two of the water signs?*

a11 From which musical show came the song, 'I'm gonna wash that man right out of my hair'?

b11 *In which show and film is the song, 'Thank heaven for little girls'?*

a12 In our solar system, what type of body is Neptune?

b12 *In which direction does the tail of a comet point?*

No. 121 Answers

a1 Kew (in Surrey)
b1 *Forsythia*
a2 A neap tide
b2 *North-north-west*
a3 Russia
b3 *Napoleon*
a4 First man to fly the English Channel
b4 *Belisha beacons (pedestrian crossings)*
a5 Switzerland, France
b5 *USA and Canada*
a6 Degas (Edgar Degas)
b6 *Venice*
a7 Verdi
b7 *Mozart*
a8 Shropshire
b8 *Lincolnshire*
a9 SHAPE
b9 *Warrant Officer*
a10 Taurus, Virgo, Capricorn
b10 *Pisces, Cancer, Scorpio*
a11 South Pacific
b11 Gigi
a12 A planet
b12 *Away from the sun*

Tie-breaker

Q For which play by Ibsen did the Norwegian composer, Edvard Grieg,
write incidental music?

A *Peer Gynt*

No. 122

a1 Is tapioca animal, vegetable, or mineral?

b1 *What are Edam, Parmesan, and Stilton?*

a2 What is calligraphy?

b2 *What is matriarchy?*

a3 In which North American city is jazz supposed to have been born?

b3 *What was the surname of the jazz musician known as 'Jelly Roll'?*

a4 What is the name of the isolated lighthouse fourteen miles south of Plymouth?

b4 *What is the name of the ancient wall which crosses England from the Solway to Wallsend?*

a5 Where in London does the Trooping of the Colour take place each June?

b5 *In which month is the annual State Opening of Parliament?*

a6 Which Mediterranean island is sometimes called George Cross Island?

b6 *On which island was Archbishop Makarios a leader?*

a7 Which song, recorded by Lale Anderson, became popular with both Rommel's troops and the Eighth Army?

b7 *In the song, which girl was invited to ride on a bicycle made for two?*

a8 In 1807, which trade was abolished in the British Empire?

b8 *What kind of famine afflicted Ireland in the 1840s?*

a9 Which country lies immediately west of Argentina?

b9 *Which country lies immediately north of Hungary?*

a10 Apart from motor-racing, in which game do we use the term chicane?

b10 *How many players are there in a netball team?*

a11 How many readings does a bill have in the House of Commons?

b11 *How many are there in a baker's dozen?*

a12 Who wrote the play *Androcles and the Lion*?

b12 *Who wrote the novel* The Mayor of Casterbridge?

No. 122 Answers

a1   Vegetable (made from the roots of cassava)
b1   *Cheeses*
a2   Handwriting
b2   *Family or society ruled by a woman*
a3   New Orleans
b3   *Morton*
a4   Eddystone
b4   *Hadrian's Wall*
a5   Horse Guards Parade
b5   *November*
a6   Malta
b6   *Cyprus*
a7   'Lili Marlene'
b7   *Daisy*
a8   Slave Trade
b8   *Potato*
a9   Chile
b9   *Czechoslovakia*
a10   Bridge (hand with no trumps)
b10   *Seven*
a11   Three
b11   *Thirteen*
a12   George Bernard Shaw
b12   *Thomas Hardy*

Tie-breaker

Q In which of Shakespeare's plays do we meet Alonso, Ferdinand, and Miranda?

A *The Tempest*

No. 123

a1 For what are the letters RNLI an abbreviation?

b1 *What do the letters QC stand for?*

a2 *What is (or was) a durbar?*

b2 *What is a shillelagh?*

a3 Can you name one of the countries in which the Caucasus mountains are situated?

b3 *In which country are the Catskill Mountains?*

a4 In the world of music, for what is Antal Dorati chiefly known?

b4 *In what sport did Dixie Dean become famous?*

a5 Can you name a country famous for its geysers?

b5 *Name a country, besides Germany, through which the River Rhine flows.*

a6 Who composed 'Alexander's Rag Time Band' and 'Annie Get Your Gun'?

b6 *Who composed 'The Entertainer' and 'The Maple Leaf Rag'?*

a7 In 1282, which principality was conquered by Edward I?

b7 *In 1349, what disaster struck England?*

a8 Which is the largest: cello, double bass, or viola?

b8 *To which section of an orchestra does a bassoon belong?*

a9 Which famous international canal was opened to traffic in 1914?

b9 *What two seas are connected by the Suez Canal?*

a10 In which English county is Bamburgh Castle?

b10 *In which county is Salisbury Plain?*

a11 Who played the title role in the film *Spartacus*?

b11 *Of which film is 'Somewhere My Love' a theme tune?*

a12 In painting, what are the three primary colours?

b12 *What do we call the art which consists of gluing objects onto canvas?*

No. 123 Answers

a1 Royal National Lifeboat Institution

b1 *Queen's Counsel*

a2 The court of an Indian ruler (*accept*: public levée of Indian prince or Anglo-Indian governor)

b2 *(Irish) oak cudgel*

a3 Russia (Russian Federation), Georgia, Azerbaijan

b3 *USA*

a4 Conductor

b4 *Soccer (Everton, in the 1920s)*

a5 New Zealand/USA/Iceland

b5 *Switzerland, Holland (it does not actually flow through France)*

a6 Irving Berlin

b6 *Scott Joplin*

a7 Wales

b7 *The Black Death (bubonic plague)*

a8 Double bass

b8 *Woodwind*

a9 Panama Canal

b9 *Mediterranean Sea and Gulf of Suez or Red Sea*

a10 Northumberland

b10 *Wiltshire*

a11 Kirk Douglas

b11 *Dr Zhivago*

a12 Red, yellow, blue

b12 *Collage*

Tie-breaker

Q Which champion jockey won his first Derby on 'Never Say Die' and has gone on to win the race eight times in all, riding such famous horses as St Paddy and Nijinsky?

A *Lester Piggott*

No. 124

a1   What would you be doing if you were using a trug?

b1   What would you place in a bassinet?

a2   In geography, what is a confluence?

b2   On a mountain, what is scree?

a3   What famous event takes place at Calgary in July?

b3   What event is commemorated by the annual flying display at Biggin Hill each September?

a4   What tax did William Pitt introduce in 1799?

b4   During which war was the Victoria Cross first awarded?

a5   Yehudi Menuhin is famous for playing which instrument?

b5   With which musical instrument do we associate Larry Adler?

a6   Who wrote the novel *The Eagle Has Landed*?

b6   Who wrote the novel You Only Live Twice?

a7   Which is the longest river in Europe?

b7   Which is the longest river in the British Isles?

a8   Who composed the opera *Das Rheingold*?

b8   Who composed the opera La Traviata?

a9   With which invention is Sir Frank Whittle chiefly associated?

b9   Who invented the petrol engine?

a10   What name was given to the 1931 mutiny of sailors over pay cuts?

b10   In which group of islands are the Old Man of Hoy and Scapa Flow?

a11   Which musical note follows *fah*?

b11   In music, what is meant by presto?

a12   In which county is the Cheddar Gorge?

b12   In which English county is Portland Bill?

No. 124 Answers

a1 Gardening (basket)
b1 *Baby (it's a wicker cradle or pram)*
a2 Joining of two rivers
b2 *Loose rock; an area of small loose rocks*
a3 The Stampede
b3 *Battle of Britain, Battle of Britain Week*
a4 Income Tax
b4 *Crimean*
a5 Violin
b5 *Harmonica*
a6 Jack Higgins
b6 *Ian Fleming*
a7 Volga
b7 *The Shannon*
a8 Wagner
b8 *Verdi*
a9 Jet engine
b9 *(Gottlieb) Daimler*
a10 Invergordon Mutiny
b10 *Orkneys*
a11 Soh
b11 *Quickly*
a12 Somerset
b12 *Dorset*

Tie-breaker

Q In which sport has Tom Watson won many championships and been described as the 'World's Number One'?
A *Golf*

No. 125

a1 What do we call the chief member of the crew of a lifeboat?

b1 *What organization supervises the lighthouses around our coasts?*

a2 What is a paragon?

b2 *What is a somnambulist?*

a3 Can you name two of the countries that border Lake Constance?

b3 *Which two countries are linked by the Brenner Pass?*

a4 From which musical came the songs, 'Memory', 'The Jellicle Ball', and 'Macavity'?

b4 *From which musical did these songs come: 'Good Morning Starshine', 'Let The Sun Shine In', and 'Aquarius'?*

a5 Can you spell pronunciation?

b5 *Can you spell effervescence?*

a6 Which actor played eight roles in the film *Kind Hearts and Coronets*?

b6 *Which former film actress married Prince Rainier of Monaco?*

a7 In which county is the New Forest?

b7 *In which county is Beachy Head?*

a8 Which group of countries has become known as the CIS?

b8 *Which country was once known as the Weimar Republic?*

a9 Which painter also invented a type of helicopter and a parachute?

b9 *Who painted the famous pictures* The Haywain *and* Flatford Mill?

a10 What meaning have the words gauche and sinister in common?

b10 *What is meant by the Latin phrase* Non sequitur?

a11 In which century did the composer Chopin live and work?

b11 *Which famous composer left a symphony unfinished in 1822?*

a12 In 1963, what happened to the island of Surtsey off Iceland?

b12 *Which island (in what is now Indonesia) exploded in 1883?*

No. 125 Answers

a1 Coxswain
b1 *Trinity House (Corporation)*
a2 A model of excellence; someone who is very good at something (*also*: a perfect diamond)
b2 *Sleepwalker*
a3 Two of: Austria, Switzerland, West Germany
b3 *Italy and Austria*
a4 Cats
b4 Hair
a5 Pro *nun* cia tion
b5 *e f f e r v e s c e n c e*
a6 (Sir) Alec Guinness
b6 *Grace Kelly*
a7 Hampshire
b7 *(East) Sussex*
a8 The former Soviet Union (Commonwealth of Independent States)
b8 *Germany (1919–33)*
a9 Leonardo da Vinci
b9 *Constable*
a10 Left-handed
b10 *It doesn't follow*
a11 Nineteenth
b11 *Schubert*
a12 It came into being (after a volcanic eruption)
b12 *Krakatoa*

Tie-breaker

Q   In order to save Eurydice, which Greek hero was said to have descended into the underworld?
A   *Orpheus*

262

No. 126

a1 What kind of trees are crack, white, and sallow?

b1 *According to the song, with which American state do we associate the Yellow Rose?*

a2 In one city, which river is crossed by the High Level, Swing, and Queen Elizabeth II bridges?

b2 *Which river is spanned by the Clifton Suspension Bridge?*

a3 Who wrote the novel *Tinker, Tailor, Soldier, Spy*?

b3 *Who wrote the novel* Where Eagles Dare?

a4 What kind of animal is driven and cared for by a mahout?

b4 *In what kind of shop would you once have found a 'Nippy' at work?*

a5 In which year did the English defeat the Spanish Armada?

b5 *What terrible disaster struck London in 1665?*

a6 Of which country was Gough Whitlam a former prime minister?

b6 *Of which country was David Ben Gurion the first prime minister?*

a7 As what did Rachmaninov achieve fame?

b7 *Who composed the* Enigma Variations?

a8 At which religious ceremony might a requiem be sung?

b8 *What is the second line of the hymn that begins 'While shepherds watched their flocks by night'?*

a9 In which country is Mount Parnassus?

b9 *In which country is the Hill of Tara?*

a10 In which industry did Sir Alastair Pilkington make important inventions?

b10 *With which industry is the inventor Henry Bessemer chiefly associated?*

a11 In which Gilbert and Sullivan comic opera do we meet 'dear little Buttercup'?

b11 *In which Gilbert and Sullivan comic opera do we meet Yum-Yum and Pooh-Bah?*

a12 Which is England's largest lake?

b12 *In Britain, which cathedral has the highest spire?*

No. 126 Answers

a1   Willows
b1   *Texas*
a2   Tyne (Newcastle)
b2   *Avon*
a3   John le Carré
b3   *Alastair MacLean*
a4   Elephant (especially in India)
b4   *Tea shop; Lyons Corner House*
a5   1588
b5   *The Great Plague*
a6   Australia
b6   *Israel*
a7   Composer
b7   *Elgar*
a8   A funeral
b8   *All seated on the ground*
a9   Greece
b9   *Ireland (Eire)*
a10   Glass
b10   *Steel*
a11   *HMS Pinafore*
b11   The Mikado
a12   Windermere
b12   *Salisbury*

Tie-breaker

Q   'Of man's first disobedience, and the fruit of that forbidden tree . . .'
These are the opening words of which famous epic poem?
A   Paradise Lost *(by John Milton)*

No. 127

a1 To whom is blood money paid?

b1 *What don't you have to pay in a free port?*

a2 In the James Bond film *Live and Let Die*, who played Bond?

b2 *Who directed the films* The Birds, Strangers on a Train, *and* Psycho?

a3 To which king was Cardinal Wolsey a chief minister?

b3 *Which historical leader was known as the 'little corporal'?*

a4 Apart from Russia and the Ukraine, which is the largest European country (in land area)?

b4 *In surface area, which is the largest lake in the British Isles?*

a5 Which area of Britain is associated with the songs 'Blaydon Races', 'Cushy Butterfield', and 'The Lambton Worm'?

b5 *In a song, with which fair in Devon is Tom Pearce associated?*

a6 On the delta of which river is the port of Alexandria?

b6 *In which country is the River Amazon mainly situated?*

a7 What nationality was the painter Rembrandt?

b7 *What nationality was the painter Picasso?*

a8 What nationality was the composer Aaron Copland?

b8 *What nationality was the composer Edvard Grieg?*

a9 Which public building in London is the monarch *not* allowed to enter?

b9 *Who first said, 'That's one small step for a man, one giant leap for mankind'?*

a10 What was the middle name of the composer John Sousa?

b10 *What was the middle name of the poet S. T. Coleridge?*

a11 Of which political party was Aneurin Bevan a leading figure?

b11 *Which trades union is known as NUPE?*

a12 In geography, what is an isthmus?

b12 *What is an atoll?*

No. 127 Answers

a1 An informer, a turncoat or anyone who betrays a member of their side to the other in return for money

b1 *Customs Duty*

a2 Roger Moore

b2 *Alfred Hitchcock*

a3 Henry VIII

b3 Napoleon I (Bonaparte)

a4 France

b4 *Lough Neagh*

a5 North-East (Tyneside, Northumberland)

b5 *Widecombe*

a6 Nile

b6 *Brazil*

a7 Dutch

b7 *Spanish*

a8 American

b8 *Norwegian*

a9 House of Commons

b9 *Neil Armstrong (when stepping onto the moon)*

a10 Philip

b10 *Taylor (Samuel Taylor)*

a11 Labour

b11 *(National Union of) Public Employees*

a12 Narrow neck of land, joining two (larger) pieces of land

b12 *Ring shaped coral reef (enclosing a lagoon)*

Tie-breaker

Q In 1875, which swimmer became the first man to swim the English Channel?

A (Captain Matthew) Webb

No. 128

a1   How did Joan of Arc die?

b1   *How was Nelson killed at Trafalgar?*

a2   Which band leader's signature tune was 'In The Mood'?

b2   *What is the title of Glen Miller's famous signature tune?*

a3   What does a farrier do?

b3   *What does a fletcher do?*

a4   Which islands does the Pentland Firth separate from the mainland of Scotland?

b4   *Which group of islands lie midway between the Shetlands and Iceland?*

a5   From which musical came the lines 'I'm getting married in the morning' and 'Why can't a woman be more like a man'?

b5   *In which musical did Liza Minnelli play Sally Bowles?*

a6   For what was Sir Jacob Epstein famous?

b6   *What nationality was the architect Frank Lloyd Wright?*

a7   What is the name of the famous radio telescope site in Cheshire?

b7   *Which English town runs its own telephone service?*

a8   What kind of plant is a biennial?

b8   *What is special about a perennial plant?*

a9   Who wrote the novels *A Farewell to Arms* and *For Whom the Bell Tolls*?

b9   *Who wrote the novels* Martin Chuzzlewit *and* Dombey and Son?

a10   Which country lies immediately south-east of Pakistan?

b10   *Picardy is in the north-east of which country?*

a11   What were the London and North Eastern and the London Midland and Scottish?

b11   *What are Ribble, Crosville, and Southdown?*

a12   Which artist painted the picture *Whistler's Mother*?

b12   *Who painted the famous picture* The Fighting Téméraire?

No. 128 Answers

a1   Burnt at the stake
b1   *By a bullet (from a French sniper)*
a2   Joe Loss
b2   *'Moonlight Serenade'*
a3   He shoes horses
b3   *He makes arrows*
a4   Orkney
b4   *The Faroes*
a5   *My Fair Lady*
b5   Cabaret
a6   Sculpture
b6   *American*
a7   Jodrell Bank
b7   *(Kingston upon) Hull*
a8   One that lasts two years (planted one year, flowers and dies the next)
b8   *It lasts for several years*
a9   Ernest Hemingway
b9   *Charles Dickens*
a10   India
b10   *France*
a11   Railways (pre-nationalization)
b11   *Bus companies*
a12   Whistler (James McNeill)
b12   *Turner (William)*

Tie-breaker

Q How long have you been married if you are celebrating your pearl wedding?
A *Thirty years*

No. 129

a1   What colour are laburnum flowers?

b1   What kind of leaves do silkworms prefer?

a2   What kind of dance is a pavan?

b2   Which kind of lamp had a mantle?

a3   For what is Woomera in Australia famous?

b3   Of what substance is the Great Barrier Reef made?

a4   In which mountain range is Annapurna?

b4   In which country is the mountain, the Jungfrau?

a5   Besides Britain, name one of the countries involved in the battle of Trafalgar.

b5   Which prince 'won his spurs' at Crecy?

a6   Who sit on the cross benches in the House of Lords?

b6   What name is given to the seat occupied by the Lord Chancellor in the House of Lords?

a7   Who composed the opera *Fidelio*?

b7   Who composed the opera Lohengrin?

a8   What is the IMF?

b8   By what name is the International Bank for Reconstruction and Development colloquially known?

a9   In a song, who was advised not to put her daughter on the stage?

b9   On radio, in which serial was Mary often worried about Jim?

a10 Which of these is the odd one out: flute, harpsichord, piccolo, oboe?

b10 Dampers, hammers, and strings can all be found in which musical instrument?

a11 What is nemesis?

b11 Who lived in Valhalla?

a12 Which city is known as 'The City of Dreaming Spires'?

b12 With which English city do you connect the name Sarum?

No. 129 Answers

a1 Yellow

b1 *Mulberry*

a2 A slow and stately one (originally Italian or Spanish)

b2 *Gas*

a3 Rocket testing; launching range (Aborigine word = spear throwing stick)

b3 *Coral*

a4 Himalayas

b4 *Switzerland*

a5 France; Spain

b5 *Edward (the Black Prince)*

a6 Members not in any political party

b6 *The Woolsack*

a7 Beethoven

b7 *Wagner*

a8 International Monetary Fund

b8 *World Bank*

a9 Mrs Worthington (by Noel Coward)

b9 *'Mrs Dale's Diary'*

a10 Harpsichord (keyboard; others woodwind)

b10 *Piano*

a11 Fate, retribution (originally: Greek goddess of retribution)

b11 *The Norse Gods; plus Norse heroes*

a12 Oxford

b12 *Salisbury*

Tie-breaker

Q What are the seven colours of the rainbow?
A *Red, Orange, Yellow, Green, Blue, Indigo, Violet*

No. 130

a1 What is a billabong?

b1 *What is mah-jong?*

a2 With which season do we primarily associate the hymn which begins 'Forty days and forty nights'?

b2 *In the hymn, which words follow: 'We plough the fields and scatter . . .'?*

a3 In which war did Admiral Jellicoe command the British fleet?

b3 *Which was the only legal political party during Germany's Third Reich?*

a4 In France, what is the Mistral?

b4 *In the West Country, what is a tor?*

a5 Who composed the music for the show *Oliver*?

b5 *Who composed the music in* West Side Story?

a6 In which English county, principally, are the Mendips?

b6 *In which English county is much of our salt mined?*

a7 What was invented by Alfred Nobel?

b7 *What was invented by George Westinghouse?*

a8 Which country almost completely surrounds the Sea of Marmara?

b8 *Name a country which borders the Dead Sea.*

a9 Where are the National Maritime Museum and the Royal Naval College?

b9 *What is the longitude of Greenwich?*

a10 What is meant in music by the term *accelerando*?

b10 *What is meant when music is marked to be played* crescendo?

a11 Who wrote the novel *Under the Greenwood Tree*?

b11 *Who wrote the novel* Fair Stood the Wind for France?

a12 Which famous French artist painted a picture *At the Moulin-Rouge*?

b12 *The artist Frans Hals painted a famous cavalier. What was he doing?*

No. 130 Answers

a1	A dried-up watercourse (or river or brook)
b1	*(Chinese) game (played with 'tiles' like dominoes)*
a2	Lent
b2	*The good seed on the land*
a3	First World War
b3	*The Nazi Party*
a4	A cold (north-west) wind (*accept*: train)
b4	*Hill, rocky peak*
a5	Lionel Bart
b5	*(Leonard) Bernstein*
a6	Somerset
b6	*Cheshire*
a7	Dynamite
b7	*(Air) brakes*
a8	Turkey
b8	*Jordan, Israel*
a9	Greenwich
b9	*0° (0 degrees)*
a10	Getting quicker
b10	*It is to get gradually louder and louder*
a11	Thomas Hardy
b11	*H. E. Bates*
a12	(Henri) Toulouse-Lautrec
b12	*Laughing*

Tie-breaker

Q Which French playwright wrote *Le Bourgeois Gentilhomme*, *Le Malade Imaginaire*, and *Tartuffe*?

A *Molière*

No. 131

a1   From which fruit is cider made?

b1   What is the fruit of the blackthorn?

a2   What was invented by the French monk, Dom Peter Perignon?

b2   In 1924, what was first manufactured by the American Clarence Birdseye?

a3   Which year is the title of an overture by Tchaikovsky?

b3   Which year is the title of a novel by George Orwell?

a4   In 1974, which new county was formed out of part of County Durham and part of the North Riding of Yorkshire?

b4   In which city are the administrative headquarters of the Lothian region in Scotland?

a5   In history, what did Luddites destroy?

b5   In the 1960s, what did the Flower People want?

a6   On retirement, who might accept the stewardship of the Chiltern Hundreds?

b6   Who summons the Commons to the House of Lords to hear the Queen's speech?

a7   Who composed the famous *Skaters' Waltz*?

b7   Who composed the Bolero *to which Torvil and Dean danced so successfully?*

a8   Where does the plant samphire grow?

b8   Where do or did troglodytes live?

a9   Who died first of Queen Victoria, Dickens, and Gladstone?

b9   Who lived longest of Queen Victoria, Michelangelo, and George Bernard Shaw?

a10   About which year is Stanley Kubrick's film that is sub-titled 'A Space Odyssey'?

b10   When Hollywood remade the film Seven Samurai *as a Western, what was its new name?*

a11   In which county is the Wrekin?

b11   In which English county is The Cheviot?

a12   Which country has the largest population?

b12   In area, which is the largest country in South America?

No. 131 Answers

a1	Apples
b1	*Sloe*
a2	Champagne
b2	*Frozen foods*
a3	1812
b3	*1984*
a4	Cleveland
b4	*Edinburgh*
a5	Machines (especially new ones)
b5	*Peace, love*
a6	An MP
b6	*Black Rod ('Gentleman Usher of the Black Rod')*
a7	Waldteufel
b7	*Ravel*
a8	On rocks; cliffs; seashore
b8	*In caves (accept: alone)*
a9	Dickens
b9	*George Bernard Shaw (94)*
a10	2001
b10	*The Magnificent Seven*
a11	Shropshire
b11	*Northumberland*
a12	China
b12	*Brazil*

Tie-breaker

Q Can you name four citrus fruits?
A *Oranges, lemons, grapefruits, limes, citrons*

No. 132

a1   What is the 'Old Lady of Threadneedle Street'?

b1   *Name the monthly magazine published by the Consumer's Association.*

a2   You've heard of the road to Mandalay — in which country is Mandalay?

b2   *Where are the Pillars of Hercules?*

a3   On which river stand the towns of Quebec and Montreal?

b3   *On which river do Chatham and Rochester stand?*

a4   Which band leader was lost in an aircraft over the English Channel on 15 December 1944?

b4   *Which star is generally associated with the song 'Somewhere Over the Rainbow'?*

a5   In 1953, besides Sir Edmund Hillary, who reached the summit of Everest?

b5   *In 1620, which group of people landed in America?*

a6   Can you spell the word 'rhythm'?

b6   *Spell 'eyrie' (the home of an eagle).*

a7   What did the Montgolfier brothers invent in Paris in 1783?

b7   *In 1939, Igor Sikorsky flew the first really successful — what?*

a8   What is a yucca?

b8   *Who first wrote about Yahoos (in Gulliver's Travels)?*

a9   Who wrote the novel *King Solomon's Mines*?

b9   *Who wrote the book Chitty Chitty Bang Bang?*

a10   Which Derbyshire town is famous for a crooked spire?

b10   *Which town in Devon is famous for carpets?*

a11   In the song, how did darling Clementine die?

b11   *In a song, what was the time of day we heard a maid sing 'O don't deceive me'?*

a12   Which French leader is buried at Colombey-les-deux-Eglises?

b12   *Where is Sir Winston Churchill buried?*

No. 132 Answers

a1   Bank of England
b1   'Which'
a2   Burma
b2   *Entrance to the Mediterranean; either side of the Straits of Gibraltar*
a3   St Lawrence
b3   *Medway*
a4   Glen Miller
b4   *Judy Garland*
a5   (Sherpa) (Norgay) Tensing
b5   *Pilgrim Fathers*
a6   R h y t h m
b6   *E y r i e*
a7   Hot-air balloon
b7   *Helicopter*
a8   Plant (American, white flowered)
b8   *Jonathan Swift*
a9   H. Rider Haggard
b9   *Ian Fleming*
a10   Chesterfield
b10   *Axminster*
a11   Drowned; 'fell into the foamy brine'
b11   *Early one morning*
a12   General de Gaulle
b12   *Bladon*

Tie-breaker

Q   Name the seven dwarfs in Disney's *Snow White*
A   *Bashful, Grumpy, Happy, Doc, Sleepy, Sneezy, Dopey*

No. 133

a1   What is mined at Kimberley in South Africa?

b1   And what is mined at Kimberley in Australia?

a2   Under whose leadership did Mafeking withstand its seven-month siege?

b2   Over whose head was a sword suspended by a single hair?

a3   Batik is a method of doing what?

b3   What do we call the making of patterns by inlaying different coloured pieces of wood?

a4   If you flew in a straight line from Tunisia to Egypt, which one intervening country would you cross?

b4   Is Mongolia north, south, east, or west of China?

a5   Who wrote the song 'We'll Gather Lilacs'?

b5   In which musical is the song 'Kansas City'?

a6   If A is Alpha and B is Bravo, what is V?

b6   What is the last letter of the Greek alphabet?

a7   About which ship, principally, is the film *A Night to Remember*?

b7   Which film featured Irving Berlin songs 'Easter Parade' and 'White Christmas'?

a8   In 1884, what was invented by Lewis Waterman?

b8   What was invented by E. G. Otis?

a9   Of which metropolitan county is Waltham Forest a borough?

b9   Of which metropolitan county is the Wirral a borough?

a10   In politics, what is a plebiscite?

b10   What is a quisling?

a11   Who was the Roman general who supported Caesar and fell in love with Cleopatra?

b11   With which famous admiral do we connect the name of Lady Hamilton?

a12   Which composer started composing at the age of five, and played before royalty the following year?

b12   Which famous composer went on composing after he had gone deaf?

No. 133 Answers

a1	Diamonds
b1	*Gold*
a2	Lord Baden-Powell
b2	*Damocles*
a3	Way of printing designs on cloth, decorating cloth (using wax and dye)
b3	*Marquetry*
a4	Libya
b4	*North*
a5	Ivor Novello
b5	Oklahoma!
a6	Victor
b6	*Omega*
a7	*Titanic*
b7	Holiday Inn
a8	Fountain pen
b8	*Lifts, elevators*
a9	(Greater) London
b9	*Merseyside*
a10	A referendum; direct vote by all the voters
b10	*A traitor; someone who co-operates with the enemy*
a11	(Mark) Antony
b11	*Nelson*
a12	Mozart
b12	*Beethoven*

Tie-breaker

Q Which English poet wrote *Samson Agonistes* and *Comus*?
A (John) Milton

No. 134

a1   What is or was a pyracantha?

b1   What is or was a diplodocus?

a2   What means of communication did Alexander Graham Bell invent?

b2   Besides Joseph Swan, who developed the first electric light bulbs?

a3   Besides being an actual star in the sky, what is a star of Bethlehem?

b3   Snap-dragon is a popular name for which flower?

a4   Who founded the London Police Force?

b4   Which famous Russian revolutionary was assassinated in Mexico?

a5   For what were Edmund Keen, David Garrick, and Henry Irving all famous?

b5   Whereabouts in a theatre are the wings?

a6   Which English city has road tunnels called Kingsway and Queensway?

b6   In which English city is the Bull Ring?

a7   What does a numismatist collect?

b7   In Britain, who is given the Privy Purse?

a8   Of which county is the national art gallery called the Prado?

b8   In which country is the Spanish Riding School?

a9   Who composed the opera Aïda?

b9   Who composed the music in the opera Peter Grimes?

a10   In area, which is the largest of these: Isle of Man, Isle of Wight, Anglesey?

b10   In surface area, which is the largest lake in Scotland?

a11   Of which country are the main political parties Fianna Fail and Fine Gael (say: Feena Foil and Feena Gale)?

b11   Of which country is the parliament the Knesset?

a12   What do we call the group of compounds containing nitrogen necessary for life and growth and found in meat, fish, and milk?

b12   In a flower, what do we call the male reproductive organ which produces pollen?

No. 134 Answers

a1   It's a shrub/bush; evergreen (*accept*: tree)
b1   *It was a dinosaur (type of extinct reptile)*
a2   Telephone
b2   *(Thomas) Edison*
a3   A plant, flower (like a lily)
b3   *Antirrhinum*
a4   Robert Peel
b4   *Trotsky*
a5   Acting
b5   *Sides of the stage*
a6   Liverpool (Merseyside)
b6   *Birmingham*
a7   Coins
b7   *Queen (or king) (money for personal use)*
a8   Spain
b8   *Austria (Vienna)*
a9   Verdi
b9   *(Benjamin) Britten*
a10   Anglesey
b10   *Loch Lomond*
a11   Irish Republic, Eire
b11   *Israel*
a12   Protein
b12   *Stamen*

Tie-breaker

Q   What date each year is United Nations Day?
A   *24 October*

No. 135

a1 Of what are Globe and Jerusalem varieties?

b1 *What kind of food is pemmican?*

a2 St Mary's, Tresco, and St Martin's all belong to which group of islands?

b2 *Of which European country are Jutland and Zealand a part?*

a3 Who succeeded Lenin as leader of the Soviet Union in 1924?

b3 *Whose mistress or wife was Eva Braun?*

a4 What is the unit of currency in India?

b4 *Which language is spoken in Brazil?*

a5 Who composed the music for *Kiss Me Kate, Can Can*, and *High Society*?

b5 *Who wrote the lyrics (the words) of* The Sound of Music?

a6 Between the wars, what was the National Anthem of Germany?

b6 *According to the song, who used to wait underneath the lantern, by the barrack gate?*

a7 Who wrote the novel *The Day of the Jackal*?

b7 *Who wrote the novel* The Big Sleep?

a8 In heraldry, what word describes an animal with its front legs raised?

b8 *In heraldry, what colour is argent?*

a9 Whose picture is on the back of an English £5 note?

b9 *Who founded London's Promenade Concerts?*

a10 Which composer wrote the *Flight of the Bumble Bee*?

b10 *Which modern composer wrote the* Fantasia on Greensleeves?

a11 In which country are the Vosges Mountains?

b11 *In which country are the Southern Alps?*

a12 In which county is the Fylde?

b12 *In which county is Romney Marsh?*

No. 135 Answers

a1 Artichoke
b1 *Dried (concentrated) meat, usually beef*
a2 The Isles of Scilly
b2 *Denmark*
a3 Stalin
b3 *Hitler's*
a4 Rupee (100 pasas = 1 rupee)
b4 *Portuguese*
a5 Cole Porter
b5 *Oscar Hammerstein II*
a6 *Deutschland Uber Alles*
b6 *Lilli Marlene*
a7 Frederick Forsyth
b7 *Raymond Chandler*
a8 Rampant
b8 *Silver*
a9 Duke of Wellington
b9 *(Sir) Henry Wood*
a10 Rimsky-Korsakov
b10 *Vaughan Williams*
a11 France
b11 *New Zealand*
a12 Lancashire
b12 *Kent*

Tie-breaker

Q The 'life cycle' of a creature is the series of changes it goes through from birth to adulthood. What is the life cycle of a frog?
A *Egg to tadpole to frog to egg*

No. 136

a1   Agnetha, Bjorn, Benny, and Frida were all members of which pop group?

b1   *Who was the main star of the film* City Lights?

a2   Who rescued Bonnie Prince Charlie by disguising him as a maid?

b2   *Who was the famous architect who rebuilt much of London after the great fire of 1666?*

a3   With what do you connect the Rothschild family?

b3   *What does a bear do to shares on the Stock Market?*

a4   What kind of stage show is *Giselle*?

b4   *In ballet, what is the* Corps de ballet?

a5   Between the World Wars, where did the League of Nations meet?

b5   *In which city are the administrative headquarters of the European Community?*

a6   On the north bank of which major river does Hull stand?

b6   *Which English county lies immediately south of the Solway Firth?*

a7   Who discovered the virus called rabies and developed an inoculation against the disease?

b7   *With which animal is the scientist Pavlov associated?*

a8   Near which holiday resort is the Great Orme?

b8   *Which Scottish city is served by Dyce airport?*

a9   At sea, when is the first watch?

b9   *On board ship when is the middle watch?*

a10   Which international organization's flag is blue with a white globe and two olive branches on it?

b10   *In Britain, in 1970, what happened to the age of majority?*

a11   How would you play a piece of music marked *adagio*?

b11   *What is meant by the musical term* largo?

a12   In population and area, which is the world's smallest sovereign country?

b12   *In area, which is the second largest country in the world?*

No. 136 Answers

a1   ABBA
b1   *Charlie Chaplin*
a2   Flora Macdonald
b2   *(Sir Christopher) Wren*
a3   Banking/finance
b3   *Sends them down in value*
a4   Ballet
b4   *The dancers who are not soloists; the equivalent of the chorus*
a5   Geneva
b5   *Brussels*
a6   Humber
b6   *Cumbria*
a7   (Louis) Pasteur
b7   *Dogs*
a8   Llandudno
b8   *Aberdeen*
a9   8pm–midnight
b9   *0000 hours to 0400 hours; Midnight to 4 a.m.*
a10   United Nations Organization
b10   *Lowered from 21 to 18; became 18*
a11   Slowly
b11   *Slowly, dignified*
a12   Vatican (City State)
b12   *Canada*

Tie-breaker

Q   Which English novelist and screenplay writer became famous before the war for his books *Mr Norris Changes Trains* and *Goodbye to Berlin*?
A   *Christopher Isherwood*

No. 137

a1   Which acid is present in tea?

b1   Belle Hélène *is a way of serving which fruit?*

a2   What would you be most likely to be buying if you were gazumped?

b2   *What does an Australian mean when he says something is played according to Rafferty's Rules?*

a3   Which former coin used to be nicknamed a joey?

b3   *How much money is meant by the slang term, a monkey?*

a4   On which lake stands the town of Montreux?

b4   *In which continent is Lake Titicaca?*

a5   Who composed the music for the musical *Cats*?

b5   *Who wrote the musical* Glamorous Night?

a6   In medieval times, what were performed in the streets of Chester, York, and Wakefield?

b6   *In the theatre, what is planned by a choreographer?*

a7   Whose ship was the first to sail right round the world?

b7   *Which famous explorer sailed on the* Golden Hind?

a8   Which of these plants are grown from bulbs: lupin, snowdrop, poppy, tulip?

b8   *Which of these are made from vegetable material: cotton, silk, linen, wool?*

a9   Who became prime minister of Britain on 5 April 1976?

b9   *In 1963, who renounced his peerage on becoming prime minister?*

a10   What is meant by albino?

b10   *Which gas in the air do plants absorb?*

a11   What nationality was the composer Franz Schubert?

b11   *Which German composer is famous for his Hungarian dances?*

a12   After China, which country has the largest population?

b12   *By population, which is the largest city in the world?*

No. 137 Answers

a1 Tannic (*allow*: tannin)
b1 *Pears (with butter and chocolate)*
a2 A house
b2 *Anything goes; there are no rules*
a3 Threepenny bit
b3 *£500 ($500 in USA)*
a4 Lake Geneva
b4 *(South) America*
a5 Andrew Lloyd Webber
b5 *Ivor Novello*
a6 (Mystery) plays (miracle plays)
b6 *Dance steps, dance routines*
a7 (Ferdinand) Magellan
b7 *(Sir Francis) Drake*
a8 Snowdrop, tulip
b8 *Cotton, linen*
a9 James Callaghan
b9 *Sir Alec Douglas-Home/Lord Home*
a10 Animal, human, or plant lacking normal colouring (in animals the hair and skin being white)
b10 *Carbon dioxide*
a11 Austrian
b11 *(Johannes) Brahms*
a12 India
b12 *Tokyo*

Tie-breaker

Q Name five of the states in Australia
A *Tasmania, Western Australia, Queensland, Northern Territory, Victoria, New South Wales, South Australia*

No. 138

a1   Which soccer team is sometimes known as the Canaries?

b1   *To see which sport would you be most likely to go to Kempton?*

a2   Gas Cooled and Fast Breeder are both types of what?

b2   *What do we call a group of stars?*

a3   On which one river stand the cities of Patna and Calcutta?

b3   *Can you name the river on which both Belgrade and Budapest stand?*

a4   Which Frenchman made popular the song 'Thank Heaven For Little Girls'?

b4   *Which singer is particularly associated with the songs, 'Sing As We Go' and 'Sally In Our Alley'?*

a5   In this country, in 1973 which tax replaced purchase tax?

b5   *Our so-called silver coins are no longer made of silver. What are they made of?*

a6   Which Russian wrote the famous novel *War and Peace*?

b6   *Who wrote the novel* Doctor Zhivago?

a7   Which is the smallest of the following: furlong, fathom, or chain?

b7   *In which of these three years were motoring tests first introduced: 1919, 1935, or 1946?*

a8   Of what is genealogy the study?

b8   *What does a megalomaniac believe?*

a9   Topiary is the art of shaping and trimming — what?

b9   *Which American tree is generally said to grow the largest?*

a10   Which is the largest musical instrument with a keyboard?

b10   *In the orchestra, which brass instrument has a sliding, adjustable tube?*

a11   Where is Transylvania?

b11   *Where was the Spanish Main?*

a12   In which Shakespeare play do we meet a monster called Caliban?

b12   *In Shakespeare, who plots Othello's downfall?*

No. 138 Answers

a1   Norwich City

b1   *Horse racing*

a2   Nuclear power reactors (*accept:* nuclear power plants or stations)

b2   *Constellation (accept: galaxy)*

a3   Ganges

b3   *Danube*

a4   Maurice Chevalier

b4   *Gracie Fields*

a5   VAT (Value Added Tax)

b5   *Cupro-nickel*

a6   Leo Tolstoy

b6   *(Boris) Pasternak*

a7   Fathom

b7   *1935*

a8   Families; family trees; history of families

b8   *That he or she is very powerful or important*

a9   Trees; bushes; hedges

b9   *Redwood*

a10   Organ

b10   *Trombone*

a11   Eastern Europe; Romania/Hungary

b11   *South America's northern coast; the Caribbean*

a12   The Tempest

b12   *Iago*

Tie-breaker

Q   Of the five classic horse races, name the two that are run at Epsom.

A   *The Derby, the Oaks*

No. 139

a1   What is special about the seeds of laburnum trees?

b1   *What is special about a bonsai tree?*

a2   What is pumpernickel?

b2   *From which part of a cow do we get tripe?*

a3   On which river stands the Lancashire town of Preston?

b3   *On which river stands the city of Durham?*

a4   Which fleet, in 1588, was commanded by the Duke of Medina Sidonia?

b4   *Which was the first nuclear powered submarine?*

a5   Which famous scientist set sail in a ship called the *Beagle*?

b5   *Which famous expedition in 1947 was led by Thor Heyerdahl?*

a6   Of what three colours is the Luxembourg flag?

b6   *Of what two colours is the Spanish flag?*

a7   In the world of newspapers, who was nicknamed 'The Beaver'?

b7   *Of which country was Campbell-Bannerman once prime minister?*

a8   What was the unit of currency in Yugoslavia?

b8   *What is the unit of currency in South Africa?*

a9   Which country lies immediately south of Albania?

b9   *Which country lies immediately north of Bulgaria?*

a10   Which composer's *Symphony No 94* is known as 'The Surprise'?

b10   *Whose* Pastoral Symphony *was first performed in 1808?*

a11   Who was the first actor to be made a lord?

b11   *Which music hall entertainer was known as the Prime Minister of Mirth?*

a12   In which human organ are there two atria and two ventricles?

b12   *In a mammal, which organ controls the amount of water in the body and takes out waste substances from the blood?*

No. 139 Answers

a1   They are poisonous

b1   *It's a miniature one (grown in a pot: Japanese)*

a2   (Rye) Bread (German)

b2   *Its stomach*

a3   Ribble

b3   *Wear*

a4   Spanish (Armada)

b4   Nautilus *(1955)*

a5   Charles Darwin

b5   *Kon Tiki*

a6   Red, white, and blue

b6   *Red and yellow*

a7   Lord Beaverbrook

b7   *Great Britain (United Kingdom)*

a8   Dinar

b8   *The rand*

a9   Greece

b9   *Romania*

a10   Haydn

b10   *Beethoven*

a11   Lord Olivier (Sir Laurence)

b11   *George Robey*

a12   Heart

b12   *Kidneys*

Tie-breaker

Q   For what purpose would a doctor prescribe an analgesic or a distalgesic?

A   *As a pain killer (drug)*

No. 140

a1   Which English sport has its headquarters in St John's Wood?

b1   *Which yacht race is sailed every two years from Cowes on the Isle of Wight to a rock off the south-west coast of Ireland and back to Plymouth?*

a2   What is an incisor?

b2   *What is meant by incisive?*

a3   Who wrote the music and words for *My Fair Lady*?

b3   *Who wrote the words and music for* Evita?

a4   For which invention is Sir Humphry Davy best remembered?

b4   *In 1935, what was invented (or pioneered) by Dr George Gallup?*

a5   In which hills is the source of the River Thames?

b5   *At the mouth of which river do we find Spurn Head and Grimsby?*

a6   Which Music Hall entertainer do you connect with the song 'Keep Right on to the End of the Road'?

b6   *Which band leader ended his broadcasts by playing 'Here's to the Next Time'?*

a7   What colour are the flowers of the mimosa tree?

b7   *What colour are the berries of the Mountain Ash tree?*

a8   Who wrote the novel *Mr Midshipman Hornblower*?

b8   *Who wrote books about triffids, krakens, and Midwich cuckoos?*

a9   In 1972, Ceylon changed its name. What is it now called?

b9   *Which colony will cease to be British after 1997?*

a10   Which famous mountain overlooks Cape Town in South Africa?

b10   *What name is given to the hill in Athens on which the Parthenon stands?*

a11   Which European country has schillings as its currency unit?

b11   *What is the unit of currency in Argentina?*

a12   In what unit is electrical resistance measured?

b12   *Of what is ballistics the science?*

No. 140 Answers

a1 Cricket (at Lords)
b1 Fastnet Race
a2 A tooth (a tooth used for cutting)
b2 Going directly to the point (of whatever is being discussed, etc.)
a3 Alan J. Lerner and Frederick Loewe
b3 Tim Rice and Andrew Lloyd Webber
a4 Miner's lamp
b4 Opinion polls; opinion surveys
a5 Cotswolds
b5 Humber
a6 Harry Lauder
b6 Henry Hall
a7 Yellow
b7 Red
a8 C. S. Forester
b8 John Wyndham
a9 Sri Lanka
b9 Hong Kong
a10 Table Mountain
b10 Acropolis
a11 Austria
b11 The peso
a12 Ohms
b12 Guns; pistols; bullets, etc.

Tie-breaker

Q How many strings has a violin (and which notes do they play)?
A *Four (G, D, A, E)*

292

No. 141 Explain Yourself!

a1   Who or what is Shanks' pony?

b1   *What is meant by walking in Indian file?*

a2   What is a cock and bull story?

b2   *What is meant by cock-eyed?*

a3   Which people originally used boomerangs?

b3   *What is a didgeridoo?*

a4   What is meant by Bristol Fashion?

b4   *What is Bristol Cream?*

a5   What is (or was) a cat o' nine tails?

b5   *Apart from being part of a cat, what is (or was) a cat's whisker?*

a6   What is terra firma?

b6   *And what is terracotta?*

a7   What is Esperanto?

b7   *What is voodoo?*

a8   To which of the senses does the word olfactory refer?

b8   *To which of the senses does the word tactile refer?*

a9   What is a pince-nez?

b9   *What is a lorgnette?*

a10   What happens to something if it is literally petrified?

b10   *What do you do if you pulverize something?*

a11   If a schoolboy goes miching, what is he doing?

b11   *What do you do if you go moonlighting?*

a12   What do we call a word that is a rearrangement of the letters of another word?

b12   *What is meant by the word penultimate?*

No. 141 Answers

a1   Walking, travelling on foot
b1   *Walking in single file (in the footprints of the man in front)*
a2   An untrue one; a made-up one
b2   *Squinting; askew (accept: stupid)*
a3   Australian Aborigines
b3   *Australian pipe-like musical instrument*
a4   Tidy; organized
b4   *A type of sherry*
a5   Whip (with nine lashes)
b5   *Part of an old-fashioned wireless (wire connected to the crystal)*
a6   Dry land
b6   *Pottery; earthenware, brown-red colour (accept: statue, ornament)*
a7   An invented language intended for international use
b7   *Magic; witchcraft (African, West Indian)*
a8   Smell
b8   *Touch*
a9   Pair of eye-glasses (held on with a nose clip, rather than side pieces)
b9   *Pair of eye-glasses (usually held by long handle; or opera glasses)*
a10   It turns to stone
b10   *Crush or grind or beat it to powder*
a11   Playing truant, hiding (West Country and Wales)
b11   *Take another job in addition to your normal one*
a12   Anagram
b12   *Next to last*

Tie-breaker

Q   What is controlled by a joystick?
A   *The movement of an aircraft in flight (accept: computer game)*

No. 142 Words, Words, Words

a1 How do we pronounce the word which is spelt: p h y s i q u e?

b1 *And how do we pronounce the word spelt: p n e u m a t i c?*

a2 By adding a prefix to the adjective normal, what word of opposite meaning can we make?

b2 *And by adding a prefix to the adjective loyal, what word of opposite meaning can be formed?*

a3 What adjective can be formed from the noun nonsense?

b3 *And what noun can be formed from the verb oblige?*

a4 What mistake did a cricket commentator make when he said that the scorer 'has done a bit of mental arithmetic with his calculator'?

b4 *What's wrong with this comment: 'Marie Scott from Fleetwood, the 17-year-old had plummeted to the top'?*

a5 And what was wrong with Jim Laker describing a cricket match as 'A unique occasion really, a repeat of Melbourne 1977'?

b5 *When commentating on darts, Sid Waddell said, 'The pendulum is swinging back and forth like a metronome.' What's wrong with that?*

a6 What was John Snagge forgetting when he said, 'I can't see who's in front, it's either Oxford or Cambridge'?

b6 *What's wrong with Richie Benaud's remark, 'The hallmark of a great captain is the ability to win the toss at the right time.'*

a7 Also talking about cricket, what's wrong with Trevor Bailey's comment, 'He's on 90, 10 away from that mythical figure'?

b7 *'Both these players seem to anticipate the play of each other almost before it happened.' Why isn't that absolutely right?*

What do the following phrases mean — and from which language do they come?

a8 Per favore

b8 *Kaput*

a9 En avant

b9 *Bona fide*

a10 Nyet

b10 *Danke schön*

a11 Arrivederci

b11 *Merci beaucoup*

a12 Muchas gracias

b12 *Anno Domini*

No. 142 Answers

a1 Physique (fizz-eek)

b1 *Pneumatic (new-matic)*

a2 Abnormal

b2 *Disloyal*

a3 Nonsensical

b3 *Obligation (accept: the legal terms obligor and obligee)*

a4 Mental arithmetic is done in your head

b4 *To plummet is to fall*

a5 Unique means one only; it can't be unique if it's happened twice

b5 *Pendulum hangs down as it swings; Metronome points up as it swings*

a6 Only Oxford and Cambridge take part in the boat race (which is what he was commenting on)

b6 *Winning the toss is luck: not ability*

a7 100 is a real, not mythical (imaginary) number

b7 *You can only anticipate something before it happens*

a8 Please (Italian)

b8 *Broken, 'bust' (German)*

a9 Forward (French)

b9 *Genuine, in good faith (Latin)*

a10 No (Russian)

b10 *Thank you very much (German)*

a11 Goodbye (Italian)

b11 *Thank you very much (French)*

a12 Thank you very much (Spanish)

b12 *In the year of our Lord (Latin)*

Tie-breaker

Q How do you spell 'subsistence'?

A *s u b s i s t e n c e*

No. 143 The Point of the Prefix

First, a group of questions, the answers to which all begin with the letters M-I-N

a1   A sweet flavoured herb, often used in a sauce with roast lamb?

b1   An item of clothing originally made famous in the 1960s and still very popular today?

a2   A soup made from a variety of vegetables and pasta?

b2   One of the states in the USA?

a3   The imperial dynasty of China which ruled from 1368 to 1644?

b3   Which word means a very small painting or portrait?

a4   Which 'min' means a wandering mediaeval singer or musician?

b4   Can you give me the word which means small, precise, or trifling?

These words all begin with M-E-D.

a5   A badge given for bravery?

b5   Something a doctor might give you to make you better?

a6   Can you give me an adjective which describes the period of time between, say, AD 500 and 1500?

b6   Can you tell me the name of the large stretch of water separating two continents, one of which is Europe?

a7   Someone who spends long periods in religious contemplation?

b7   Something which is merely of middling or medium quality?

a8   A mixture or succession of several tunes or pieces of music?

b8   Someone who tries to reconcile in a dispute between two or more different people or groups might be described as a — what?

And now a group of words beginning C-E-L.

a9   A stringed musical instrument?

b9   A room, usually underground?

a10   A plant whose stems are sometimes used as a cooked vegetable or in a salad?

b10   An alternative to the word Centigrade?

a11   A person who is famous — perhaps in the world of show-business?

b11   Something heavenly, divine or a body up in the sky?

a12   A transparent wrapping material made from viscose?

b12   Someone who remains unmarried, especially by religious vow?

No. 143 Answers

a1	Mint
b1	*Miniskirt*
a2	Minestrone
b2	*Minnesota*
a3	Ming
b3	*Miniature*
a4	Minstrel
b4	*Minutiae or Minute*
a5	Medal/Medallion (allow either)
b5	*Medicine or Medication*
a6	Mediaeval
b6	*Mediterranean*
a7	Meditation/Meditating
b7	*Mediocre*
a8	Medley
b8	*Mediator*
a9	'Cello (Violoncello)
b9	*Cellar*
a10	Celery
b10	*Celsius*
a11	Celebrity
b11	*Celestial*
a12	Cellophane
b12	*Celibate*

Tie-breaker

Q Which C-E-L word means swiftness?
A *Celerity*

No. 144 Round Britain Quiz

a1   What name is given to someone who comes from the Scilly Isles?

b1   *Off which headland is the Longships Lighthouse?*

a2   Which is the most southerly point on the English mainland?

b2   *On the south coast, which county lies between Hampshire and Devon?*

a3   In which county are the Quantock Hills?

b3   *In which English town did Romans once take the waters and later Beau Nash became a leader of fashion?*

a4   What is special about the White Horse of Uffington?

b4   *On which river does Southampton stand?*

a5   In which Berkshire town is the Royal Military Academy?

b5   *In which English city is the Fitzwilliam Museum?*

a6   On which river stands the city of Norwich?

b6   *Burnham, Thorpe, in Norfolk, is the birthplace of which famous admiral?*

a7   Until 1974, which was the smallest county in England?

b7   *Which fuel is brought ashore from West Sole and the Lemon Field in the North Sea?*

a8   Which great house in Derbyshire is sometimes called the Palace of the Peak?

b8   *Which is the smallest cathedral city in Britain?*

a9   Which English city did the Romans call Deva?

b9   *Which hill in Lancashire is particularly associated with witches?*

a10   In which English town or city is the Land of Green Ginger?

b10   *For what is Fylingdales in Yorkshire now famous?*

a11   Which cathedral city is especially associated with the Venerable Bede?

b11   *Which stretch of water separates Scotland from the north east coast of Cumbria?*

a12   In which Scottish region is Dundee?

b12   *Which is the Granite City?*

No. 144 Answers

a1   A Scillonian

b1   Land's End

a2   The Lizard

b2   Dorset

a3   Somerset

b3   Bath

a4   It's carved into the hillside (350 feet long) (Said to commemorate Alfred's victory over the Danes)

b4   River Test (or River Itchen)

a5   Sandhurst

b5   Cambridge

a6   Wensum

b6   Lord Nelson

a7   Rutland

b7   (Natural) Gas

a8   Chatsworth House

b8   St David's

a9   Chester

b9   Pendle

a10   Hull (Kingston upon Hull)

b10   Early warning radar station

a11   Durham

b11   Solway Firth

a12   Tayside

b12   Aberdeen

Tie-breaker

Q   What and where is the North Minch?

A   An area (or 'arm') of sea; that part of the Atlantic Ocean that separates the Outer Hebrides from the Scottish mainland.

No. 145 Top of the Form

History:

a1   In which war did Florence Nightingale tend the wounded?

b1   Which president of Egypt was assassinated in 1981?

a2   In which country were there groups of warriors known as Samurai?

b2   What is the OAU?

a3   Of which country was Kemal Attaturk a leader?

b3   Which American president resigned over the Watergate scandal?

Geography:
What is the capital city of each of these countries:

a4   Kenya?

b4   Afghanistan?

a5   Jordan?

b5   Zaire?

a6   Lithuania?

b6   Sudan?

a7   Zambia?

b7   Bangladesh

Mathematics:

a8   What do we call an eight sided polygon?

b8   How many angles has a decagon?

a9   Leo is 50 per cent older than Roy. By what percentage is Roy younger than Leo?

b9   What is the square root of 625?

Science:

a10   What is the opposite of an alkali?

b10   What is the name of that gas that is used to make fizzy drinks fizzy?

a11   What common substance is manufactured from silicates of lime, soda, and potash?

b11   How many colours are there in the spectrum?

a12   Which of these is not a metal: Uranium, Neon, Copper?

b12   On a map, what places are joined by isotherms?

No. 145 Answers

a1   The Crimean War
b1   President Anwar Sadat
a2   Japan
b2   *The Organization for African Unity*
a3   Turkey
b3   *(Richard) Nixon*
a4   Nairobi
b4   *Kabul*
a5   Amman
b5   *Kinshasa*
a6   Vilnius
b6   *Khartoum*
a7   Lusaka
b7   *Dacca*
a8   Octagon
b8   *Ten*
a9   33⅓
b9   *25*
a10 An acid
b10 *Carbon dioxide*
a11 Glass
b11 *Seven*
a12 Neon (it is a gas)
b12 *Places that have the same temperature*

Tie-breaker

Q   And finally in this round, who can spell 'scintillating'?
A   *scin till a ting*

No 146 Names and Nouns

a1   For what first name is Hal an abbreviation?

b1   *Giovanni is the Italian equivalent of which English first name?*

a2   What would you do on a pogo-stick?

b2   *Of what is a pommel a part?*

a3   Many Scottish surnames begin with Mac: what does Mac mean?

b3   *What is the English equivalent of the Irish name Sean?*

a4   If a Brecon Buff hisses, what does a Khaki Campbell do?

b4   *What is a Portuguese Man o' War?*

a5   What would you be most likely to do with a hassock?

b5   *What would you normally do at an escritoire?*

a6   On what would you be most likely to find a ferrule?

b6   *For what would you be most likely to use a swizzle stick?*

a7   Originally, in which country was the word sahib once a form of address?

b7   *Who traditionally received a dowry?*

a8   What would you be arranging if you were doing *ikebana*?

b8   *What do you use to make patterns in macramé?*

a9   Originally, what was a kaleidoscope?

b9   *What kind of precious stone is the Koh-i-noor?*

a10   Why is a hamburger so called, even though there is no ham in it?

b10   *What's the difference between a hornbeam and a hornbill?*

a11   If you suffered the bastinado, which part of you would be affected?

b11   *What are Evzones?*

a12   If you're an arctophile, what do you like or collect?

b12   *Of what is cartography the science?*

No. 146 Answers

a1   Henry (*accept*: Harry)

b1   *John*

a2   Bounce along; jump up and down

b2   *Saddle (rounded part) or sword (ball-shaped handle)*

a3   Son of

b3   *John*

a4   It quacks (it's a duck; a Brecon Buff is a goose)

b4   *Jellyfish*

a5   Kneel on it

b5   *Write*

a6   Walking stick; cane; umbrella

b6   *Mixing drinks (especially cocktails)*

a7   India

b7   *A husband (when he married his wife) (accept: widow, on death of her husband)*

a8   Flowers, twigs, etc.

b8   *String*

a9   Toy (tube with mirrors in which are seen patterns of coloured glass)

b9   *Diamond*

a10   It was invented in Hamburg (in Germany)

b10   *Hornbeam is a tree; hornbill is a bird*

a11   Feet (oriental method of caning)

b11   *Greek soldiers (riflemen; they wear skirts)*

a12   Teddy bears

b12   *Map-making*

Tie-breaker

Q What can a polyglot do?
A *Speak or understand many languages*

No. 147 Quickly, please!

a1 What is a sheepshank?

b1 *What is a spinney?*

a2 Who would be most likely to have a woggle?

b2 *What is or was an Eton crop?*

a3 What is a game (or gammy) leg?

b3 *What is the wife of a sultan called?*

a4 What is Reuters?

b4 *What is Tass?*

a5 Where would you find a watermark?

b5 *If a woman at a dance is described as a wallflower, what does she lack?*

a6 What would you do with a flageolet?

b6 *What two things would you expect to do at a* thé dansant?

a7 What does a bibliophile love?

b7 *What is a portmanteau?*

a8 In Japan, what is hara-kiri?

b8 *Where would you usually find an epitaph written?*

a9 Originally, on what did we ring changes?

b9 *In olden times, what was a Gentleman of the Road?*

a10 What is a tercentary?

b10 *What is a termagent?*

a11 Of what is linguistics the science?

b11 *What is nitrous oxide colloquially known as?*

a12 What is a Shangri-La?

b12 *What kind of material is shantung?*

No. 147 Answers

a1   Knot; hitch used to shorten rope
b1   *Small wood, thicket*
a2   Boy Scout
b2   *Hairstyle*
a3   A lame one (Celtic dialect)
b3   *Sultana*
a4   News agency
b4   *A Russian news agency*
a5   In paper (or banknotes, postage stamps)
b5   *A partner*
a6   Blow it (small flute)
b6   *Dance, drink tea*
a7   Books
b7   *Trunk (accept: suitcase)*
a8   (Ritual) suicide
b8   *On a tomb or gravestone*
a9   (Church) bells
b9   *Highwayman*
a10   Three-hundredth anniversary
b10   *A noisy or quarrelsome woman*
a11   Languages; words
b11   *Laughing gas*
a12   A place where everything is beautiful, pleasant
b12   *Silk*

Tie-breaker

Q   In Chicago, in gangster days, what was the purpose of a Mickey Finn?
A   *To drug you, make you unconscious*

No. 148 Who Said That?

Who first said the following?

a1   'Let's do it, let's fall in love'

b1   *'Dance, dance, dance little lady'*

a2   'Wakey-wakey! Rise and shine!'

b2   *'Give him the money, Barney'*

a3   'Whatever goes upon two legs is an enemy. Whatever goes upon four legs, or has wings, is a friend.'

b3   *'Wish me luck as you wave me goodbye'*

a4   'Miss Otis regrets she's unable to lunch today'

b4   *'My goodness, those diamonds are lovely!' 'Goodness had nothing to do with it'*

a5   'To be or not to be, that is the question'

b5   *'Once more unto the breach, dear friends'*

a6   'Hath not a Jew eyes? Hath not a Jew hands, organs, dimensions, senses, affections, passion?'

b6   *'Ill met by moonlight, proud Titania'*

And in history, who said:

a7   'I have the body of a weak and feeble woman'

b7   *'We are not amused'*

a8   'Who will rid me of this turbulent priest?'

b8   *'How is the Empire?'*

a9   'Let them eat cake'

b9   *'Because it is there'*

a10 'The whole of Gaul is divided into three parts'

b10 *'Let not poor Nelly starve'*

a11 'I believe it is peace in our time'

b11 *'An iron curtain has descended across the continent'*

a12 In which Gilbert and Sullivan opera are the words 'My object all sublime, I shall achieve in time. — To let the punishment fit the crime'?

b12 *In which Gilbert and Sullivan opera are the words 'I'm called Little Buttercup, dear little Buttercup'?*

No. 148 Answers

a1   Cole Porter

b1   *Noel Coward*

a2   Billy Cotton (in his 'Bandshow')

b2   *Wilfred Pickles (in 'Have a Go!')*

a3   Snowball (in *Animal Farm* by George Orwell)

b3   *Gracie Fields*

a4   Cole Porter

b4   *Mae West*

a5   Hamlet

b5   *Henry V*

a6   Shylock

b6   *Oberon*

a7   Elizabeth I

b7   *Victoria*

a8   Henry II (of Thomas à Becket)

b8   *George V (supposedly these were his last words before his death. Others say his last words were 'Bugger Bognor')*

a9   Marie Antoinette (attributed to her; in fact the remark had been made before)

b9   *Sir Edmund Hillary (on being asked why he climbed Everest)*

a10   Julius Caesar

b10   *Charles II*

a11   Neville Chamberlain

b11   *Winston Churchill*

a12   *The Mikado*

b12   HMS Pinafore

Tie-breaker

Q   Who wrote the lines: 'A little learning is a dangerous thing; Drink deep, or taste not the Pierian Spring'?

A   (Alexander) Pope

No. 149 Mainly for Linguists!

a1   What do the Latin words *Deo volente* mean?

b1   *What is the meaning of 'hoo ha' adopted from the Yiddish?*

a2   What does the Latin phrase *in loco parentis* mean?

b2   *In Spain, if someone said* Vamose, *what would he mean?*

a3   To what does the Australian term pom or pommie refer?

b3   *In America, what is a chowder?*

a4   What is the American phrase 'fifty cards in the pack' used to imply of someone?

b4   *Which is larger, an English or an American billion?*

a5   If you were in a car in America, how would you probably be travelling?

b5   *In America, what is the Old Glory?*

a6   In which country is Tamil a native language?

b6   *Which language has derived from that of Dutch settlers in South Africa?*

a7   Which language superseded the dead Semitic language of Aramaic?

b7   *What is the main language spoken in Thailand?*

a8   Where might you expect the Bantu family of languages to be spoken?

b8   *What is the official language of Venezuela?*

a9   In grammar, what is a gerund?

b9   *What is a Spoonerism?*

a10   What is a hyperbole (say: *hy-per-bo-lee*)?

b10   *What is tautology?*

a11   What is alliteration?

b11   *What is parenthesis?*

a12   Which language is Dansk in its own language?

b12   *What is the main language of Bangladesh?*

No. 149 Answers

a1 God willing

b1 *Fuss and bother*

a2 In the place of a parent

b2 *Let's go!*

a3 An Englishman, especially one who has come to settle in Australia

b3 *Famous clam stew*

a4 Mental deficiency; 'something missing'

b4 *English: 1,000,000,000,000; American: 1,000,000,000*

a5 By rail

b5 *American flag*

a6 India, Ceylon

b6 *Afrikaans*

a7 Arabic

b7 *Thai*

a8 Central Africa

b8 *Spanish*

a9 Verbal noun; noun formed from verb by adding -ing; a noun with the form of a present participle

b9 *Inversion of initial letters of words, eg. saying 'the town drain' when you mean 'the down train'*

a10 Exaggeration for emphasis

b10 *Unnecessary repetition*

a11 Sequence of words with same initial letter

b11 *One or more words added or introduced as an added explanation (or afterthought), often separated from the rest of the sentence by a pair of commas or brackets*

a12 Danish

b12 *Bengali*

Tie-breaker

Q What is onomatopoeia? (say: on-o-mat-o-pe-ah)

A *Words whose sound is their meaning (for example: crash, bang, cuckoo . . .)*

No. 150 More Spellings!

a1   Can you spell 'committee'?

b1   *Spell 'desperate'*

a2   Who can spell 'colander' (the kitchen utensil for draining things) (*say*: cull-ender)?

b2   *Can you spell 'delicatessen'?*

a3   Spell 'paraffin'

b3   *Who can spell 'phosphorus'?*

a4   Who can spell 'archipelago'?

b4   *Who can spell 'guarantee'?*

a5   How do you spell 'privilege'?

b5   Who can spell 'fluorescent'?

a6   How do you spell 'sciatica'?

b6   *Can you spell 'obstreperous'?*

a7   Can you spell 'innocuous'?

b7   *Spell 'resistance'*

a8   Spell 'acoustics'

b8   *Can you spell 'Antarctic', the area round the South Pole?*

a9   Spell 'antediluvian'

b9   Spell 'impeccable'

a10   Spell 'fuchsia'

b10   *Can you spell 'Mississippi'?*

a11   Can you spell 'pseudonym'?

b11   *Spell 'phlegmatic'*

a12   Spell 'predominance'

b12   *Spell 'reminiscence'*

No. 150 Answers

a1 committee
b1 desperate
a2 colander
b2 delicatessen
a3 paraffin
b3 phosphorus
a4 archipelago
b4 guarantee
a5 privilege
b5 fluorescent
a6 sciatica
b6 obstreperous
a7 innocuous
b7 resistance
a8 acoustics
b8 antarctic
a9 antediluvian
b9 impeccable
a10 fuchsia
b10 mississippi
a11 pseudonym
b11 phlegmatic
a12 predominance
b12 reminiscence

Tie-breaker

Q Can you spell 'iridescent'?
A IRIDESCENT

312

No. 151

a1   What are cherubim and seraphim?

b1   *What is a warlock?*

a2   Where in Wales is the International Music Festival held each year?

b2   *What sort of show is held in late May each year, in the Royal Hospital grounds, London?*

a3   What kind of creature was Tyrannosaurus Rex?

b3   *What do we call the hardened remains of a prehistoric plant or creature that has been preserved in a rock?*

a4   By what name was Lord Avon known when he was prime minister?

b4   *Of which political party was Hugh Gaitskill a leader?*

a5   Which British film told the story of Eric Liddell and Harold Abrahams?

b5   *Which early film star was called* The Great Lover *and starred in the film* The Sheik?

a6   Which English general rode a horse called Copenhagen?

b6   *In a zoo, what sort of animals were An-An and Chi-Chi?*

a7   What does an etymologist study?

b7   *What does an entomologist study?*

a8   For which month of the year is emerald the birthstone?

b8   *For which month of the year is ruby the birthstone?*

a9   Which country has a Union Jack and four stars of the Southern Cross in red on its flag?

b9   *Which New Zealand scientist was the first man to split the atom?*

a10   In Roman mythology, who was the god of war?

b10   *In classical mythology, who was the messenger of the gods?*

a11   Which planet is nearest the Earth?

b11   *Which is the largest planet in our solar system?*

a12   Which playing card is sometimes called 'The Curse of Scotland'?

b12   *In Scotland, what is 'the roaring game'?*

No. 151 Answers

a1   Angels
b1   A male witch or wizard
a2   Llangollen
b2   (Chelsea) Flower show
a3   Dinosaur
b3   Fossil
a4   (Sir) Anthony Eden
b4   Labour
a5   *Chariots of Fire*
b5   Rudolph Valentino
a6   Duke of Wellington
b6   Pandas (giant pandas)
a7   Words (their derivations)
b7   Insects
a8   May
b8   July
a9   New Zealand
b9   (Ernest) Rutherford
a10 Mars
b10 Hermes (Greek) or Mercury (Roman)
a11 Venus
b11 Jupiter
a12 Nine of Diamonds
b12 Curling

Tie-breaker

Q   Following the rising of 1715, in which year was the Second Jacobite Rising in Scotland?
A   1745

No. 152

a1   Why would you be happy to pay a peppercorn rent?

b1   *Where used you to get your money back by pressing Button B?*

a2   Of which political party was Benjamin Disraeli a leader?

b2   *Of which political party was Stanley Baldwin a leader?*

a3   In 1853, what everyday snack was supposedly invented by a Red Indian Chief?

b3   *What was invented by W. L. Judson in 1891?*

a4   What drug is obtained from foxglove leaves?

b4   *What is the proper name for marsh gas?*

a5   Which famous pin-up of the Second World War was especially famous for her shapely legs?

b5   *In the Second World War, what was Sir Claude Auchinleck's nickname?*

a6   Near which Canadian city are the Plains of Abraham?

b6   *Which Australian city is named after the wife of William IV?*

a7   Who first said 'The wind of change is blowing through the continent'?

b7   *Who first said, 'Patriotism is the last refuge of a scoundrel'?*

a8   As what is Orlando Gibbons remembered?

b8   *In what job has David Lean achieved fame?*

a9   In legend, how did Tam o' Shanter escape from some witches?

b9   *What was Cyrano de Bergerac's outstanding feature?*

a10   Who was the first bowler to take 300 test match wickets?

b10   *Who was the first jockey to be knighted?*

a11   In the Old Testament, who was David's father?

b11   *Which biblical hero slew the Philistines with the jawbone of an ass?*

a12   Birds: What is the other name for the peewit?

b12   *Which bird is sometimes called the laverock?*

No. 152 Answers

a1   Because it's very small; nominal

b1   *Telephone box*

a2   Tory (Conservative)

b2   *Conservative*

a3   Potato chips

b3   *Zip*

a4   Digitalis

b4   *Methane*

a5   Betty Grable

b5   *The Auk*

a6   Quebec

b6   *Adelaide*

a7   Harold Macmillan (speaking about Africa)

b7   *Dr Johnson*

a8   Composer (church music)

b8   *Film director (Bridge on the River Kwai, Lawrence of Arabia)*

a9   By crossing a river (*or* on horseback)

b9   *His nose*

a10   Fred Trueman

b10   *Sir Gordon Richards*

a11   Jesse

b11   *Samson*

a12   Lapwing (*or*: green or black plover, pyewipe)

b12   *Lark*

Tie-breaker

Q   Off the coast of which continent are the Ross Sea, the Weddell Sea, and Amundsen Sea?

A   *Antarctica*

No. 153

a1   In which continent is the Gobi Desert?

b1   *In which continent is the country of Chad?*

a2   In Australia, what kind of animal is a brumby?

b2   *Of which Australian state is Adelaide the capital?*

a3   With which game do you associate Spasky, Korchnoi, and Karpov?

b3   *Which suit in a pack of cards is named after the Spanish word for sword?*

a4   From which musical comes the song 'Tomorrow'?

b4   *Which dance band leader used to introduce his programme with a slow, slow, quick, quick, slow?*

a5   In mythology, what did Jason and the Argonauts go seeking?

b5   *In mythology, King Midas had the ears of which animal?*

a6   In poetry, which fish asked a snail to walk a little faster?

b6   *What sex are oysters?*

a7   Before blotting paper was invented, did people use linen, sand, or cotton to dry the ink on their letters?

b7   *What was invented by John Napier?*

a8   What item of clothing was originally made from serge made in the French town of Nîmes?

b8   *Around the home, for what did we once use hay boxes?*

a9   What is the everyday name for the Collegiate Church of St Peter in London?

b9   *In which London institution is the Lutine bell?*

a10   Who was the first emperor of what came to be known as the Holy Roman Empire?

b10   *In France, to whom was the title Dauphin given?*

a11   Of which chemical element is the symbol the letter K?

b11   *Of which chemical element is the symbol Zn?*

a12   With which festival do we primarily associate the hymn which begins: 'On Jordan's bank, The Baptist's cry'?

b12   *With which festival do we primarily associate the hymn which begins: 'Christ the Lord is risen today'?*

No. 153 Answers

a1   Asia
b1   *Africa*
a2   (Wild) Horse
b2   *South Australia*
a3   Chess
b3   *Spades (espada)*
a4   *Annie*
b4   *Victor Sylvester*
a5   The Golden Fleece
b5   *An ass*
a6   Whiting ('The Walrus and the Carpenter' by Lewis Carroll)
b6   *Male one year, female next (accept: hermaphrodites)*
a7   Sand
b7   *Logarithms*
a8   Jeans (serge de Nîmes = denim)
b8   *To keep food warm*
a9   Westminster Abbey
b9   *Lloyd's*
a10   Charlemagne
b10   *Eldest son of the king; a prince*
a11   Potassium
b11   *Zinc*
a12   Advent
b12   *Easter*

Tie-breaker

Q Who composed the famous *Hungarian Rhapsodies*?
A *(Franz or Ferencz) Liszt*

No. 154

a1 What kind of fruit is a morello?

b1 *By what other name is the mountain ash tree generally known?*

a2 What is meant by saying a person is hirsute?

b2 *What do we mean if we say a person is poker-faced?*

a3 Which child film star sang 'On the good ship Lollipop'?

b3 *Who wrote the line, 'Mad dogs and Englishmen go out in the midday sun'?*

a4 Who became prime minister in May 1940?

b4 *What nationality was the war-time traitor Vidkun Quisling?*

a5 By what other name is St Stephen's Day generally known?

b5 *Which festival celebrates the coming of the Wise Men to the infant Jesus?*

a6 Which of these railway stations is *not* in London: Blackfriars, Paddington, Temple Meads?

b6 *Where was London's first international airport?*

a7 Something said to be cupric contains which metal?

b7 *Into what two elements is water divided by electrolysis?*

a8 Which politician devised a scheme for sending boys down the mines during the Second World War?

b8 *Who is remembered as the architect of the British Welfare State?*

a9 In which Welsh county is Swansea?

b9 *In which Welsh county is Snowdon?*

a10 A bull bellows, but which animal 'bells'?

b10 *Of which animal is ermine the fur?*

a11 For what did Holman Hunt achieve fame?

b11 *As what did Etherege, Wycherley, and Congreve all achieve fame?*

a12 Which code of football is played with eighteen men on each team?

b12 *How many players are there on a British lacrosse team?*

No. 154 Answers

a1 Cherry

b1 *Rowan*

a2 He's hairy

b2 *His face shows no expression*

a3 Shirley Temple

b3 *Noël Coward*

a4 Winston Churchill

b4 *Norwegian*

a5 Boxing Day

b5 *Epiphany (Twelfth Night)*

a6 Temple Meads (Bristol)

b6 *Croydon*

a7 Copper

b7 *Hydrogen and oxygen*

a8 (Ernest) Bevin ('The Bevin Boys')

b8 *Sir William Beveridge*

a9 *West* Glamorgan

b9 *Gwynedd*

a10 A deer (*accept*: stag)

b10 *Stoat*

a11 Painting (especially *The Light of the World*)

b11 *Dramatists; playwrights*

a12 Australian

b12 *Twelve*

Tie-breaker

Q What is the distinguishing feature of a marsupial animal?
A *It has a pouch (in which to carry its young)*

No. 155

a1   What is meant by the word diurnal?

b1   *If something is said to be ecclesiastical, what is it to do with?*

a2   Of which political party was Gladstone a leader?

b2   *Of which political party was Lloyd George a leader?*

a3   To see which sport would you be most likely to go to Towcester?

b3   *Which university cricket team plays at home at Fenner's?*

a4   In fable, which large bird is said to sing beautifully just before it dies?

b4   *According to a song, which creature had 'great big googly eyes'?*

a5   Who was the first Christian martyr?

b5   *What was the original profession of St Luke?*

a6   Who wrote the play *Look Back in Anger*?

b6   *Who wrote the play* Hedda Gabler?

a7   Of the Seven Wonders of the World, where was the Temple of Diana?

b7   *In which exhibition was there a skylon and a Dome of Discovery?*

a8   With which form of power is Sizewell in Suffolk associated?

b8   *What are pinnipeds?*

a9   Margaret Hookham is a famous British ballerina. What is her stage name?

b9   *Which dancer starred in the ballet film* The Red Shoes?

a10   By what name is Nyasaland now known?

b10   *What was Zaïre formerly called?*

a11   With which English city are the painters Cotman and Crome particularly associated?

b11   *Which British landscape artist painted* Rain, Steam and Speed *and* Snowstorms?

a12   In space, what is a quasar?

b12   *What causes a solar eclipse?*

No. 155 Answers

a1	Daily
b1	*The Church*
a2	Liberal (Whig)
b2	*Liberal*
a3	Horse racing
b3	*Cambridge*
a4	Swan
b4	*Lambton Worm*
a5	St Stephen
b5	*Physician, doctor of medicine*
a6	John Osborne
b6	*Ibsen*
a7	Ephesus
b7	*Festival of Britain (South Bank, 1951)*
a8	Nuclear
b8	*Animals with flippers (instead of normal limbs, e.g. seals)*
a9	(Dame) Margot Fonteyn
b9	*Moira Shearer*
a10	Malawi
b10	*(Belgian) Congo*
a11	Norwich
b11	*(Joseph Mallord William) Turner*
a12	Source of energy/light/radio waves
b12	*The moon passing between the Earth and the Sun*

Tie-breaker

Q For which acid is the chemical symbol H_2SO_4?
A *Sulphuric acid*

No. 156

a1   At the start of a game, how many pawns are there on a chess board?

b1   *In which ancient board game does the board gradually fill up with black and white stones as players win territory?*

a2   On which item of clothing would you find a welt?

b2   *What is meant by welching?*

a3   In Paris, what is the Bourse?

b3   *In which city is the Rialto Bridge?*

a4   For what precious metal are the letters Au the chemical symbol?

b4   *Which metal is represented by the chemical symbol Pb?*

a5   Terpsichore is the art of . . . what?

b5   *What, in music, is a nocturne?*

a6   Which is the longest river which flows entirely in England?

b6   *Into which other river does the river Trent flow?*

a7   As what is Thomas Tallis remembered?

b7   *What was John Speed famous for making?*

a8   Of what did Thomas Sheraton become a famous designer?

b8   *In the world of antiques, for what is Meissen famous?*

a9   In which book does Christian meet Hopeful and Mr Worldly-Wiseman?

b9   *In Gulliver's Travels, what did the Little Endians quarrel with the Big Endians about?*

a10   Which saint is said to have been crucified upside down?

b10   *Which saint was supposedly crucified on a diagonal cross?*

a11   In mythology, of what was Minerva the goddess?

b11   *In mythology, of what was Morpheus the god?*

a12   Which English king couldn't speak English?

b12   *Who was the last English king to lead his troops into battle?*

No. 156 Answers

a1   Sixteen

b1   Go

a2   A shoe (strip of leather used to attach the 'upper' to the sole)

b2   Move off without paying debts or bets

a3   The French Stock Exchange

b3   Venice

a4   Gold

b4   Lead

a5   Dancing

b5   A sad/dreamy/gentle piece of music in keeping with night-time

a6   Thames (the Severn is also in Wales)

b6   Humber

a7   Composer

b7   Maps

a8   Furniture

b8   Porcelain (china)

a9   Pilgrim's Progress

b9   Which end you should open a boiled egg

a10   St Peter

b10   St Andrew

a11   Wisdom

b11   Sleep (or dreams)

a12   George I

b12   George II

Tie-breaker

Q   How many times does a normal long-playing record revolve in one minute?

A $33\frac{1}{3}$

No. 157

a1   What is a brisket?

b1   *What is bric-à-brac?*

a2   Colloquially speaking, what is horse-trading?

b2   *How would you be feeling if you were cock-a-hoop?*

a3   According to a traditional rhyme, which day's child is 'full of woe'?

b3   *Solomon Grundy, born on Monday, christened on Tuesday — according to this rhyme what happened to him on Wednesday?*

a4   For what sort of story is the French writer La Fontaine, famous?

b4   *What is an author's magnum opus?*

a5   Of which political party was Ramsay MacDonald a leader?

b5   *Who succeeded Winston Churchill as prime minister in 1945?*

a6   In ancient British legend, what was Avalon?

b6   *In legend, what was Excalibur?*

a7   In the hymn, which words follow: 'Abide with me . . .'?

b7   *In a famous hymn, what line comes before 'Our hope for years to come'?*

a8   What game was first played by Red Indians (then by Canadians) and came to England in 1865?

b8   *Which type of football is played on an oval pitch?*

a9   Which Welsh poet wrote a famous play set in the village of Llareggub?

b9   *Which peninsula lies between Swansea Bay and Carmarthen Bay, in South Wales?*

a10   What do we call the storey of a building which is between two main floors?

b10   *In British history and architecture, which period is known as Regency?*

a11   Which pop singer starred in the films *The Man Who Fell to Earth* and *Merry Christmas, Mr Lawrence*?

b11   *Which American actor was famous for starring in swashbuckling roles in such films as* The Thief of Baghdad *and* The Three Musketeers?

a12   In which field of science did John Dalton make discoveries?

b12   *Who is known as the father of chemistry?*

No. 157 Answers

a1   Joint of meat (especially the breast)

b1   Oddments (old furniture, china, antiques, etc.)

a2   Shrewd dealing; bargaining

b2   Cheerful; boastful; on top of the world

a3   'Wednesday's child is full of woe'

b3   Married

a4   Fables (*accept*: stories in verse)

b4   His major work

a5   Labour

b5   Clement Attlee

a6   Paradise; island of the blessed, where heroes went (*accept*: Glastonbury)

b6   A sword; King Arthur's sword

a7   'Fast falls the eventide'

b7   'O God, our help in ages past'

a8   Lacrosse

b8   Australian

a9   Dylan Thomas (*Under Milk Wood*)

b9   Gower Peninsular

a10   Mezzanine

b10   Early nineteenth century (1811–1820)

a11   David Bowie

b11   Douglas Fairbanks (Senior)

a12   Chemistry, the atom

b12   (Robert) Boyle (1627–91)

Tie-breaker

Q   Who wrote *Tristram Shandy*?

A   *(Laurence) Sterne*

No. 158

a1   Two British prime ministers were father and son. What was their surname?

b1   *Who was prime minister at the time of the present Queen's Coronation?*

a2   The velocipede was an early form of which kind of vehicle or transport?

b2   *Which side of a ship is the leeward side?*

a3   Which film star was widely known as 'The World's Sweetheart'?

b3   *Which star made her name in the film* The Blue Angel?

a4   On which island is the port of Holyhead?

b4   *In which island is the House of Keys?*

a5   How many players are there on a baseball team?

b5   *How long is a cricket pitch?*

a6   Of which book is the Vulgate a Latin translation?

b6   *Which famous book still in print was published in English for the first time in 1549?*

a7   For what purpose did the ancient Egyptians build the Pyramids?

b7   *Which is the largest ancient circle of standing stones in Europe?*

a8   In 1984, Kathy Sullivan became the first woman to do . . . what?

b8   *Which scientist first said the earth moved round the sun?*

a9   Which Flemish artist painted *Children's Games, Village Wedding,* and *Hunters in Snow, February*?

b9   *In which Italian city is the Uffizi Gallery (say:'you-fitz-y')?*

a10   In the Bible, what was the name of Adam and Eve's firstborn son?

b10   *What food did God provide for the Children of Israel on their journey to the Promised Land?*

a11   As what did Sir James Jeans achieve fame?

b11   *For what did Philip Larkin become famous?*

a12   In mythology, what was Elysium?

b12   *Across which legendary river are souls said to be carried into Hades?*

No. 158 Answers

a1 Pitt

b1 *Sir Winston Churchill*

a2 Bicycle

b2 *Side sheltered from the wind*

a3 Mary Pickford

b3 *Marlene Dietrich*

a4 Holy Island (off Anglesey)

b4 *Isle of Man*

a5 Nine

b5 *22 yards (20.12 metres) (accept: 1 chain)*

a6 The Bible

b6 *Book of Common Prayer; Prayer Book*

a7 Tombs for their rulers (also to house their belongings after death)

b7 *Avebury*

a8 Walk in space

b8 *Copernicus*

a9 (Pieter) Brueghel

b9 *Florence*

a10 Cain

b10 *Manna*

a11 Physicist; astronomer

b11 *Poetry*

a12 Paradise; a kind of heaven

b12 *Styx*

Tie-breaker

Q Which English king was murdered in 1327 in Berkeley Castle in Gloucestershire?

A *Edward II*

No. 159

a1 What do you do if you go on a peregrination?

b1 *What is a peregrine?*

a2 What is sometimes followed by an aftershock?

b2 *Of which metal is pinchbeck an imitation?*

a3 Who wrote the plays *Roots* and *Chips With Everything*?

b3 *Who wrote the Aldwych farces, such as* Rookery Nook *and* A Cuckoo in the Nest?

a4 Of which country was Andrew Jackson twice president?

b4 *Which American president succeeded Richard Nixon?*

a5 In England, who came to the throne on the death of Edward III?

b5 *Which royal prince was killed in a plane crash during the last war?*

a6 In which county is the radio telescope, Jodrell Bank?

b6 *The architect Sir Basil Spence designed which cathedral?*

a7 What job did Frank Phillips, John Snagge, and Stuart Hibberd have in common?

b7 *Who played the piano on radio's 'Have a Go' and Ena Sharples in 'Coronation Street'?*

a8 In which country is the source of the River Danube?

b8 *Into which sea does the River Volga flow?*

a9 Which is the oldest university in Britain?

b9 *In 1878, what revolutionary step was taken by London University?*

a10 Who wrote the novel *A Kind of Loving*?

b10 *Who wrote the poems 'Upon Westminster Bridge' and 'The Daffodils'?*

a11 On which date each year does All Saints Day fall?

b11 *On what day of the week does Ascension Day always occur?*

a12 Which legendary king had a sister called Morgan le Fay?

b12 *In legend, who beheaded the Green Knight?*

No. 159 Answers

a1   Go on a journey; go on your travels

b1   *Type of falcon (accept: Type of hawk)*

a2   An earthquake

b2   *Gold*

a3   (Arnold) Wesker

b3   *Ben Travers*

a4   USA (*accept*: America)

b4   *Gerald Ford*

a5   Richard II

b5   *Duke of Kent*

a6   Cheshire

b6   *Coventry*

a7   Newsreaders (radio) or radio announcers

b7   *Violet Carson*

a8   Germany

b8   *Caspian Sea*

a9   Oxford (founded about 1167)

b9   *It admitted women as students*

a10   Stan Barstow

b10   *(William) Wordsworth*

a11   1 November

b11   *Thursday*

a12   King Arthur

b12   *(Sir) Gawain*

Tie-breaker

Q   In science, of what is genetics the study?

A   *Genes; heriditary characteristics*

No. 160

a1 What do you do if you exonerate a person?

b1 *What do you do if you exorcise a place or building?*

a2 In legend, for what was King Croesus famous?

b2 *Which Roman god gave his name to January?*

a3 In films, who was the famous 'It' girl?

b3 *Who starred in the film* Limelight?

a4 In which American state is Chicago?

b4 *Of which American state is Jackson the capital?*

a5 In 1819, in which English city did the 'Battle of Peterloo' take place?

b5 *In which country were the Black-and-Tans deployed by the British government?*

a6 Which cross was the symbol of the Free French during the Second World War?

b6 *What are the two main colours of the Argentinian flag?*

a7 Who first sailed alone around the world?

b7 *Who first sailed non-stop round the world?*

a8 According to the Bible, what kind of a woman has a 'price far above rubies'?

b8 *Who first spoke the words known as the Magnificat?*

a9 In the Burgess and Maclean spy scandal, who was the so-called Third Man?

b9 *Eva and Maria Estela were both wives of which Argentinian president?*

a10 What do we call a triangle which has two sides (but only two) of equal length?

b10 *How many degrees are contained in each angle of an equilateral triangle?*

a11 For what is the writer Holinshed famous?

b11 *While imprisoned in the Tower of London, who wrote a history of the world?*

a12 Of which country is Uttar Pradesh a part?

b12 *Of which country is Sumatra a part?*

No. 160 Answers

a1	Free them from blame; 'let them off'
b1	*Free it from evil spirits; rid it of ghosts, etc.*
a2	Wealth ('as rich as Croesus')
b2	*Janus*
a3	Clara Bow
b3	*Charlie Chaplin*
a4	Illinois
b4	*Mississippi*
a5	Manchester
b5	*Ireland*
a6	Cross of Lorraine
b6	*Blue and white*
a7	(Joshua) Slocum (1895–8)
b7	*Robin Knox-Johnson*
a8	A virtuous woman
b8	*Mary (the mother of Jesus)*
a9	Kim Philby
b9	*Peron*
a10	Isosceles
b10	*Sixty*
a11	His chronicles, histories (Shakespeare's source material)
b11	*Sir Walter Ralegh*
a12	India
b12	*Indonesia*

Tie-breaker

Q In which Shakespeare play is there a famous speech which begins, 'The quality of mercy is not strained . . .'?

A *The Merchant of Venice*

No. 161

a1   What is campanology?

b1   *What is campanile (say: cam-pan-ee-lay)?*

a2   Tyrone Guthrie, Peter Hall, and Trevor Nunn have all achieved fame as what?

b2   *Besides being a batsman, why did Alan Knott win his place on the England cricket team?*

a3   On which river are the Niagara Falls?

b3   *On which famous river is Kinshasa situated?*

a4   In which American state is there a city called Birmingham?

b4   *In area, which is the largest of the United States of America?*

a5   Who composed the musicals *Annie Get Your Gun* and *Call Me Madam*?

b5   *Which hit musical is about dancers auditioning for a new show?*

a6   Which English city is named after a saint who was originally a Roman soldier?

b6   *Which Roman emperor was converted to Christianity when he saw a cross shining in the sky?*

a7   In mythology, what was special about Adonis?

b7   *Who was the Greek Goddess of love and beauty?*

a8   In 1948, which general assembly drew up the Declaration of Human Rights?

b8   *Which black township near Johannesburg became famous after demonstrations there in 1976?*

a9   Which known planet in our solar system is usually furthest from the sun?

b9   *Phobos and Deimos are moons of which planet?*

a10   For which month of the year is topaz the birthstone?

b10   *For which month of the year is amethyst the birthstone?*

a11   What is the name of the old Roman road that ran from the Channel ports by way of London to Shropshire?

b11   *From where did the Jutes come, before they invaded the south of England?*

a12   Which Greek dramatist wrote the plays *The Frogs* and *The Birds*?

b12   *Which statesman and politician wrote the novel* Savrola?

No. 161 Answers

a1   Art of bell-ringing (the whole subject of bells)
b1   *Bell tower*
a2   Theatre directors
b2   *As a wicket-keeper*
a3   River Niagara
b3   *Zaïre (accept: Congo)*
a4   Alabama
b4   *Alaska*
a5   Irving Berlin
b5   *'A Chorus Line'*
a6   St Albans
b6   *Constantine*
a7   Very handsome (loved by Venus)
b7   *Aphrodite*
a8   United Nations
b8   *Soweto*
a9   Pluto
b9   *Mars*
a10   November
b10   *February*
a11   Watling Street
b11   *Jutland (accept: Germany, Frankish territory)*
a12   Aristophanes
b12   *Winston Churchill*

Tie-breaker

Q When you visit a doctor, he might use a sphygmomanometer on you. If he did, what would he be measuring?
A *Your blood pressure (particularly of the arteries)*

No. 162

a1   Who was the wife of Hiawatha?

b1   *As what did Elizabeth Barrett and her husband Robert both achieve fame?*

a2   What is a bullace?

b2   *What is bullion?*

a3   In poetry, how many lines has a limerick?

b3   *In poetry, how many lines has a sonnet?*

a4   In which war was the siege of Dien Bien Phu?

b4   *In which country did Mau Mau guerillas fight for liberation?*

a5   In geography, what is savannah?

b5   *In geography, what are the doldrums?*

a6   What is a tangent?

b6   *What do we call the side of a triangle that is opposite a right angle?*

a7   Which pianist's greatest hit was 'Blueberry Hill'?

b7   *In song, whose Rag-time Band was 'The Best Band in the Land'?*

a8   To which prime minister was Lady Falkender once secretary?

b8   *Politics: who was Jenny Lee's husband?*

a9   In which war was Robert E. Lee a distinguished general?

b9   *In the USA, which line is (or was) popularly regarded as dividing the North from the South?*

a10   Who first said 'I think, therefore I am'?

b10   *Who said, on arriving in New York, 'I have nothing to declare but my genius'?*

a11   Who was king of the Greek gods?

b11   *By what Roman name is the greek god of wine, Dionysus, also known?*

a12   In the Bible, in which village did Martha and Mary live?

b12   *Who was the father of the disciples, James and John?*

No. 162 Answers

a1	Minnehaha
b1	*Poets*
a2	A kind of plum (tree or fruit)
b2	*Gold or silver before it is made into coins. (Bullion is also gold or silver thread)*
a3	Five
b3	*Fourteen*
a4	Vietnam War
b4	*Kenya*
a5	(Tropical) grassland (a dry, dusty region)
b5	*Areas (near equator) with very little wind*
a6	A straight line which *touches* a circle at one point, but does not cross the circle
b6	*Hypotenuse*
a7	Fats Domino
b7	*Alexander's*
a8	Harold Wilson
b8	*Aneurin (Nye) Bevan*
a9	American Civil War
b9	*The Mason-Dixon Line*
a10	Descartes (*say*: Day-cart)
b10	*Oscar Wilde*
a11	Zeus (Jupiter was King of the Roman gods)
b11	*Bacchus*
a12	Bethany
b12	*Zebedee*

Tie-breaker

Q Which city became capital of Wessex and then later also became capital of England?

A *Winchester*

No. 163

a1   In the south of which continent are the Straits of Magellan?

b1   *In which continent is the Cape of Good Hope?*

a2   In everyday usage, what is ozone?

b2   *If flotsam is things found floating on the sea after a shipwreck, what is jetsam?*

a3   In America, for what did Grandma Moses achieve fame, late in life?

b3   *The North American Indian chief Uncas is famous as being the last of which tribe?*

a4   Who wrote the play *French Without Tears*?

b4   *Who wrote the novel* Stalky and Co?

a5   In politics, what did the party known as the Whigs become after 1832?

b5   *Which famous bill was carried through parliament in 1832?*

a6   Who was the legendary strong man compelled to support the heavens upon his head and shoulders?

b6   *What was supposed to happen when you pulled a mandrake root out of the earth?*

a7   According to the song, who was a zealous High Churchman in 'good King Charles's golden days'?

b7   *In a song, who is delighted 'on a shinging night, in the season of the year'?*

a8   Which two countries fought at the Battle of Tannenberg in 1914?

b8   *In the Second World War, what were Gold, Juno, and Sword?*

a9   For which art did Walter Richard Sickert become famous?

b9   *For what product has the village of Capo di Monte become famous?*

a10   Which apostle was chosen to replace Judas Iscariot?

b10   *In the Bible, what is meant by an epistle?*

a11   George and Weedon Grossmith wrote a famous diary. What was it called?

b11   *In 1963, which report resulted in the reorganization of the railways?*

a12   For what would you use a hygrometer?

b12   *What is measured by a hydrometer?*

No. 163 Answers

a1 America
b1 *Africa*
a2 Pleasant air (usually near the sea or river)
b2 *Things deliberately thrown from a ship to lighten it*
a3 Artist, painter
b3 *Mohicans*
a4 Terence Rattigan
b4 *Rudyard Kipling*
a5 The Liberals
b5 *Reform Bill*
a6 Atlas
b6 *Either: (a) the plant screamed or (b) you would die*
a7 Vicar of Bray
b7 *The Lincolnshire Poacher*
a8 Germany and Russia
b8 *The Allied invasion beaches in Normandy*
a9 Painting
b9 *Porcelain, porcelain figures (accept: pottery, ceramics)*
a10 Matthias
b10 *A letter*
a11 *Diary of a Nobody*
b11 *Beeching Report*
a12 To measure the humidity in the air
b12 *The density of a liquid*

Tie-breaker

Q In mythology, of where was Priam king?
A *Troy*

No. 164

a1 What are nomads?

b1 What or who was a shogun?

a2 Of which country is New Brunswick a province?

b2 Of which republic is the Transvaal a province?

a3 For what was Capability Brown famous?

b3 For what has Sir Michael Tippett achieved fame?

a4 In 1830, a very early railway was opened — between which two towns?

b4 In 1897, which royal celebration took place?

a5 In mythology, Pan was half man and half animal. What animal?

b5 Which legendary beast was half man, half bull?

a6 From which island did the actress Lillie Langtrey come?

b6 Which music hall star sang 'I'm one of the ruins Cromwell knocked about a bit'?

a7 Which of these metals has the lowest melting point: iron, mercury, lead?

b7 When a ray of light passes from air to water, is it reflected, refracted, or retracted?

a8 Which Liberal politician was coalition prime minister from 1916 to 1922?

b8 Who was the first Labour member of the House of Commons?

a9 Which rock star appeared in the films Ned Kelly and Performance?

b9 In which film did Simon and Garfunkel sing 'Mrs Robinson'?

a10 In the world of finance what do the initials MLR stand for?

b10 For what is, or was, CWS the abbreviation?

a11 Which season of the Church's year is associated with the hymn 'Hail the day that sees Him rise'?

b11 With which festival do we primarily associate the hymn which begins 'Come, Holy Ghost, our souls inspire'?

a12 Who captained the MCC cricket team for the notorious 'Body Line' tour of Australia in 1932–3?

b12 Who was the oldest player ever to play cricket in test matches?

No. 164 Answers

a1   Wandering people
b1   *A Japanese military ruler (pre-1868)*
a2   Canada
b2   *South Africa*
a3   Landscape gardening
b3   *Composer (musician)*
a4   Liverpool and Manchester
b4   *Queen Victoria's diamond jubilee*
a5   Goat
b5   *Minotaur*
a6   Jersey
b6   *Marie Lloyd*
a7   Mercury
b7   *Refracted*
a8   Lloyd George
b8   *Keir Hardie*
a9   Mick Jagger
b9   *The Graduate*
a10   Minimum Lending Rate
b10   *Co-operative Wholesale Society (The Co-op)*
a11   Ascension
b11   *Whitsun*
a12   D. R. Jardine
b12   *(Wilfred) Rhodes (52 years 165 days; for England)*

Tie-breaker

Q   What is the famous advice of the three monkeys of Nikko?
A   *Speak no evil, hear no evil, see no evil*

No. 165

a1   In which religion is Ramadan a holy month?

b1   *In which religion is Hannukah a festival?*

a2   For what was Sarah Siddons famous?

b2   *In which art did Edith Sitwell become famous?*

a3   For the Ancient Greeks, what were the four elements?

b3   *About what did Euclid write a study?*

a4   What is foolscap?

b4   *What is fire-damp?*

a5   What is the name of the hot southerly wind that blows from the Sahara across southern Italy?

b5   *In geography, what do we call the treeless plains that border the Arctic Ocean?*

a6   For what purpose did the French use Devil's Island, from 1854 to 1938?

b6   *Which famous building in Berlin was burned down, probably by the Nazis, in 1933?*

a7   Who is usually credited with being the first man to reach the North Pole in 1909?

b7   *Who first reached the South Pole?*

a8   In Greek legend, whom did Narcissus love?

b8   *Who was Venus?*

a9   What kind of book was edited by the French writer Diderot?

b9   *What kind of reference book was Bradshaw's?*

a10   In printing, in which colour were rubrics originally printed?

b10   *What colour is cyan?*

a11   The American president — Harry S. Trueman: what did the 'S' stand for?

b11   *Which American President had the first names Thomas Woodrow?*

a12   According to the song, on which hill lived a lass so neat, with a smile so sweet?

b12   *Which song begins: 'Down yonder green valley, where streamlets meander'?*

No. 165 Answers

a1   Islam (the Muslim religion)
b1   *Hebrew (Jewish)*
a2   Acting
b2   *Literature/poetry*
a3   Earth, Air, Fire, and Water
b3   *Geometry*
a4   A size of paper (originally had a fool's cap as watermark)
b4   *(Dangerous) mixture of gases (especially in mines)*
a5   The Sirocco *or* Khamsin
b5   *The Tundra*
a6   Prison (penal colony)
b6   *Reichstag*
a7   Commander Peary
b7   *Roald Amundsen (Scott reached it a month later)*
a8   Himself
b8   *(Roman) goddess of love (or beauty)*
a9   Encyclopaedia
b9   *Railway timetable*
a10   Red
b10   *Blue/green*
a11   Nothing — just an initial
b11   *Wilson*
a12   Richmond Hill
b12   *'The Ash Grove'*

Tie-breaker

Q   Name the seven deadly sins.
A   *Pride, Lust, Avarice, Envy, Gluttony, Sloth, Wrath (Anger)*

No. 166

a1   What, originally, was a hotch-potch?

b1   *What is a giant sequoia?*

a2   What is the total number of degrees of the angles of a triangle?

b2   *What is special about the temperature −273.16 degrees centigrade?*

a3   In 1348, a great plague spread over Britain causing many deaths. By what name is this plague popularly known?

b3   *The Battles of Worcester, Edgehill, and Marston Moor all took place during the same war. Which war?*

a4   As what did W. H. Auden achieve fame?

b4   *As what did Le Corbusier achieve fame?*

a5   In which group of islands is San Carlos Bay?

b5   *Can you name the island in the Indian Ocean which is 223 miles north of Java Head?*

a6   Properly speaking, what is a pagoda?

b6   *Of which religious faith would you be if you worshipped in a gurdwara?*

a7   In mythology, what monster lived in a labyrinth on the island of Crete?

b7   *In mythology, who swam the Hellespont every night to see his lover?*

a8   To which political party did Herbert Asquith belong?

b8   *Of which political party was Jo Grimond once leader?*

a9   In which war was the Battle of Bunker Hill?

b9   *Who was King of England when the American colonies were lost?*

a10   Who composed the opera *Madam Butterfly*?

b10   *Who composed the opera* William Tell?

a11   Who wrote the novel *Love Story*?

b11   *Who wrote the novel* Peyton Place?

a12   What do we call three painted panels, hinged together?

b12   *Which art did Goethe describe as 'frozen music'?*

No. 166 Answers

a1 A thick broth containing meat and vegetables
b1 *A tree (from USA)*
a2 180
b2 *Absolute zero; lowest temperature which can exist*
a3 The Black Death
b3 *English Civil War*
a4 Poet
b4 *Architect*
a5 Falklands
b5 *Christmas Island*
a6 Temple (or sacred tower) (Buddhist)
b6 *Sikh*
a7 The minotaur
b7 *Leander*
a8 Liberal
b8 *Liberal*
a9 American War of Independence
b9 *George III*
a10 Puccini
b10 *Rossini*
a11 Erich Segal
b11 Grace Metalious
a12 Triptych
b12 *Architecture*

Tie-breaker

Q Through which artery does blood flow to the lungs?
A *Pulmonary*

344

No. 167

a1 What is the word taxi short for?

b1 'Salop' is the abbreviated name of which English county?

a2 What is Sanskrit?

b2 What is vetch?

a3 Which two French provinces were annexed by Germany in 1871 and returned to France in 1919 (and again in 1945)?

b3 Last century, which Prussian statesman was largely responsible for unifying Germany?

a4 In geography, what do we call the broad, treeless plains of southern Russia?

b4 What are the Horse Latitudes?

a5 For what was Sir Malcolm Sargent famous?

b5 In which art did George Romney achieve fame?

a6 Who wrote the novel *Our Man in Havana*?

b6 Who wrote the novel Clayhanger?

a7 In mythology, of what was Vulcan the god?

b7 Of what sport was Diana the goddess?

a8 Temple, Fisher, and Ramsey have all held which high office?

b8 To whom does the Swiss Guard form an escort?

a9 Who was President of the United States of America immediately before Ronald Reagan?

b9 Which American president launched a famous 'New Deal'?

a10 Who composed the opera *La Bohème*?

b10 Who composed the opera The Bartered Bride?

a11 In which area of biology did the scientist Mendel make important discoveries?

b11 Where do we find geothermal energy?

a12 In heraldry, what colour is sable?

b12 In heraldry, what colour is azure?

No. 167 Answers

a1	Taximeter
b1	*Shropshire*
a2	Language (of Ancient India; literally 'without writing')
b2	*Wildflower, plant (of the pea family)*
a3	Alsace and Lorraine
b3	*Bismarck*
a4	The Steppes
b4	*A sub-tropical region of calm weather (around 30 degrees north and south)*
a5	Conductor (music)
b5	*Painting*
a6	Graham Greene
b6	*Arnold Bennett*
a7	Fire (*accept*: metal working, volcanoes)
b7	*Hunting*
a8	Archbishop of Canterbury
b8	*The Pope*
a9	Jimmy Carter
b9	*(Franklin D.) Roosevelt*
a10	Puccini
b10	*Smetana*
a11	Hereditary; genetics; inherited factors (*accept*: hybridity)
b11	*In the earth; in rocks*
a12	Black
b12	*Blue*

Tie-breaker

Q The Pomegranate is the national emblem of which European country?
A *Spain*

No. 168

a1 In cricket, for what do the initials MCC stand?

b1 *If someone has the letters BD after their name, what have they studied?*

a2 Which Prussian was known as the Iron Chancellor?

b2 *After which Soviet Minister was an explosive cocktail named?*

a3 What does a Job's comforter do to you?

b3 *What is meant by the word prodigal?*

a4 Which country lies immediately south of Belgium?

b4 *Which European capital city is near a port called Piraeus?*

a5 Which explorer sailed to Australia in a ship called the *Endeavour*?

b5 *In 1642, which island was discovered by the explorer Tasman?*

a6 In which city is James Joyce's novel *Ulysses* set?

b6 *In which novel are there 'three rings for the Elven-Kings under the sky'?*

a7 Who is the patron saint of Czechoslovakia?

b7 *St Crispin is the patron saint of whom?*

a8 Which father and son designed and built early railway locomotives?

b8 *In the days of steam railway engines, what two things were kept in an engine's tender?*

a9 Which American state was purchased from the Russians in 1867?

b9 *Which American state is sometimes called 'The Green Mountain'?*

a10 Which American star had a number one hit in 1970 with 'Wandrin' Star'?

b10 *Back in 1966, who had a hit with the tune 'Spanish Flea'?*

a11 What is the name of R. C. Sherriff's famous play about the First World War?

b11 *Arthur Miller's play* The Crucible *deals with witchcraft in which American town?*

a12 What would you fear if you suffered from pyrophobia?

b12 *Of what is hydrostatics the study?*

No. 168 Answers

a1 Marylebone Cricket Club
b1 *Divinity (Bachelor of Divinity)*
a2 Von Bismarck
b2 *Molotov*
a3 Makes you feel worse, more miserable
b3 *Wasteful (recklessly wasteful)*
a4 France
b4 *Athens*
a5 Captain Cook
b5 *Tasmania* or *New Zealand (accept: Van Dieman's Land)*
a6 Dublin
b6 Lord of the Rings
a7 St Wenceslas *(accept:* St Procopius; and John of Nepumuk*)*
b7 *Shoemakers*
a8 George and Robert Stephenson
b8 *Coal, water*
a9 Alaska
b9 *Vermont*
a10 Lee Marvin
b10 *Herb Alpert*
a11 *Journey's End*
b11 *Salem*
a12 Fire
b12 *Liquids (and their pressures and forces)*

Tie-breaker

Q Why did people travelling by ship to India prefer a cabin on the port side going out and the starboard side coming home; and what word has this habit given us?
A *To be away from the sun/heat; POSH (Port out, starboard home)*

No. 169

a1   Normally, how often is a census taken in this country?

b1   *Who might have the right of primogeniture?*

a2   Which European capital was virtually destroyed by an earthquake in 1755?

b2   *In 1704 which Mediterranean rocky promentary was captured by England?*

a3   For what did Dame Sybil Thorndike become famous?

b3   *In what area was Marie Stopes a pioneer?*

a4   Name the ship in which Captain Scott made his first Antarctic expedition?

b4   *Who was the famous medieval traveller who left Venice in 1271 to explore Asia?*

a5   Which author created the character Phileas Fogg?

b5   *Which writer created the detective Lord Peter Wimsey?*

a6   For what type of books did Karl Baedeker become famous?

b6   *For what information would you consult* Groves Dictionary?

a7   If someone is lachrymose, what do they do a lot?

b7   *If you're sanctimonious, what are you pretending to be?*

a8   Off the coast of which islands is Scapa Flow?

b8   *On which island is or was Carisbrook Castle?*

a9   In which language was the novel *Don Quixote* (say: 'Kee-hoh-tay') originally written?

b9   *In which language did St Paul write his epistles?*

a10   In which country did people once worship the god Osiris?

b10   *Which Hindu god's name now describes a large, heavy lorry?*

a11   If you landed at La Guardia Airport in which city would you be?

b11   *Which city is served by Schiphol Airport?*

a12   Who was the Swedish film actress who became a Hollywood legend and starred in such films as *Mata Hari, Grand Hotel* and *Queen Christina*?

b12   *In the Pink Panther films, who played Inspector Clouseau?*

No. 169 Answers

a1	Every ten years
b1	*First born: eldest son*
a2	Lisbon
b2	*Gibraltar*
a3	Acting (especially the part of St Joan)
b3	*Birth control*
a4	Discovery
b4	*Marco Polo*
a5	Jules Verne
b5	*Dorothy L. Sayers*
a6	Guidebooks
b6	*Music and musicians*
a7	Cry; are tearful
b7	*Devout/holy*
a8	The Orkneys
b8	*Isle of Wight*
a9	Spanish
b9	*Greek*
a10	Egypt
b10	*Juggernaut (a name for Krishna)*
a11	New York
b11	*Amsterdam*
a12	Greta Garbo
b12	*Peter Sellers*

Tie-breaker

Q Can you name the four full English quarter days?
A *Lady Day, Midsummer, Michaelmas, Christmas (25 March, 24 June, 29 September, 25 December)*

No. 170

a1   What is meant by the phrase 'Hobson's Choice'?

b1   *What is meant by the Persian word Baksheesh?*

a2   Which state in Australia is an island?

b2   *In which ocean is New Guinea?*

a3   In Roman history, whose wife was Calpurnia?

b3   *Who was the first Emperor of Rome?*

a4   Which country was invaded by Russian tanks and toops in November 1956?

b4   *In 1960, who killed 67 Africans at Sharpeville?*

a5   What kind of transport was a diligence?

b5   *What kind of transport is or was a trolley bus?*

a6   As what has Malcolm Williamson achieved fame?

b6   *As what did Molière achieve fame?*

a7   In the novel by Jack London, what kind of creature is White Fang?

b7   *With which mammal is the book* Ring of Bright Water *chiefly concerned?*

a8   Which American hit-singer starred in the television series 'The Partridge Family'?

b8   *By what name was the pop singer Peter Noone once known?*

a9   What date is Candlemas Day?

b9   *In which country is 6 February or Waitangi Day the national day?*

a10   Which artist painted the famous picture *Guernica*?

b10   *Which artist painted the famous picture* The Anatomy Lesson*?*

a11   Where in France in 1858 was there a famous vision of the Virgin Mary?

b11   *Whose official residence is Fulham Palace?*

a12   Up to nationalization, which railway company ran the east coast main line to York and Scotland?

b12   *Between which two towns was the railway line that carried Stephenson's first steam locomotive?*

No. 170 Answers

a1   You have no choice at all

b1   *A gratuity; a tip; a 'backhander'*

a2   Tasmania

b2   *(Western) Pacific*

a3   Julius Caesar's

b3   *Augustus*

a4   Hungary

b4   *The South African Police*

a5   (Stage) coach (horse-drawn coach)

b5   *Electrically powered bus; bus that runs on electricity provided by a pair of overhead wires*

a6   Composer (Master of the Queen's Musick)

b6   *Playwright*

a7   Wolf

b7   *Otters*

a8   David Cassidy

b8   *Herman (of the Hermits)*

a9   2 February

b9   *New Zealand*

a10   (Pablo) Picasso

b10   *Rembrandt*

a11   Lourdes

b11   *Bishop of London*

a12   London, North-Eastern (Railway)

b12   *Stockton and Darlington*

Tie-breaker

Q   There used to be a road sign which was a picture of a burning torch. What did it mean?

A   *School ahead*

No. 171

a1   What is an abyss?

b1   *What is an adage?*

a2   Off which coast of Africa is the island of Madagascar?

b2   *In which ocean is the island of Tristan da Cunha?*

a3   In what unusual place did Simeon Stylites live for thirty years?

b3   *For what are Trappist monks noted?*

a4   What sort of person is a carpet-bagger?

b4   *What is, or was, a footpad?*

a5   In 1949, which defensive alliance was formed by the Western nations?

b5   *In which year was the Six Day War between Israel and the Arab states?*

a6   Which dramatist wrote the play called *The Caretaker*?

b6   *Who wrote the play* Waiting for Godot?

a7   In the sixteenth century, in which country were Protestants called Huguenots?

b7   *In Britain, from 1649 to 1653, what was nicknamed 'The Rump'?*

a8   Paderewski was once prime minister of Poland. For what else was he famous?

b8   *In which branch of science did Edward Jenner make famous discoveries?*

a9   In mythology, who was Polyphemus?

b9   *In Roman mythology, of what was Pluto king?*

a10   Who is the patron saint of music?

b10   *In the song, by which river lived a jolly miller?*

a11   For which month of the year is agate the birthstone?

b11   *For which month of the year is opal the birthstone?*

a12   In fiction, Sancho Panza served whom?

b12   *Which author created the character Soames Forsyte?*

No. 171 Answers

a1   A great depth; chasm (appears to have no bottom)
b1   Proverb; saying; piece of wisdom
a2   South-East (*accept*: East)
b2   Atlantic (South)
a3   On top of a stone pillar; up a pole
b3   Their vow of silence
a4   Politician moving in on another area
b4   A highwayman; a thief
a5   NATO (North Atlantic Treaty Organization)
b5   1967
a6   Harold Pinter
b6   Samuel Beckett
a7   France
b7   Parliament (sixty radical MPs)
a8   Concert pianist
b8   Medicine; vaccination
a9   One-eyed giant (chief of the Cyclops in the *Odyssey*)
b9   The Underworld or the dead
a10   St Cecilia (feast day: 22 November)
b10   The River Dee
a11   June
b11   October
a12   Don Quixote
b12   John Galsworthy

Tie-breaker

Q   What is unique about British postage stamps?
A   They do not carry the name of their country of origin on them. (Britain is the only country in the world not to put its name on its stamps.)

No. 172

a1 In the hope of preserving international friendship, which organization was founded in 1920?

b1 *Of which larger, international organization is the Security Council a part?*

a2 In which comic could you once read about the Bruin Boys?

b2 *What do you do if you bowdlerize a book?*

a3 What do you get from someone if you debrief them?

b3 *What can you do if you're ambidextrous?*

a4 Which is the largest island in the Caribbean Sea?

b4 *Which is the highest of these: Mount McKinley, K2, Mont Blanc?*

a5 She became a missionary in China and led many children to safety. Who was she?

b5 *Whose law says that work expands so as to fill the time available for its completion?*

a6 Of which Shakespeare play is *Kiss Me, Kate* a musical version?

b6 *Which Shakespeare play is about three caskets?*

a7 In which religion is Rosh Hashanah a festival?

b7 *For what religious festival is Pentecost another name?*

a8 In mythology, whose wings melted when he flew too close to the sun?

b8 *Which Greek hero was the husband of Penelope?*

a9 Who invented the 'bouncing bomb' used by the Dambusters?

b9 *Which east German city was devastingly bombed by the Allies on the night of 13 February 1945?*

a10 In which country might you live and work on a kibbutz?

b10 *Which day of the week is named after the Norse goddess of love?*

a11 Whom did the Egyptians fight at the battle of Actium in 31 BC?

b11 *Which ancient Mexican people were overthrown by Cortez?*

a12 Soccer now. 1928, 1930, and 1952. In which of these years was the World Cup first held?

b12 *In which country were the finals of the 1978 World Cup played?*

No. 172 Answers

a1   League of Nations
b1   *United Nations*
a2   *Rainbow (Tiger Tim, Jumbo the Elephant, Joey, Fido, Bobby Bear, etc.)*
b2   *Remove the naughty bits*
a3   Information
b3   *Use either hand equally well (especially for writing)*
a4   Cuba
b4   *K2 (second highest mountain in the world)*
a5   Gladys Aylward
b5   *(Professor) Parkinson (C. Northcote Parkinson)*
a6   *The Taming of the Shrew*
b6   The Merchant of Venice
a7   Jewish (New Year)
b7   *Whitsun (Jewish Harvest Festival)*
a8   Icarus
b8   *Odysseus (Ulysses)*
a9   Barnes Wallis
b9   *Dresden*
a10   Israel
b10   *Friday (Frigg or Freya)*
a11   Romans
b11   *Aztecs*
a12   1930
b12   *Argentina*

Tie-breaker

Q   Which is the oldest university in the United States?
A   Harvard

No. 173

a1 In which country is the famous landmark Ayer's Rock?

b1 *In which country is Lake Winnipeg?*

a2 What are 747s and DC-8s?

b2 *Rump, T-bone, and sirloin are joints of which meat?*

a3 Is argon a gas, metal, or an alkali?

b3 *And is tungsten a gas, metal, or an alkali?*

a4 In which sport would you perform a double axel?

b4 *Which game would you be playing if you were 'at the oche' (say: okky)?*

a5 What fraction of a gross is three dozen?

b5 *After the number 53, which is the next highest prime number?*

a6 Where in your home might you find the gas freon?

b6 *If some rubbish is biodegradable, what will eventually happen to it?*

a7 Who established the first English printing press at Westminster in 1477?

b7 *In 1517, who nailed 95 theses to the church door at Wittenberg?*

a8 Of which country was Cadwalader a prince and hero?

b8 *Which king was called 'The wisest fool in Christendom'?*

a9 Who wrote the poem *Jabberwocky*?

b9 *Which poet wrote a long poem about Hiawatha?*

a10 Who write *The Day of the Triffids*, *The Chrysalids*, and *Chocky*?

b10 *In which novel by J. D. Salinger does the character Holden Caulfield appear?*

a11 With which day of the year do we particularly associate simnel cake?

b11 *What name is given to food prepared according to Jewish law?*

a12 In mythology, what did Prometheus steal from heaven and give to mankind?

b12 *In mythology, what did Cassandra prophesy?*

No. 173 Answers

a1   Australia
b1   *Canada*
a2   Airliners (*accept:* aircraft)
b2   *Beef* (accept *steak*)
a3   Gas (a noble gas)
b3   *Metal*
a4   Ice skating (*or* free skating; figure skating)
b4   *Darts*
a5   A quarter
b5   *59*
a6   In a fridge, freezer (*or* aerosol)
b6   *It will rot away*
a7   William Caxton
b7   *Martin Luther*
a8   Wales
b8   *James I (of England, VI of Scotland)*
a9   Lewis Carroll
b9   *(Henry Wadsworth) Longfellow*
a10   John Wyndham
b10   Catcher in the Rye
a11   Mothering Sunday (*accept:* Easter or Christmas)
b11   *Kosher*
a12   Fire
b12   *Doom; disasters (especially the Fall of Troy)*

Tie-breaker

Q What is the standard gauge of British railway tracks? (the distance between a pair of running lines)
A 4 feet 8½ inches

No. 174

a1   Besides sugar, from what are meringues made?

b1   *Of which religion was Guru Nanak a founder?*

a2   What do we call a chain of molecules bonded together?

b2   *As what did Spencer Tracy achieve fame?*

a3   Which country lies immediately south of Egypt?

b3   *By what initials was the Soviet Committee of State Security known?*

a4   In computing, what is meant by 'mega' (as in 'megabyte')?

b4   *In electronics, what is a PC board?*

a5   What have the following in common: Festiniog, Ravenglass & Eskdale, and Romney, Hythe & Dymchurch?

b5   *And what have these three kings in common: Edward II, Richard II, and Edward VIII?*

a6   Sumatra, Borneo, and Java are all part of which country?

b6   *In which country is Mount Ararat (on which Noah's ark is said to have come to rest)?*

a7   For what is Cézanne famous?

b7   *In which language did Euripides write his plays?*

a8   Which poet wrote a famous poem about John Gilpin?

b8   *Which poet wrote a love song to Miss Joan Hunter Dunn?*

a9   Of which ancient city was Pericles a statesman?

b9   *How did Socrates die?*

a10   In Christianity, which bird is sometimes used as a symbol of the Holy Spirit?

b10   *With which festival do we primarily associate the hymn which begins 'Come, ye thankful people come'?*

a11   What is the name of the calendar we use in the Western World?

b11   *Will the year 2000 be a leap year?*

a12   What is shown by a flowchart?

b12   *And what is shown by a pie chart?*

No. 174 Answers

a1	Egg whites
b1	*Sikhism*
a2	Polymer
b2	*(Film) actor*
a3	Sudan
b3	*KGB*
a4	One million
b4	*Printed circuit*
a5	All are (narrow gauge) railways
b5	*All abdicated*
a6	Indonesia
b6	*Turkey*
a7	Painting, an artist
b7	*Greek*
a8	William Cowper (*say*: Cooper)
b8	*(Sir John) Betjeman*
a9	Athens
b9	*He drank hemlock (was made to do so)*
a10	The dove
b10	*Harvest*
a11	Gregorian calendar
b11	*Yes (although 1700, 1800, and 1900 were not leap years)*
a12	(Continuous) sequence of operations or events *or* computer programs
b12	*The proportions of the components of the whole; how something is divided up*

Tie-breaker

Q In the computer language BASIC, why is it important to know when and when not to use the command 'NEW' (N-E-W)?

A *Because it wipes the entire program contents from the memory*

No. 175

a1   Which part of an animal is its muzzle?

b1   *What kind of animal is a predator?*

a2   What is a parka?

b2   *Whereabouts would you wear a ruff?*

a3   If the pound were to equal $1.50, how many dollars would you get for £10.50?

b3   *If you get 230 Spanish pesetas for a pound, how many pesetas would you get for £12?*

a4   Of which county is the Isle of Sheppey a part?

b4   *On which island does a Battle of the Flowers take place?*

a5   In mythology, who was the god of the sea?

b5   *In Roman mythology, who is the equivalent of the Greek god Hermes?*

a6   In the eleventh century, which Spanish national hero championed Christianity against the Moors?

b6   *In medieval times, what was the name of the famous league of trading cities in North Germany?*

a7   When talking of watches and calculators, for what do the letters LCD stand?

b7   *And in physics, what is UVR?*

a8   Who is known as the father of English history?

b8   *Who is known as the father of English poetry?*

a9   Who was the mother of the Blessed Virgin Mary?

b9   *In the Good Friday ceremony, how many Stations of the Cross are there?*

a10   Sinology is the study of which language and country?

b10   *Which language uses the Cyrillic alphabet?*

a11   For what is Palestrina famous?

b11   *Of which country is Taliesin a famous poet (say: Tal-ee-ess-in)?*

a12   In 1829, what did George Shillibeer introduce in London?

b12   *In 1844, W. C. T. Dobson is said to have sent the first . . . what?*

No. 175 Answers

a1 Nose *and* mouth
b1 *One that hunts/kills/feeds on other animals*
a2 Anorak; loose coat with hood
b2 *Round your neck*
a3 $15.75
b3 *2,760*
a4 Kent
b4 *Jersey*
a5 Poseidon (Greek); Neptune (Roman)
b5 *Mercury*
a6 El Cid (Roderigo Diaz de Bivar)
b6 *Hanseatic League*
a7 Liquid Crystal Display
b7 *Ultra Violet Ray*
a8 Bede (the Venerable Bede)
b8 *Chaucer*
a9 St Anne
b9 *Fourteen*
a10 China
b10 *Russian (or Bulgarian, Slav, Mongolian)*
a11 Composer (*accept*: choir master, conductor)
b11 *Wales*
a12 A bus service (horse bus)
b12 *The first Christmas card*

Tie-breaker

Q From the Straits of Dover up to the English-Scottish border, there are eleven English counties which border the North Sea. How many of them can you name?

A *Northumberland, Tyne and Wear, Durham, Cleveland, North Yorkshire, Humberside, Lincolnshire, Norfolk, Suffolk, Essex, and Kent.*

No. 176

a1 In a car, what does the sump contain?

b1 *And which device disconnects the drive from the engine to the gear box?*

a2 What is the plural of 'court martial'?

b2 *What is the plural of octopus?*

a3 In which sport would you use a Malibu board?

b3 *Which island is famous for puffins and has its own stamps?*

a4 Which film star was originally named Alexander Archibald Leach?

b4 *And which film director and actor was born Allen Stewart Konigsberg?*

a5 What are North and South Utsire (say: Ut-sir-a)?

b5 *Where are the shipping areas Rockall and Shannon?*

a6 In which country is the Nullarbor Plain?

b6 *In which country is Tuscany?*

a7 In which battle did Richard III lose his crown and the throne?

b7 *In 1381, during which revolution was Wat Tyler killed?*

a8 For what theory is Albert Einstein famous?

b8 *For what is Milton Friedman famous?*

a9 Which novelist wrote the book *Westward Ho*?

b9 *Who wrote* The Beggars Opera?

a10 Which famous poet was made a peer in 1884?

b10 *Which poet laureate died in 1984?*

a11 In which religion is Diwali a festival (sometimes written Divali)?

b11 *In which religion is Sukkot a festival?*

a12 What is a palindrome?

b12 *What does a mnemonic help you to do?*

No. 176 Answers

a1   (Lubricating) oil
b1   *Clutch*
a2   Courts martial
b2   *Octopuses*
a3   Surfing
b3   *Lundy*
a4   Cary Grant
b4   *Woody Allen*
a5   Shipping areas; sea areas; weather forecasting areas
b5   *West of Ireland*
a6   Australia
b6   *Italy*
a7   Battle of Bosworth Field (1485)
b7   *The Peasants' Revolt*
a8   Theory of Relativity
b8   *Economics (monetarism)*
a9   Charles Kingsley
b9   *John Gay*
a10   (Alfred, Lord) Tennyson
b10   *Sir John Betjeman*
a11   Hindu
b11   *Jewish*
a12   Word (or words) that read the same forwards and backwards (Madam, I'm Adam)
b12   *Remember something*

Tie-breaker

Q   The Roman system of numbering uses seven different letters. Can you name them all and also say what number each letter stands for?

A   I = 1, V = 5, X = 10, L = 50, C = 100, D = 500, M = 1,000

No. 177

a1 Which birds do we sometimes describe as making a honking noise?

b1 *Which bird is famous for laying its eggs in other birds' nests?*

a2 Which television series featured the character Kate Longton?

b2 *And in which TV series do the characters Daisy, Enos, and Uncle Jesse appear?*

a3 In the world of aviation, what is meant by your ETA?

b3 *And also in the world of flying, for what do the letters VTOL stand?*

a4 In which religion has there traditionally been a caste system?

b4 *And in which religion are the faithful supposed to observe 'the five pillars'?*

a5 In which novel do we read about Ralph, Simon, and Piggy?

b5 *And in which novel do we meet Napoleon, Snowball, and Boxer?*

a6 On which river delta stands the city of Karachi?

b6 *Tanganyika and Zanzibar now form which one country?*

a7 Who discovered the sea route to India via South Africa?

b7 *Which famous explorer sailed to the West Indies in the* Santa Maria?

a8 Who wrote the lines, 'I wandered lonely as a cloud that floats on high o'er vales and hills'?

b8 *Upon which bridge did he write the poem which begins: 'Earth hath not anything to show more fair'?*

a9 In 1265, who summoned what is often called the first English parliament?

b9 *Which English prince fought at the Battle of Crecy?*

a10 Which religious movement was founded by George Fox?

b10 *Which people's collection of laws is called the Talmud?*

a11 In mythology, who is partner to Gog?

b11 *In mythology, which riddle was solved by Oedipus?*

a12 In heraldry, dexter is the right hand side of a shield. What is the left-hand side?

b12 *In heraldry, what is meant by couchant?*

No. 177 Answers

a1   Goose (*accept*: heron)
b1   *Cuckoo*
a2   *Juliet Bravo*
b2   Dukes of Hazzard
a3   Estimated Time of Arrival
b3   *Vertical Take Off and Landing*
a4   Hinduism
b4   *Islam*
a5   *Lord of the Flies* (William Golding)
b5   Animal Farm *(George Orwell)*
a6   Indus
b6   *Tanzania*
a7   (Vasco) da Gama
b7   *(Christopher) Columbus*
a8   William Wordsworth
b8   *Westminster Bridge (London)*
a9   Simon de Montfort
b9   *Edward, the Black Prince (son of Edward III)*
a10 Quakers (Society of Friends)
b10 *Jewish*
a11 Magog
b11 *The Riddle of the Sphinx*
a12 Sinister
b12 *Lying down*

Tie-breaker

Q   Who conducted the government operations at the Sidney Street Siege in Stepney in 1911?
A   Winston Churchill (then Home Secretary)

No. 178

a1 In chess, in the move known as castling, which two pieces are involved?

b1 In cricket, how many balls are there usually in an over?

a2 In the rhyme, who killed Cock Robin?

b2 In which country is the province of Manitoba?

a3 As what are phosphates used?

b3 In computing, what is remotely moved by a mouse?

a4 The Granta is another name for which English river?

b4 What must Muslims do during Ramadan?

a5 What is the unit of currency in the Netherlands?

b5 What kind of animal is a Kerry Blue?

a6 In pantomime, who is Aladdin's mother?

b6 In which sport is or was Christy O'Connor Junior a champion?

a7 If something is porous, what can pass through it?

b7 If something is translucent, what can pass through it?

a8 In which sea is the island of Heligoland?

b8 On which island is Snaefell?

a9 In which year was the Crystal Palace built?

b9 In which part of the British Empire was there a mutiny in 1857?

a10 What nationality was Christopher Columbus?

b10 What nationality was the explorer Ferdinand Magellan?

a11 Who wrote the poem 'Tintern Abbey Revisited'?

b11 Who wrote the poem 'A Shropshire Lad'?

a12 What is the meaning of the Greek word *eureka*?

b12 What is homo sapiens?

No. 178 Answers

a1   Castle (= rook) *and* King
b1   *Six*
a2   The Sparrow
b2   *Canada*
a3   As fertilizers
b3   *Cursor*
a4   The Cam
b4   *Fast (during daylight hours)*
a5   Guilder
b5   *Dog (terrier)*
a6   Widow Twankey
b6   *Golf*
a7   Liquids or gas
b7   *Light*
a8   North Sea
b8   *Isle of Man*
a9   1851 (for the Great Exhibition)
b9   *India*
a10   Italian
b10   *Portuguese*
a11   (William) Wordsworth
b11   *A. E. Housman*
a12   'I have found it'
b12   *The human species; human beings*

Tie-breaker

Q   How many human beings were there in the ark (and who were they)?
A   *Eight: Noah and his wife, his three sons (Ham, Shem, and Japheth) and their wives*

No. 179

a1 What is a haiku?

b1 *And what is a sari?*

a2 Can you tell us what a sitar is (*spelt* s-i-t-a-r)?

b2 *What kind of food is pilau?*

a3 What is a junk?

b3 *What is a dhoti?*

a4 To which country does Corsica belong?

b4 *Of which country is the Isle of Tiree a part?*

a5 What is (or was) a sackbut?

b5 *Furniture: what is or was a tester?*

a6 Who wrote these words: 'The truth is rarely pure and never simple'?

b6 *Whom did Oscar Wilde describe as 'the Unspeakable in pursuit of the Uneatable'?*

a7 Besides the Carthaginians, who fought the Punic Wars?

b7 *Of the Seven Wonders of the World, what was the Pharos of Alexandria?*

a8 Which large island is said to have been discovered by Eric the Red?

b8 *Which part of the American continent was explored by John Cabot?*

a9 In physics, what is measured in joules?

b9 *And also in physics, what is measured in hertz?*

a10 Which Shakespearean play includes Andrew Aguecheek and Toby Belch?

b10 *Which play by Bernard Shaw is about an officer in the Salvation Army?*

a11 Nicholas Breakspear is the only Englishman ever to achieve which high religious office?

b11 *When the Presbyterian Church in England and the Congregational Church united in 1972, by what name did they become known?*

a12 Edith, Osbert, and Sacheverell were all writers. What was their surname?

b12 *Edward II, Dr Faustus, and* The Jew of Malta *were all plays by which playwright?*

No. 179 Answers

a1 Poem (Japanese, three lines, usually seventeen syllables)

b1 *Woman's garment/dress (one long piece of cloth wrapped round the body; Indian)*

a2 Musical instrument (stringed; Indian)

b2 *Rice (mixed with ghee [clarified butter] and spices)*

a3 (Chinese sailing) boat

b3 *Men's garment (wrapped around the body and between the legs)*

a4 France

b4 *Scotland*

a5 (Early) musical instrument (rather like a trombone)

b5 *Canopy (e.g. over a four-poster bed or pulpit)*

a6 Oscar Wilde

b6 *Fox hunters*

a7 Romans

b7 *(Marble) watch tower/lighthouse*

a8 Greenland

b8 *Newfoundland, Labrador (accept: Canada)*

a9 Energy; work or quantity of heat

b9 *Wave frequencies; frequencies of a periodic phenomenon*

a10 Twelfth Night

b10 *Major Barbara*

a11 Pope (1154–9)

b11 *United Reformed Church*

a12 Sitwell

b12 *Christopher Marlowe*

Tie-breaker

Q Name the four provinces of Ireland

A *Leinster, Munster, Ulster, Connaught*

No. 180

a1 In which television serial did we meet the characters Gladys and Ted Bovis?

b1 *In which television serial did Miss Ellie appear?*

a2 Which other animal did the now extinct mammoth look like?

b2 *Which sea mammal has tusks and a moustache?*

a3 In which city is there a famous Western (or Wailing) Wall?

b3 *Can you give us an example of a fossil fuel?*

a4 Which American state is nicknamed the Bluegrass State?

b4 *In rugby union, what colour jerseys are worn by the Welsh team?*

a5 Who wrote *A Child's Garden of Verses*?

b5 *In a poem, who looked up at the stars above and sang to a small guitar?*

a6 In which continent are there grasslands known as the Pampas?

b6 *In which part of the world is grass or scrubland called the Veld?*

a7 What are Grandsire Triples and Plain Bob Minor?

b7 *What is the Greek equivalent of the letter 's'?*

a8 For what sport is Henley famous?

b8 *What are bangers and hot rods?*

a9 Who wrote the novel *Jewel in the Crown*?

b9 *Which nurse became famous at Scutari?*

a10 Who built the defensive dyke that ran from the Dee to the Wye?

b10 *Of which tribe or people was Boadicea (or Boudicca) the queen?*

a11 What does a psephologist study?

b11 *What work is done by a lapidary?*

a12 In the Bible, how many psalms are there?

b12 *In legend, what is the name for the cup from which Jesus drank at the Last Supper?*

No. 180 Answers

a1 Hi-de-Hi!
b1 Dallas
a2 Elephant (furry)
b2 *Walrus*
a3 Jerusalem
b3 *Coal; oil; natural gas (made from the remains of living matter)*
a4 Kentucky
b4 *Red*
a5 Robert Louis Stevenson
b5 *The Owl (in 'The Owl and the Pussy Cat' by Edward Lear)*
a6 (South) America
b6 *South Africa*
a7 Methods (or changes) of bell-ringing
b7 *Sigma*
a8 Rowing
b8 *(Saloon) cars used for racing*
a9 Paul Scott
b9 *Florence Nightingale*
a10 Offa
b10 *Iceni*
a11 Elections; the way people vote
b11 *He cuts or polishes gems*
a12 150
b12 *The Holy Grail*

Tie-breaker

Q Kepler's Laws cover the movement of which bodies?
A *Planets*

No. 181

a1   With which emblem do MGM films begin?

b1   Of which bank is a black horse the emblem?

a2   What can be either aneroid or mercury?

b2   What's special about osmium?

a3   Which animal is feline?

b3   Which animal is equine?

a4   For which art is David Hockney famous?

b4   In which sport is Pat Edery famous?

a5   In which country is Gdansk?

b5   Which are the three Benelux countries?

a6   For which month of the year is garnet the birthstone?

b6   For which month of the year is turquoise the birthstone?

a7   Who designed and engineered the Suez Canal?

b7   Who was the Greek scientist who discovered the laws of floating objects?

a8   By what title was the military leader Arthur Wellesley better known?

b8   Which duke was drowned in a butt of malmsey wine?

a9   Who wrote the poems 'The Rainbow' and 'The Solitary Reaper'?

b9   Who wrote the poems 'Ozymandias' and 'Ode to the West Wind'?

a10   Name two countries which border Lake Tanganyika.

b10   Name two countries which border Lake Victoria.

a11   Of which religion was Vishnu one of the chief deities?

b11   Which religion was founded just over 400 years ago, to reconcile Hindus and Muslims?

a12   Who is the author of the 'Foundation' science fiction novels?

b12   Which novel by Evelyn Waugh features Sebastian Flyte and Charles Ryder?

No. 181 Answers

a1 A (roaring) lion
b1 *Lloyds*
a2 A barometer
b2 *It's the heaviest or densest metal*
a3 The cat
b3 *The horse*
a4 Painting or photography
b4 *Horse racing*
a5 Poland
b5 *Belgium, Netherlands, Luxembourg*
a6 January
b6 *December*
a7 (Ferdinand) de Lessseps
b7 *Archimedes*
a8 Duke of Wellington
b8 *(George, Duke of) Clarence*
a9 (William) Wordsworth
b9 *(Percy Bysshe) Shelley*
a10 Tanzania, Zambia, Zaire, Burundi
b10 *Uganda, Kenya, Tanzania*
a11 Hinduism (*accept:* 'Followers of Krishna')
b11 *The Sikh faith*
a12 Isaac Asimov
b12 *Brideshead Revisited*

Tie-breaker

Q Can you name the nine known planets in our solar system?
A *Mercury, Venus, Earth, Mars, Jupiter, Saturn, Uranus, Neptune, Pluto*

No. 182

a1   In the Army, what is a QMG?

b1   In Army slang, what is a rookie?

a2   What is the modern equivalent for the old fashioned word kin? (as in 'kith and kin')?

b2   In the world of antiques, what is a tallboy?

a3   Of which county is the Isle of Thanet a part?

b3   Ronaldsway is an airport on which island?

a4   At what age can you give blood, vote, and see an X-rated film?

b4   What is the youngest age you can be sent to prison?

a5   What is meant by the phrase *quid pro quo*?

b5   In which continent does the language Gujarati originate?

a6   What kind of product was featured in the first commercial shown on ITV?

b6   In film or television, what is meant by panning?

a7   *Iota, kappa*, and *lambda* are letters in which alphabet?

b7   Which Greek letter denotes the mathematical constant 3.14159?

a8   Holi is a spring religious festival. In which religion?

b8   Winter sees the festival of Hannukah. In which religion is Hannukah observed?

a9   In which year did the English Civil War begin?

b9   In which year was the Restoration of the British monarchy?

a10   Who is the oldest man mentioned in the Bible?

b10   In the Bible, of Esau and Jacob, which was the hairy man?

a11   What nationality was the explorer Vasco da Gama?

b11   What nationality was the mathematician Pythagoras?

a12   Which Greek poet wrote *The Odyssey*?

b12   Which Persian poet wrote the poem, the Rubaiyat?

No. 182 Answers

a1   Quarter Master General (in charge of stores, provisions)

b1   *A new recruit; an 'innocent'*

a2   Relations: family

b2   *(Double) chest of drawers*

a3   Kent

b3   *Isle of Man*

a4   Eighteen

b4   *Seventeen*

a5   An equivalent; something being given in return

b5   *Asia*

a6   Toothpaste ('Gibbs SR')

b6   *Swivelling of a stationary camera sideways*

a7   Greek

b7   *Pi*

a8   Hinduism

b8   *Jewish*

a9   1642

b9   *1660*

a10   Methuselah (he died when he was 969)

b11   *Esau (Genesis 27: 2)*

a11   Portuguese

b11   *Greek*

a12   Homer

b12   *Omar Khayyam*

No. 183

a1   What were once called Light, Home, and Third?

b1   *What have the following in common: Mugwort, Ragged Robin, and Meadowsweet?*

a2   On which sea is the Ukranian port of Odessa situated?

b2   *In which country is the port of Esbjerg?*

a3   On which country was the Ottoman Empire based?

b3   *In which country was the 'Night of the Long Knives'?*

a4   In 1938, which country was taken over in Hitler's *Anschluss*?

b4   *In 1945, whom did Truman and Churchill meet at Potsdam?*

a5   What is meant by your *alma mater*?

b5   *What is meant by the Latin phrase in camera?*

a6   Which famous actress had the first name of Tallulah?

b6   *Sandy Macpherson was a popular performer in cinemas in the 1930s. What did he do?*

a7   Which philosopher was a pupil of Socrates and author of *The Republic*?

b7   *What organization was founded by the Revd Chad Varrah?*

a8   Who wrote the books *Good Wives* and *Little Women*?

b8   *A collection of stories called Kiss Kiss and the book Charlie and the Chocolate Factory were both written by whom?*

a9   According to the Bible, what shall the meek inherit?

b9   *In the Bible, what is said to be the root of all evil?*

a10   In which Shakespearean play do we meet Goneril, Regan, and Cordelia?

b10   *According to Shakespeare, who killed Macbeth?*

a11   In Greek mythology, who is the sun god?

b11   *In Greek mythology, what is Hades?*

a12   In which country were the finals of the 1974 World Cup played?

b12   *In which country were the finals of the 1978 World Cup played?*

No. 183 Answers

a1 BBC radio networks (later renamed Radios 2, 3, and 4)

b1 *Wild flowers*

a2 Black Sea

b2 *Denmark*

a3 Turkey

b3 *Germany (1934; Hitler arranged the murder of some of the Brownshirts)*

a4 Austria

b4 *Stalin*

a5 Foster Mother (*or*: school or college)

b5 *Secretly; in private*

a6 Tallulah Bankhead

b6 *Played the organ*

a7 Plato

b7 *Samaritans*

a8 Louisa M. Alcott

b8 *Roald Dahl*

a9 The earth

b9 *Love of money (accept: money)*

a10 *King Lear*

b10 *Macduff*

a11 Helios (*accept*: Apollo, often associated with the sun)

b11 *The Underworld*

a12 West Germany

b12 *Argentina*

Tie-breaker

Q Which novelist is associated with the towns of Rochester, Ipswich, and Broadstairs?

A *Charles Dickens*

No. 184

a1   If A is Alpha and B is Bravo, what is D?

b1   What is unusual about this sentence: The quick brown fox jumps over the lazy dog?

a2   Of which country is the Peloponnese a part?

b2   In which country is the Camargue?

a3   For what is the scientist Lord Rutherford chiefly remembered?

b3   For what form of entertainment was 'Lord' George Sanger famous?

a4   Who are the *hoi polloi*?

b4   What is meant by the Latin phrase Felo de se?

a5   What is special about the planet Saturn?

b5   Which country has a Union Jack and five white stars of the Southern Cross on its flag?

a6   Who wrote *It Shouldn't Happen to a Vet*?

b6   Hindley, Heathcliff, and Linton are characters in which novel?

a7   Canary Wharf and Heron Quays are part of which London development?

b7   What is controlled or supervised by the Corporation of Trinity House?

a8   In Scotland, what is or was the tawse?

b8   What same meaning have the French word après-midi and the German word Nachmittag?

a9   What did Joseph have put in Benjamin's sack?

b9   In the Bible, which is the City of David?

a10   When was the last successful land invasion of Britain?

b10   In which year were the parliaments of England and Scotland united?

a11   In astronomy, what are nebulae?

b11   For what is Na the chemical symbol?

a12   Who wrote the poems 'Cargoes' and 'Sea Fever'?

b12   Who wrote the poems 'Venus and Adonis' and 'The Rape of Lucrece'?

No. 184 Answers

a1   Delta
b1   *It contains all the letters of the alphabet*
a2   Greece
b2   *France*
a3   Work in physics; study of atoms
b3   *Circus*
a4   The common people; everybody; the 'ordinary' people
b4   *Suicide*
a5   It is surrounded by rings (probably of millions of separate solid particles) (*accept*: has several moons/satellites)
b5   *Australia*
a6   James Herriot
b6   *Wuthering Heights*
a7   Isle of Dogs (accept: Docklands)
b7   *Lighthouses (the marking of coastal waters, wrecks) (accept: pilots)*
a8   Strap; leather belt (with which children were beaten)
b8   *Afternoon*
a9   A silver cup (*accept*: A chalice or goblet)
b9   *Jerusalem*
a10   1066
b10   *1707*
a11   Clouds of dust and gas *or* systems of stars and interstellar matter
b11   *Sodium*
a12   John Masefield
b12   *Shakespeare*

Tie-breaker

Q   Which group of animals or creatures have three pairs of legs attached to the thorax and (usually) two pairs of wings?
A   *Insects*

No. 185

a1   In which country did paper originate?

b1   *What form of transport was developed by Igor Sikorsky?*

a2   Which part of speech describes how an action is performed?

b2   *What is an addendum?*

a3   What is a euphemism?

b3   *What is the difference in meaning of these two words: 'among and between'?*

a4   Where does the International Court of Justice normally meet?

b4   *In what building was Maria Marten supposedly murdered?*

a5   Which earl was known as the Kingmaker?

b5   *In which town was Archbishop Cranmer burnt at the stake?*

a6   Which king ruled England from the year 1100 until his death in 1135, (when the crown was seized by Stephen)?

b6   *Of which country was Donald Bane a King?*

a7   Alice Liddell became the heroine of a famous book. Which?

b7   *As what did Isadora Duncan achieve fame?*

a8   In which country did the dance, the Samba, originate?

b8   *In which country did the dance, the Rumba, originate?*

a9   Which angel foretold Jesus' birth?

b9   *Which king tried to get the child Jesus put to death?*

a10   Who wrote the poem that begins: 'Oh to be in England, Now that April's there . . .'?

b10   *Who wrote the lines: 'They shall grow not old, as we that are left grow old: Age shall not weary them, nor the years condemn'?*

a11   In mythology, what job was done by Charon?

b11   *In mythology, what kind of animal was Cerberus?*

a12   Which country won the World Cup in 1970?

b12   *Which country won the World Cup in 1982?*

No. 185 Answers

a1   China

b1   *Helicopter*

a2   An adverb

b2   *An addition (especially an extra section at the end of a book)*

a3   A polite or 'nice' way of saying something rude or unpleasant

b3   *'Among' involves three or more people or things (e.g. among friends = among three or more friends) while 'between' involves only two.*

a4   The Hague

b4   *The Red Barn (at Polstead, near Ipswich)*

a5   Warwick (Richard Neville)

b5   *Oxford*

a6   Henry I

b6   *Scotland*

a7   Alice's Adventures in Wonderland

b7   *Dancer*

a8   Brazil

b8   *Cuba*

a9   Gabriel

b9   *Herod*

a10   Robert Browning ('Home Thoughts from Abroad')

b10   *(Lawrence) Binyon*

a11   Ferried dead across the river Styx; a boatman

b11   *Dog*

a12   Brazil

b12   *Italy*

Tie-breaker

Q   Who was the author of *The Spoils of Poynton*, *The Golden Bowl* and the famous ghost story 'The Turn of the screw'?

A   Henry James

a1   What is German for the number five?

b1   *What is the English for the French number* vingt-et-un?

a2   What is sarsaparilla?

b2   *What is retsina?*

a3   Around 1850, what was invented by a London shopkeeper called John Bowler?

b3   *With what article of clothing was Anthony Eden associated?*

a4   In which sport might an eight, a four, or a pair take part?

b4   *How many times did the famous horse Red Rum win the Grand National?*

a5   As what did Sir George Gilbert Scott achieve fame?

b5   *In which art did Sarah Bernhardt achieve fame?*

a6   In the children's stories, which bear cannot resist marmalade?

b6   *Which writer created Sam Weller?*

a7   What is meant by the Latin phrase *semper fidelis*?

b7   *What does the Latin phrase* pax vobiscum *mean?*

a8   W. B. Yeats: what do the initials 'W.B.' stand for?

b8   *As what did Ivy Benson, Jack Hylton, and Victor Silvester all achieve fame?*

a9   In which year did Julius Caesar first invade Britain?

b9   *In which year did Columbus discover the West Indies?*

a10   Who wrote the sequence of novels called *The Alexandria Quartet*?

b10   *Who wrote the novel* The French Lieutenant's Woman?

a11   In art, which painter is usually thought of as having invented Cubism?

b11   *The German artist, Hans Holbein painted a famous portrait of an English king. Which king?*

a12   Medicine: what is the most important component of red blood cells?

b12   *History: which group supporting the rights of property owners were led by John Lilburne and others?*

No. 186 Answers

a1   Fünf
b1   21 (accept: pontoon)
a2   Drink (made from the roots of the plant Smilax)
b2   Wine (Greek, resinated)
a3   Bowler hat
b3   Hat (homburg)
a4   Rowing
b4   Three
a5   Architect (also designed the classic red telephone box)
b5   Acting: theatre
a6   Paddington
b6   Charles Dickens (in The Pickwick Papers)
a7   Always faithful; forever faithful
b7   Peace be with you
a8   William Butler
b8   Bandleaders
a9   55 BC
b9   1492
a10   Lawrence Durrell
b10   John Fowles
a11   Picasso (or Braque)
b11   Henry VIII
a12   Haemoglobin
b12   The Levellers

Tie-breaker

Q   Fourteen American Presidents have held office since World War I ended. Name seven of them.
A   *George Bush, Ronald Reagan, Jimmy Carter, Gerald Ford, Richard Nixon, Lyndon Johnson, John Kennedy, Dwight Eisenhower, Harry Truman, Franklin Roosevelt, Herbert Hoover, Calvin Coolidge, Warren Harding, Woodrow Wilson*

No. 187

a1   If you're good at stenography, what can you write?

b1   What do you do if you exonerate a person?

a2   Traditionally, who would wear a cap and bells?

b2   In the tropics, why are white clothes preferred to black ones?

a3   In a children's book, who said he was a bear of 'Very little brain'?

b3   Which story-book doctor was able to talk to the animals?

a4   *Uisge beatha* is Gaelic for 'Water of Life'. By what name do we call this drink?

b4   From which grain is whisky usually made?

a5   In 1827, of what was John Macadam appointed general surveyor?

b5   With what in particular do you associate the engineer James Brindley?

a6   Of which book was the Authorized Version published in 1611?

b6   In which year was the American Declaration of Independence?

a7   Gloriana was a name given to which English queen (by the poet Spenser)?

b7   What is the difference between a queen regent and a queen consort?

a8   Which poet wrote the lines, 'The curfew tolls the knell of parting day'?

b8   Who wrote the poem that begins: 'Season of mists and mellow fruitfulness'?

a9   Kalends, nones, and ides were fixed points each month in which calendar?

b9   In ancient times, what was the Rubicon?

a10 In heraldry, what is a chevron?

b10 In heraldry, what colour is gules? (say: goulz)

a11 Chemistry: what do we call the particle formed when a neutral atom or group of atoms has gained or lost electrons?

b11 Astronomy: which planet has moons called Io, Ganymede, and Callisto?

a12 Theatre: Peter Shaffer is a well-known playwright. Can you name *one* of his plays?

b12 History: for ten months following his victory at Stirling Bridge in 1297, who was Guardian of Scotland and commander of its army?

No. 187 Answers

a1 Shorthand

b1 *Free them from blame; 'let them off'*

a2 A jester

b2 *White reflects heat rays, black absorbs them*

a3 Winnie-the-Pooh

b3 *Dr Dolittle*

a4 Whisky

b4 *Barley (accept: rye or maize)*

a5 Roads

b5 *Canal building; canals; aqueducts*

a6 Bible

b6 *1776*

a7 Elizabeth I

b7 *A queen regent is queen in her own right (like Elizabeth I and II or Victoria); a queen consort is the wife of a king*

a8 (Thomas) Gray

b8 *John Keats*

a9 The Roman

b9 *River (between Gaul and Italy)*

a10 Bent (or angled) stripe (like an arrow head), point upwards

b10 *Red*

a11 Ion (An*ion* = negative, cation = positive)

b11 *Jupiter*

a12 One of: *Royal Hunt of the Sun, Equus, Amadeus, Five Finger Exercise, Black Comedy, The White Liars, The Battle of Shriving* (or *Shrivings*)*, The Private Ear and the Public Eye*

b12 *(William) Wallace*

Tie-breaker

Q The first five books of the Old Testament are sometimes called the Books of Moses, or the Pentateuch. What are their names?

A *Genesis, Exodus, Leviticus, Numbers, Deuteronomy*

No. 188

a1   Spell currant (as found in a cake)

b1   *Spell the word compliment, when it means 'words of praise'*

a2   What musical instrument did Sparky play?

b2   *In woodwork, into what does a tenon fit in order to form a joint?*

a3   What is a pomander?

b3   *What colour is pompadour?*

a4   For what drink is Vichy famous?

b4   *From which town does the drink port take its name?*

a5   Children's books: What sort of animal is Babar?

b5   *In which book does a rabbit say, 'By my ears and whiskers, I shall be late'?*

a6   Which English Admiral is sometimes described as 'The Hero of the Nile'?

b6   *Who sailed round the world in the yacht Gypsy Moth IV?*

a7   Who wrote the poem 'Don Juan'?

b7   *Who wrote the poem 'The Charge of the Light Brigade'?*

a8   What is meant by the phrase *al fresco*?

b8   *What is meant by the phrase* caveat emptor?

a9   Of which language is Walloon a type?

b9   *Yiddish, Hebrew, and Arabic are all languages of which state?*

a10   What is the Magnificat?

b10   *The* Mahabharata *and the* Ramayana *are both great Indian . . . What? (say: Ma-hab-a-rata; Rama-ya-na)*

a11   Aviation: by what name is the Boeing E3A Sentry aircraft often known?

b11   *Maths: What do we call the pictorial representation of a set?*

a12   In classical mythology, what kind of danger was Charybodis (say: Ka-rib-dis)?

b12   *In the* Odyssey, *into what did the witch Circe (say: sir-sey) change the sailors?*

No. 188 Answers

a1 Currant
b1 *Compliment*
a2 (Magic) piano
b2 *Mortise*
a3 A ball shaped container, holding perfume
b3 *Claret, purple*
a4 (Mineral) water
b4 *Oporto*
a5 An elephant
b5 Alice's Adventures in Wonderland
a6 Lord Nelson
b6 *(Sir Francis) Chichester*
a7 Lord Byron
b7 *(Alfred, Lord) Tennyson*
a8 'In the open air'
b8 *'Let the buyer beware'*
a9 French (Belgian French)
b9 *Israel*
a10 Hymn or words spoken by the Virgin Mary, used as part of Evening Prayer in church
b10 *Poems (accept: stories or legends)*
a11 AWACS (Airborne Warning and Control System)
b11 *Venn diagram*
a12 A whirlpool
b12 *Pigs*

Tie-breaker

Q In the seventeenth century, which architectural or artistic style was characterized by extravagant decoration?

A *The Baroque (accept: Rococo)*

No. 189

a1   What was a clipper?

b1   *What was a clippie?*

a2   Which monster first made the headlines in 1933?

b2   *What kind of monster or person was Polyphemus (say: Polly-fee-mus)?*

a3   At what number in Downing Street is the Chief Whip's office?

b3   *What is the name of the prime minister's country home?*

a4   Athene and Minerva are the Greek and Roman goddesses of . . . what?

b4   *Eros and Cupid are the Greek and Roman gods of . . . what?*

a5   What was tested on the Bikini Atoll in 1946?

b5   *In May 1900, which South African town was 'relieved'?*

a6   If you were having a holiday in Marrakesh, in which country would you be?

b6   *In which country is the holiday resort of Acapulco?*

a7   What is French leave?

b7   *If you are suffering from* ennui *how are you feeling?*

a8   In which of Dickens' novels does Pip meet a convict?

b8   *Which of Charles Dickens' novels is about the French Revolution?*

a9   For what is Sir Osbert Lancaster best remembered?

b9   *As what did Sir Edwin Lutyens achieve fame?*

a10   In which year did the 10-shilling note cease to be legal tender?

b10   *Last century, what was the face value of a groat coin?*

a11   In which sport has Great Britain's women's team been captained by Mary Eckersall?

b11   *In netball, when are you offside?*

a12   Who wrote the poem that begins: 'Is there anybody there? said the Traveller'?

b12   *Who wrote the poem that begins: 'If I should die, think only this of me'?*

No. 189 Answers

a1 A fast sailing ship (colloquially, also a stylish or beautiful woman)
b1 *Bus conductress (especially during the Second World War)*
a2 Loch Ness Monster
b2 *One-eyed giant (in the Odyssey)*
a3 Number 12
b3 *Chequers*
a4 Wisdom
b4 *Love*
a5 Atom bomb
b5 *Mafeking*
a6 Morocco
b6 *Mexico*
a7 Absence
b7 *Bored, fed up*
a8 *Great Expectations*
b8 Tales of Two Cities
a9 Cartoons (also stage design)
b9 *Architect (designed the Cenotaph, Liverpool RC cathedral)*
a10 1970
b10 *4d (four old pence)*
a11 Hockey
b11 *If you enter an area of the court not assigned to your position*
a12 Walter de la Mare
b12 *Rupert Brooke*

Tie-breaker

Q Which is the longest musical note?
A *Breve*

No. 190

a1 What does a Spaniard mean when he says *hasta manana*?

b1 *What does the Latin word* salve *mean?*

a2 What have these in common: Snowdon, Vale of Rheidol, and Talyllyn?

b2 *William Hartnell, Tom Baker, and Jon Pertwee have all played which television character?*

a3 What is meant by deportment?

b3 *What is legerdemain?*

a4 Which kind of animals figure largely in the novel *Watership Down*?

b4 *In which book did George, Harris, and J. appear?*

a5 In which year was the Battle of Agincourt?

b5 *In which year was the Battle of Bosworth Field?*

a6 Which famous lexicographer was born at Lichfield?

b6 *A famous English poet is buried at Grasmere in the Lake District, Who?*

a7 What was (or is) the job of the fuller?

b7 *Historically, what was the job of a beadsman?*

a8 In which story do we hear about Never-Never Land?

b8 *How was Peter Pan different from all other boys?*

a9 Grendel is a monster in which epic early English poem?

b9 *Who became the hero of plays by Marlowe and Goethe and an opera by Gounod (say: Gur-te; Gou-no)?*

a10 Which religious order was founded by a monk who has given his name to a liqueur still made in a French abbey?

b10 *Which religious order was founded by St Ignatius Loyola?*

a11 What was the surname of the poet whose first names were Thomas Stearns?

b11 *What was the surname of the poet whose first names were Gerard Manley?*

a12 What is the capital of Pakistan?

b12 *What is the capital of Indonesia?*

No. 190 Answers

a1 'Till tomorrow'
b1 *'Welcome; hail; greetings'*
a2 Railways (narrow gauge; in Wales)
b2 *Dr Who*
a3 The way a person walks, carries him or herself (or should do)
b3 *Sleight of hand*
a4 Rabbits
b4 *Three Men in a Boat*
a5 1415
b5 *1485*
a6 (Dr Samuel) Johnson
b6 *(William) Wordsworth*
a7 To clean or thicken cloth
b7 *To say prayers*
a8 *Peter Pan*
b8 *(a) He never grew up; (b) He could fly*
a9 *Beowulf*
b9 *Faust (or Faustus)*
a10 Benedictines
b10 *Jesuits; Society of Jesus*
a11 Eliot
b11 *Hopkins*
a12 Islamabad
b12 *Jakarta*

Tie-breaker

Q Name the four people or creatures present at the Mad Hatter's tea party
A *Alice, the Mad Hatter, the March Hare, and the Dormouse*

No. 191

a1   By what name is the African country, the Gold Coast, now called?

b1   *Which European country invaded and conquered Ethiopia (or Abyssinia) between 1935 and 1937?*

a2   In the American West, what was James Butler Hickock's nickname?

b2   *Sheriff Pat Garrett killed a young outlaw who had formerly been his friend. Who was he?*

a3   For what event is 1989 remembered in Berlin?

b3   *In 1959, which spiritual leader was forced to leave his homeland?*

a4   Which political party do you support if you're 'true blue'?

b4   *At which political party conference might you hear 'The Red Flag'?*

a5   On television, who plays Lovejoy?

b5   *On television, of which hotel was the manager called Basil?*

a6   With which sport do you associate Ray Reardon?

b6   *For what has Ogden Nash achieved fame?*

a7   Which brothers once had hits with 'Bye Bye Love' and 'Cathy's Clown'?

b7   *What are the Christian names of the two brothers who formed the group Bros?*

a8   Who wrote the play *Brief Encounter*?

b8   *Who wrote the play* Cat on a Hot Tin Roof?

a9   In 1979, who was elected president of the USA?

b9   *In 1979, which London embassy was stormed by SAS troops?*

a10   In which year did Hitler invade Russia?

b10   *Which German ship sank* HMS Hood?

a11   Whose visit to America inspired him to compose a New World symphony?

b11   *Which of these was not a French: composer Debussy, Delius, Delibes?*

a12   In which year did the state of Israel officially come into being?

b12   *Who became prime minister of India in 1947?*

No. 191 Answers

a1   Ghana
b1   *Italy*
a2   Wild Bill Hickock
b2   *Billy the Kid*
a3   Opening up of the Berlin Wall; free travel between East and West Berlin
b3   *Dalai Lama (Tibet)*
a4   Conservative
b4   *Labour/Socialist (accept: Communist)*
a5   Ian McShane
b5   *'Fawlty Towers'*
a6   Snooker
b6   *(Humorous) poetry*
a7   The Everly Brothers
b7   *Matt and Luke*
a8   Noël Coward
b8   *Tennessee Williams*
a9   Ronald Reagan
b9   *Iranian*
a10   1941
b10   *The battleship* Bismarck
a11   Anton Dvorák (say: Vor-jhak)
b11   *Delius (he was British)*
a12   1948
b12   *Jawaharlal (Pandit) Nehru*

Tie-breaker

Q   Haroun al-Raschid made his court a centre of art and learning. In which work of literature does it figure?
A   *A Thousand and One Nights*

No. 192

a1 Which singer had hits with 'Summer Holiday' and 'Congratulations'?

b1 *Which group first had hits with 'Can't Get No Satisfaction' and 'Jumpin' Jack Flash'?*

a2 What is lady's slipper?

b2 *What is a prickly pear?*

a3 What have the Haymarket, the Globe, and Her Majesty's in common?

b3 *What do Canada, Walker, and Ryder have in common?*

a4 What is the clay, meerschaum, used to make?

b4 *Of what is snuff a powdered form?*

a5 Which politician do you associate with a yacht called *Morning Cloud*?

b5 *What post in the House of Commons was once held by George Thomas MP?*

a6 On television, in 'Last of the Summer Wine', what part is or was played by Kathy Staff?

b6 *Which television comedy show came from 'Beautiful Downtown Burbank'?*

a7 In which American city were the 1984 Olympic Games held?

b7 *In which city were the 1980 Summer Olympics held?*

a8 Which British city has railway stations called Central and Queen Street?

b8 *What is the name of the tube line that opened in London in 1979?*

a9 Which pope died in August, 1978?

b9 *Which international movement was popularized by the Maharishi Mahesh Yogi?*

a10 Whose last words (according to Shakespeare) were 'Et tu, Brute'?

b10 *Which naval officer ended his life by saying 'I thank God I have done my duty'?*

a11 Who was the first criminal 'caught by wireless'?

b11 *Mr Parker and Mr Longbaugh were train robbers. How are they better known (especially since there was a film retelling their adventures)?*

a12 When Canada was French, what was it called?

b12 *Who was Canada's first prime minister?*

No. 192 Answers

a1	Cliff Richard
b1	*Rolling Stones*
a2	(Wild) flower
b2	*Cactus*
a3	All (London) theatres
b3	*They are all cups awarded for Golf*
a4	Pipes
b4	*Tobacco*
a5	Edward Heath
b5	*Speaker*
a6	Nora Batty
b6	*'Rowan and Martin's Laugh-in'*
a7	Los Angeles
b7	*Moscow*
a8	Glasgow or Cardiff
b8	*Jubilee Line*
a9	Paul (VI) (Giovanni Batista Montini)
b9	*Transcendental Meditation (TM)*
a10	Julius Caesar
b10	*Lord Nelson*
a11	Dr Crippen (while fleeing to America, by ship)
b11	*Butch Cassidy and the Sundance Kid*
a12	New France
b12	*Sir John MacDonald*

Tie-breaker

Q What happened to the Ninth Legion of the Roman army after it left York to march northwards?

A It vanished

No. 193

a1   What is samphire?

b1   What kind of plant is marjoram?

a2   Of which church is the Archbishop of Westminster a leader?

b2   By what title is the Bishop of Rome usually known?

a3   On which course is the Lincolnshire Handicap run?

b3   In which sport do Featherstone and Hull Kingston Rovers compete?

a4   In which museum is the painting the Mona Lisa?

b4   In a museum in which city is Michelangelo's statue of David?

a5   What is the capital of the Canadian province of Ontario?

b5   And of the Canadian province, Newfoundland?

a6   When something is galvanized, with what is it covered or coated?

b6   What is measured by a Geiger counter?

a7   Which pop star had hits with 'All Shook Up', 'Love Me Tender', and 'Hound Dog'?

b7   Which popular singer was once particularly associated with a rocking chair?

a8   In which country did General Jaruzelski once impose martial law?

b8   In which industry is or was Ray Buckton a union leader?

a9   On which television series were Napoleon Solo and Illya Kuryakin the stars?

b9   In which television serial did we meet the characters Sarah Layton and Guy Perron?

a10   In which year did the French Revolution begin?

b10   Which French King was called 'The Sun King'?

a11   Who composed The Young Person's Guide to the Orchestra?

b11   Who wrote the music that was later given the words, 'Land of Hope and Glory'?

a12   Besides Hadrian, which Roman emperor had a wall built across Britain?

b12   Who was Rome's great enemy, who came from Carthage in the third century BC?

No. 193 Answers

a1   Plant, seashore plant (*accept*: flower) (edible)
b1   Herb
a2   (Roman) Catholic
b2   The Pope
a3   Doncaster
b3   Rugby League
a4   The Louvre, Paris
b4   Florence
a5   Toronto
b5   St John's
a6   Zinc
b6   Radioactivity (chiefly alpha, beta, and gamma rays)
a7   Elvis Presley
b7   Val Doonican
a8   Poland
b8   Railways (ASLEF, train drivers)
a9   The Man from UNCLE
b9   Jewel in the Crown
a10 1789
b10 Louis XIV
a11 Benjamin Britten
b11 Edward Elgar
a12 Antoninus
b12 Hannibal

Tie-breaker

Q   Which Shakespearean play is said to have been written at the request
    of Queen Elizabeth, so she could see more of Falstaff?
A   *The Merry Wives of Windsor*

No 194

a1   With which sport has Tony Jacklin been associated?

b1   In which sport has Sue Barker been a star?

a2   How many leaves are there on a shamrock?

b2   Which flower is sometimes known as the woodbind?

a3   Which early rock star's group was called The Comets?

b3   Of which pop group was Johnny Rotten the leader?

a4   In which country was Gomulka a political leader?

b4   Of which country has Malcolm Fraser been the prime minister?

a5   In 1980, which president of Yugoslavia died?

b5   In 1980, why did 64 countries boycott the Olympics?

a6   On television, who played Callan?

b6   In which television serial did Kevin Banks marry Glenda Brownlow?

a7   Which political party was founded by Roy Jenkins?

b7   In 1981, who headed the inquiry into the Brixton riots?

a8   What do we call a positive electrode?

b8   What do we call a negative electrode?

a9   In which Shakepearean play does a king's ghost walk on the castle ramparts?

b9   In which Shakespearean play is there a famous sleep-walking scene?

a10   What was Drake's ship *The Golden Hind* originally called?

b10   Who took command of the British fleet after Nelson died at Trafalgar?

a11   Which of Beethoven's symphonies is the Choral?

b11   Which of Verdi's operas is set in ancient Egypt?

a12   Verulamium was the Roman name of which English city?

b12   Which English archbishop signs himself Ebor?

No. 194 Answers

a1	Golf
b1	*Tennis*
a2	Three
b2	*Honeysuckle (wild)*
a3	Bill Haley
b3	*The Sex Pistols*
a4	Poland
b4	*Australia*
a5	Tito
b5	*Because of Russia's invasion of Afghanistan*
a6	Edward Woodward
b6	*'Crossroads'*
a7	Social Democrat (SDP)
b7	*Lord Scarman*
a8	An anode
b8	*A cathode*
a9	*Hamlet*
b9	Macbeth
a10	*The Pelican*
b10	*Admiral Collingwood*
a11	Ninth
b11	Aïda
a12	St Albans
b12	York

Tie-breaker

Q What do we call a value on a scale from 0 to 14 that shows how strongly acid or alkaline water or a chemical solution is?

A *The Ph value (0–7 is acidic; 7–14 is alkaline; pure water has a Ph value of 7)*

No. 195

a1   In the 1960s, which pop group was led by Ray Davies?

b1   *Which group once had a hit with 'You Won't Find Another Fool Like Me'?*

a2   For which country did Kapil Dev play cricket?

b2   *In which sport has Roger Clark been a champion?*

a3   In which television series were two detectives played by John Thaw and Dennis Waterman?

b3   *On television, which 'Professionals' were played by Lewis Collins and Martin Shaw?*

a4   Where in Britain is the monument known as Cleopatra's Needle?

b4   *In which city is Leonardo da Vinci's famous painting* The Last Supper?

a5   What is the capital of the Australian state of Queensland?

b5   *And what is the capital of the Australian state of Victoria?*

a6   For what does the abbreviation SALT stand?

b6   *For what does the abbreviation ROM stand?*

a7   Of which political party was Jeremy Thorpe once leader?

b7   *Of which political party was Peter Shore once a leading member?*

a8   At which Cheshire town did the London and North Western Railway have its main locomotive works?

b8   *Swindon was an important railway station and works on which pre-nationalization railway?*

a9   In words like geography and geology, what does the 'geo' part mean?

b9   *And in words like photography and photoelectric, what does the 'photo' part mean?*

a10   Which queen spoke of having the name 'Calais' in her heart?

b10   *Which French leader made famous the remark that the British are a 'nation of shopkeepers'?*

a11   The Latin word *io* (spelt I-O) was a shout of joy. Which punctuation has it turned into?

b11   *In which town or city is a street called 'Land of Green Ginger'?*

a12   Which English county has the longest coastline?

b12   *Which towers were built on the south-east coastline for defence against a Napoleonic invasion?*

No. 195 Answers

a1 The Kinks

b1 The New Seekers

a2 India

b2 Rally driving; motor sport

a3 *The Sweeney*

b3 Bodie and Doyle

a4 The Embankment (London)

b4 Milan

a5 Brisbane

b5 Melbourne

a6 Strategic Arms Limitation Talks

b6 Read Only Memory (computer terminology)

a7 Liberal (accept: Social Liberal Democrat)

b7 Labour

a8 Crewe

b8 Great Western Railway

a9 Earth

b9 To do with light

a10 Mary

b10 Napoleon

a11 Exclamation mark

b11 Hull (Kingston upon Hull)

a12 Cornwall

b12 Martello Towers

Tie-breaker

Q What is the capital of Zaïre?

A *Kinshasa*

No. 196

a1   On television, who was the original compère on *Juke Box Jury*?

b1   *What job on American television was done by Walter Cronkite?*

a2   In which country is Gaelic Football chiefly played?

b2   *What kind of sport is Kendo?*

a3   Which comedian plays the character Dame Edna Everage?

b3   *Who wrote and made famous the songs, 'I Love a Lassie' and 'Stop Yer Ticklin', Jock'?*

a4   In horse racing in Britain, who has been the most successful jockey?

b4   *What sporting achievement was made in 1979 by 12-year-old Marcus Hooper?*

a5   On which island was Dom Mintoff a leading politician?

b5   *Which great English statesman had his 'Wilderness Years'?*

a6   For which group was 'Bohemian Rhapsody' a No 1 hit?

b6   *Which rock artist had hits with 'Tutti Frutti', 'Ready Teddy', and 'Baby Face'?*

a7   In which Shakespearean play does Petruchio marry Kate?

b7   *In which Shakespearean play does Puck 'put a girdle round about the Earth'?*

a8   In which English city are streets called Deansgate, Oxford Road, and John Dalton Street?

b8   *And in which English city are streets called Corporation Street, New Street, and the Moor Street?*

a9   Who directed the films *Dr Strangelove* and *2001: A Space Odyssey*?

b9   *And who directed the films* North by Northwest *and* The Birds?

a10   In which ship did the Pilgrim Fathers sail to America in 1620?

b10   *What was the great achievement of Joshua Slocum, completed in 1898?*

a11   Name the two English counties known as 'counties palatine'?

b11   *Which two Scottish regions border England?*

a12   What do we call the hormone produced in vertebrates at time of fear or exercise which makes the body react quickly to danger?

b12   *What do we call the condition of the blood when it has a shortage of red blood cells or haemoglobin (say: hee-mo-glo-bin)?*

No. 196 Answers

a1   David Jacobs
b1   *Newscaster (news editor)*
a2   Ireland
b2   *Japanese sword fighting (bamboo 'swords')*
a3   Barry Humphries
b3   *Sir Harry Lauder*
a4   (Sir) Gordon Richards
b4   *Swam the Channel (then the youngest person to do so)*
a5   Malta
b5   *Winston Churchill*
a6   Queen
b6   *Little Richard*
a7   *The Taming of the Shrew*
b7   A Midsummer Night's Dream
a8   Manchester
b8   *Birmingham*
a9   Stanley Kubrick
b9   *Alfred Hitchcock*
a10   *The Mayflower*
b10   *Sailing alone around the world*
a11   Cheshire and Lancashire (a count palatine had powers similar to those of a sovereign. Durham was once a county palatine.)
b11   *The Borders* and *Dumfries and Galloway*
a12   Adrenalin
b12   *Anaemia*

Tie-breaker

Q   In the nineteenth century, whose visit to the Galapagos islands helped him to develop a revolutionary theory?

A   *Charles Darwin (Theory of Evolution)*

No. 197

a1   In Britain, where is the Isle of Dogs?

b1   *In which English county can the world's first iron bridge be seen?*

a2   Which highwayman is said to have had a horse called Black Bess?

b2   *Mazzini and Garibaldi did much to help unite which country?*

a3   In Britain, where is the Tomb of the Unknown Soldier?

b3   *In Paris, where is the Tomb of the Unknown Soldier?*

a4   Which actor played Captain Mainwaring in the TV series *Dad's Army*?

b4   *In the original* Avengers *series, who played Emma Peel?*

a5   Of which country was Javed Miandad once its cricket captain?

b5   *With which sport do you connect the name Sam Snead?*

a6   Who was the oldest ever British prime minister?

b6   *Who became prime minister at the age of 24?*

a7   Which group made the record albums 'Abbey Road' and 'Let it Be'?

b7   *Which group first had hits with 'Good Vibrations' and 'Sloop John B'?*

a8   What do you do if you genuflect?

b8   *With what part of the day are vespers associated?*

a9   Who first wrote, 'A thing of beauty is a joy for ever'?

b9   *Which blind English poet wrote about the fall of Satan?*

a10   Mrs Bandaranaike was the world's first woman prime minister — of which country?

b10   *Who was Britain's first Jewish prime minister?*

a11   For the discovery of which chemical element is Henry Cavendish remembered?

b11   *Which scientist discovered the laws of heredity after conducting experiments with peas?*

a12   How do we define the word biomass?

b12   *What is meant by a geostationary orbit?*

No. 197 Answers

a1   London's Docklands
b1   *Shropshire*
a2   Dick Turpin
b2   *Italy*
a3   Westminster Abbey
b3   *Arc de Triomphe*
a4   Arthur Lowe
b4   *Diana Rigg*
a5   Pakistan
b5   *Golf*
a6   Gladstone (84 when he retired in 1894)
b6   *Pitt (William Pitt the Younger)*
a7   The Beatles
b7   *The Beach Boys*
a8   Bend the knee (as in worship) (*accept:* curtsey)
b8   *Evening*
a9   Keats
b9   *Milton*
a10   Ceylon (now Sri Lanka)
b10   *Disraeli (1868)*
a11   Hydrogen
b11   *Gregor Mendel*
a12   The total amount of animal and plant life on the Earth
b12   *It is when a satellite orbits the Earth at a speed of exactly the same as the Earth, so the satellite always stays above the same point on the Earth's surface.*

Tie-breaker

Q   Can you name the six 'Noble Gases'?
A   *Helium, Neon, Argon, Krypton, Xenon, and Radon*

No. 198

a1 Which group of mammals are known as the primates?

b1 *What are plankton?*

a2 What did King John lose in the Wash?

b2 *Who was King of Great Britain at the time of the American War of Independence?*

a3 In which building is Lord Nelson buried?

b3 *Where is Winston Churchill buried?*

a4 What was the title of Tom Jones' first big hit?

b4 *What connection has the singer Kate Bush with the novelist Emily Brontë?*

a5 With which sport is Nick Faldo associated?

b5 *In which sport has Buster Mottram achieved fame?*

a6 On television, in *Upstairs, Downstairs*, who played the butler, Hudson?

b6 *And in television's* The Professionals, *who did Gordon Jackson play?*

a7 Of which country is Kathmandu the capital?

b7 *And of which country is Accra the capital?*

a8 Who, in 1949, was elected first president of Israel?

b8 *Who was the American general whose post-war European aid programme is known by his name?*

a9 What is attacked by caries?

b9 *Also in the human body, where are your carpals?*

a10 Whose last words are said to have been 'I shall hear in Heaven'?

b10 *Which Victorian prime minister said, 'Die, my dear doctor! That's the last thing I shall do' — and then died?*

a11 To whom is the Dunmow Flitch (of bacon) awarded each year?

b11 *Which three cathedral choirs are involved in the Three Choirs Festival?*

a12 What is the chemical symbol for the element tin?

b12 *What is the chemical symbol for the element iron?*

No. 198 Answers

a1   Monkeys, apes, and humans

b1   *Small, microscopic organisms that float near the surface of the sea*

a2   His jewels (and entire baggage train)

b2   *George III*

a3   St Paul's Cathedral, London

b3   *Blaydon, Oxfordshire (in Blaydon churchyard)*

a4   'It's not unusual'

b4   *Wuthering Heights (Kate Bush had a hit with a song of this title; Emily Brontë wrote the novel)*

a5   Golf

b5   *Tennis*

a6   Gordon Jackson

b6   *George Cowley*

a7   Nepal

b7   *Ghana*

a8   Chaim Weizmann

b8   *General Marshall (Marshall Plan)*

a9   Teeth (the decay of teeth by bacteria)

b9   *In the wrist (they are the small bones that join the forearm to the hand)*

a10   Beethoven

b10   *Lord Palmerston*

a11   The couple who best prove they have not regretted their marriage that year (Dunmow is in Essex)

b11   *Gloucester, Hereford, and Worcester*

a12   Sn

b12   *Fe*

Tie-breaker

Q   What does the acronym laser stand for?

A   Light Amplification by Stimulated Emission of Radiation

No. 199

a1 Of which country has Bob Hawke been prime minister?

b1 *Of which country was Mr Andropov the president?*

a2 Which television policeman was played by the late Jack Warner?

b2 *On television, in the New Avengers, which character was played by Patrick MacNee?*

a3 With which sport is Nancy Lopez associated?

b3 *In which sport did Terry Spinks become famous?*

a4 Which British group first had a hit with the song 'Nights In White Satin'?

b4 *Which pop group first had a hit with 'Penny Lane'?*

a5 On which part of a flower are the pollen grains deposited during pollination?

b5 *Which organ in a flower produces pollen?*

a6 In which year was Nicholas II, the last tsar of Russia, murdered?

b6 *Which English king was killed by an arrow in the New Forest?*

a7 What is the capital of Barbados?

b7 *What is the capital of the Bahamas?*

a8 Which duke owns or is associated with Woburn Abbey?

b8 *Which duke owns Chatsworth House?*

a9 Of which county is Holy Island or Lindisfarne a part?

b9 *Which is the third largest of the Channel Islands?*

a10 Only one American president held office four times. Who was he?

b10 *Which American president was born in a log cabin in 1809?*

a11 East Bergholt in Suffolk is the birthplace of which famous painter?

b11 *Huntingdon is the birthplace of which ruler of England?*

a12 Who wrote the novel *Kipps*?

b12 *Who wrote the novel Tom Jones?*

No. 199 Answers

a1	Australia
b1	*Soviet Union (USSR)*
a2	Dixon of Dock Green
b2	*Steed*
a3	Golf
b3	*Boxing*
a4	The Moody Blues
b4	*The Beatles*
a5	The stigma
b5	*The stamen*
a6	1918 (the year after the Russian Revolution)
b6	*William II (accept: William Rufus)*
a7	Bridgetown
b7	*Nassau*
a8	Duke of Bedford
b8	*Duke of Devonshire*
a9	Northumberland
b9	*Alderney*
a10	Franklin D. Roosevelt
b10	*Abraham Lincoln*
a11	Constable
b11	*Oliver Cromwell*
a12	H. G. Wells
b12	*Henry Fielding*

Tie-breaker

Q How long does it take the Earth to travel round the sun?
A *365¼ days; 1 year*

No. 200 Topical Questions

a1   Who is the Chancellor of the Exchequer?

b1   *Who is the Home Secretary?*

a2   Besides the leaders of the Conservative and Labour parties, name the leader of a British political party and his or her party.

b2   *In the House of Commons, who is the leader of the Opposition?*

a3   Who is the Foreign Secretary?

b3   *Who is the present Irish taoiseach or prime minister?*

a4   When is the next leap year?

b4   *In which year was the last General Election held?*

a5   How much does it cost to send an ordinary letter (under 60 grams) by first class post?

b5   *For an ordinary family car, how much is the Road Fund Licence for one year?*

a6   Who is the manager of England's soccer team?

b6   *Which soccer team won this year's English league championship?*

a7   Who is the French president?

b7   *Who is Vice-President of the USA?*

a8   Who is the Secretary of State for Education?

b8   *Who is Secretary of State for Employment?*

a9   Who is the Secretary of State for Industry?

b9   *Who is Secretary of State for Defence?*

a10   At Wimbledon, last summer, who was the men's singles champion?

b10   *At Wimbledon, last summer, who was the women's singles champion?*

a11   Which country won the Rugby Union Grand Slam this year?

b11   *Who won this year's Boat Race (from Putney to Mortlake)?*

a12   Who is the poet laureate?

b12   *Who is general secretary of the TUC?*

No. 200 Answers

Any answers we supplied to this round would soon be out of date! Answers can be found in various reference books — especially the current Whitaker's Almanack.

Tie-breaker

Q. Name the ruling kings or queens of three European countries (excluding the United Kingdom)
(For example: Belgium, Denmark, the Netherlands, Norway)

The 20th Century Quizbook
David Self

Find out how much you and your friends know about the most world-changing century ever!

David Self's new bumper collection of 5000 fully researched questions provides all quiz organizers with a superb ready-to-use quiz kit.

- 200 quizzes of 24 graded questions each (plus a tie-breaker)
- quizzes arranged in order of increasing difficulty
- suitable for two teams of 3, 4 or 6 contestants
- general knowledge and special 'theme' rounds — all related to the twentieth century and designed to appeal to young and old alike
- pronunciation guides for tricky words and hints to help questionmasters and quiz organizers

How To Develop A Super Power Memory

Harry Lorayne

There is no such thing as a poor memory — only a trained or untrained one. This book proves it by showing with what speed and ease anyone can accomplish seemingly amazing memory feats.

'I don't care how poor you may think your memory is now! I believe that you have a memory 10 to 20 times more powerful than you realize today!'

Harry Lorayne's unique system of memory builders provides a quick and easy remedy for forgetfulness. Read Chapter 5 today and you will learn how to recall twenty important facts that you have never been able to memorize before. Tomorrow you will be able to plan your entire day in your mind — no longer will you need to rely on reminders, notes or other paper crutches!

Allow Harry Lorayne to share his secret with you, and you can build yourself a fabulous memory from scratch. Here at last is your chance to gain the super-powered, filing cabinet memory you've always dreamed about!

Double Your Learning Power

Geoffrey Dudley

Do you often forget the very things you want to remember — names of people you have just met, important addresses, useful contacts, telephone numbers? Are you embarrassed in business and social life by your inability to recall facts that should be on the tip of your tongue? If so, then you will realize that forgetfulness is an exasperating habit.

Yet inside your head you are equipped with an instrument which has a potential for remembering far more remarkable than the most advanced computer. All you need to do is learn how to fully tap its resources.

Here, at last, is a book to help you. After detailed research into modern scientific experiments Geoffrey Dudley reveals what psychologists have discovered about the process of learning and suggests practical ways of using this knowledge to your advantage.